PRIMATE FIELD STUDIES

Series Editors:

Robert W. Sussman, Washington University
Natalie Vasey, Portland State University

Series Editorial Board:

Simon Bearder, Oxford-Brookes University
Marina Cords, Columbia University
Agustin Fuentes, Notre Dame University
Paul Garber, University of Illinois
Annie Gautier-Hion, Station Biologique de Paimpont
Joanna Lambert, University of Wisconsin
Robert D. Martin, Field Museum
Deborah Overdorff, University of Texas
Jane Phillips-Conroy, Washington University
Karen Strier, University of Wisconsin

Series Titles:

The Spectral Tarsier
Sharon L. Gursky, Texas A&M University

Strategies of Sex and Survival in Hamadryas Baboons: Through a Female Lens
Larissa Swedell, Queens College, The City University of New York

The Behavioral Ecology of Callimicos and Tamarins in Northwestern Bolivia
Leila M. Porter, Northern Illinois University

The Socioecology of Adult Female Patas Monkeys and Vervets
Jill D. Pruetz, Iowa State University

Apes of the Impenetrable Forest: The Behavioral Ecology of Sympatric Chimpanzees and Gorillas
Craig B. Stanford, University of Southern California

Forthcoming Titles:

A Natural History of the Brown Mouse Lemur
Sylvia Atsalis, Brookfield Zoo

The Gibbons of Khao Yai
Thad Q. Bartlett, The University of Texas at San Antonio

PRIMATE FIELD STUDIES

Many of us who conduct field studies on wild primates have witnessed a decline in the venues available to publish monographic treatments of our work. As researchers we have few choices other than to publish short technical articles on discrete aspects of our work in professional journals. Also in vogue are popular expositions, often written by non-scientists. To counter this trend, we have begun this series. Primate Field Studies is a venue both for publishing the full complement of findings of long-term studies, and for making our work accessible to a wider readership. Interested readers need not wait for atomized parts of long-term studies to be published in widely scattered journals; students need not navigate the technical literature to bring together a body of scholarship better served by being offered as a cohesive whole. We are interested in developing monographs based on single or multi-species studies. If you wish to develop a monograph, we encourage you to contact one of the series editors.

About the Editors:

Robert W. Sussman (Ph.D. Duke University) is currently Professor of Anthropology and Environmental Science at Washington University, St. Louis, Missouri and past Editor-in-Chief of *American Anthropologist,* the flagship journal of the American Anthropological Association. His research focuses on the ecology, behavior, evolution and conservation of nonhuman and human primates, and he has worked in Costa Rica, Guyana, Panama, Madagascar and Mauritius. He is the author of numerous scientific publications, including *Biological Basis of Human Behavior,* Prentice Hall (1999), *Primate Ecology and Social Structure* (two volumes), Pearson Custom Publishing (2003), and *The Origin and Nature of Sociality,* Aldine de Gruyter (2004).

Natalie Vasey (Ph.D. Washington University) is currently assistant professor of anthropology at Portland State University in Portland, Oregon. Her work explores the behavioral ecology, life history adaptations, and evolution of primates, with a focus on the endangered and recently extinct primates of Madagascar. She has presented her research at international venues and published in leading scientific journals. She is dedicated to educating students and the public-at-large about the lifestyles and conservation status of our closest relatives in the animal kingdom.

The Spectral Tarsier

Sharon L. Gursky

Texas A&M University

Upper Saddle River, New Jersey 07458

BOWLING GREEN STATE
UNIVERSITY LIBRARY

Library of Congress Cataloging-in-Publication Data

Gursky, Sharon

The spectral tarsier/submitted by Sharon Gursky.
   p.   cm — (Primate field series)
   ISBN 0-13-189332-7
   1. Tarsius spectrum.   I. Title.   II. Series.

QL737.P965G87 2007
599.8'3—dc22

2006040599

Publisher: Nancy Roberts
Supplements Editor: LeeAnn Doherty
Editorial Assistant: Lee Peterson
Full Service Production Liaison: Joanne Hakim
Marketing Director: Brandy Dawson
Senior Marketing Manager: Marissa Feliberty
Manufacturing Buyer: Ben Smith
Cover Art Director: Jayne Conte
Cover Design: Kiwi Design
Cover Photos: *Main image front cover and image on back cover* courtesy of Sharon L. Gursky; *top band images 1-4* courtesy of Robert W. Sussman/Washington University of St. Louis
Director, Image Resource Center: Melinda Patelli
Manager, Rights and Permissions: Zina Arabia
Manager, Visual Research: Beth Brenzel
Photo Coordinator: Annette Linder
Full-Service Project Management: Bharath Parthasarathy/TexTech International
Composition: TexTech International
Printer/Binder: RR Donnelley & Sons Company

Credits and acknowledgments borrowed from other sources and reproduced, with permission, in this textbook appear on appropriate page within text.

Copyright © 2007 by Pearson Education, Inc., Upper Saddle River, New Jersey, 07458. Pearson Prentice Hall. All rights reserved. Printed in the United States of America. This publication is protected by Copyright and permission should be obtained from the publisher prior to any prohibited reproduction, storage in a retrieval system, or transmission in any form or by any means, electronic, mechanical, photocopying, recording, or likewise. For information regarding permission(s), write to: Rights and Permissions Department.

Pearson Prentice Hall™ is a trademark of Pearson Education, Inc.
Pearson® is a registered trademark of Pearson plc
Prentice Hall® is a registered trademark of Pearson Education, Inc.

Pearson Education LTD., London
Pearson Education Singapore, Pte. Ltd
Pearson Education, Canada, Ltd
Pearson Education—Japan
Pearson Education Australia PTY, Limited

Pearson Education North Asia Ltd
Pearson Educación de Mexico, S.A. de C.V.
Pearson Education Malaysia, Pte. Ltd
Pearson Education, Upper Saddle River, New Jersey

10 9 8 7 6 5 4 3 2 1
ISBN 0-13-189332-7

*Dedicated to my Nana, Lucille Pusar,
and in loving memory of my Popop, Louis Pusar*

⟩

Contents

List of Figures

List of Tables

Acknowledgments

Many people were critical to the development of this book and to the research that led up to it. It is here that I would like to acknowledge their pivotal role. The story begins at Hartwick College in Oneonta, New York. Under the guidance of Connie Anderson, I had the privilege to spend the summer conducting an internship at the Duke University Primate Center (DUPC) in Durham, New Colarado. Working under the supervision of David Haring, Patricia Wright, and Elwyn Simons, it was at the DUPC that I was first introduced to tarsiers. After learning about the DUPC's problems maintaining a breeding colony of tarsiers, I was convinced that the best way to maintain tarsiers in captivity was to study them in their natural environment.

I entered graduate school with the intention of studying the most endangered tarsier species, *Tarsius syrichtu*, in its natural environment, the Philippines. While at the University of New Mexico (UNM) I met Jatna Supriatna, a fellow primatology graduate student, who happened to be from Indonesia. Jatna, Jeff Froehlich, and colleagues were organizing a group of scientists to study the primates throughout the island of Sulawesi in Indonesia. Jatna convinced me to join the Sulawesi Primate Project and study tarsiers there instead of the Philippines. During my first trip to Indonesia, Jatna, Yoppy Muskita, and I visited several sites searching for tarsiers. My experience was so rewarding that I decided to complete my dissertation on the spectral tarsiers, *Tarsius spectrum*, instead of the Philippine tarsiers. Over many years, Jatna has continued to support and sponsor my research in Sulawesi, and his letter-writing efforts cannot go unappreciated! Noviar Andayani has also been very supportive, sponsoring my research and encouraging me to continue studying these enigmatic primates.

While at UNM, I realized that I would be better off studying under the guidance of a professor who was familiar with the trials and tribulations of studying tarsiers. Thus, I transferred from UNM to the State University of New York at Stony Brook to study tarsiers with Patricia Wright. While at Stony Brook, Patricia Wright and John Fleagle were especially encouraging of my research endeavors and I thank them.

Texas A&M University has also provided a tremendous amount of resources toward my research. In particular, I would like to thank the Anthropology Department Head, David Carlson, for providing time off from my teaching responsibilities, and Dean Johnson for his support of spousal hiring.

A number of organizations have also been generous with their support. The Indonesian Institute for Sciences (LIPI) regularly granted me permission for my research, and the Department of Forestry in Jakarta and Manado regularly gave me permission to conduct my research in protected forest. The National Science Foundation, Fulbright Foundation, LSB Leakey Foundation, Wenner Gren Foundation, Sigma Xi, PSC-CUNY, the Chicago Zoological Society, Douroucouli Foundation, and Primate Conservation Inc. all provided various amounts of financial support for my research.

In addition to the intellectual, logistic, and financial support provided by the above individuals and organizations, I could never have conducted my research without the help and guidance of my many Batuputian field assistants: Nestor, Petros, Uri, Celsius, Franz, Ben, Felik, Lende, and Yunus. Without their help, I'd be lost in the forest, walking in circles around the same tree—*literally*!

I would also like to thank the anonymous reviewers, Natalie Vasey, and Bob Sussman for the time and effort they put into this manuscript.

Lastly, I would like to acknowledge my family. My husband Michael regularly took care of our children while I conducted research, both when I was in the field and when I was home. He not only supports my research, but he recognizes how important it is to me. My words cannot begin to express my thanks for his assistance and support. To my children, Noah and Hannah . . . thank-you for putting up with cold baths and eating rice for every meal while in Indonesia!

The Spectral Tarsier

1

Taxonomic History

(Photo by Ben Batuputih)

Tarsiers first became known to Western scientists because of an account given to Petiver by a missionary, J. G. Camel, based on the latter's discussions with an individual from Luzon, Philippines (Hill 1955). Camel described the Philippine tarsier as a small monkey with big round eyes that never or rarely closed; skinny, hairless ears; mouselike fur: and a tail and hind feet almost the same as its length body. (One interesting note: Philippine tarsiers are restricted to the southern Philippine islands; consequently, the individual whom Camel met could not have been from Luzon!) Petiver published his description in the Philosophical Transactions of the Royal Society in 1705 and named the animal *Cercopithecus luzonis minimus* because of its primatelike features. In 1765, Buffon also described a tarsier, which he gave the name *Didelphis macrotarsus; Didelphis* because he believed tarsiers were related to opossums, and *macrotarsus* because of the extremely long tarsal bones exhibited by this animal. Erxleben (1777) was the first scientist to recognize the similarities between tarsiers and other prosimian primates, and consequently he named them *Lemur tarsier*.

Soon, though, these names were invalidated. The names *Cercopithecus, Didelphis*, and *Lemur* had already been used for Old World monkeys, opossums, and lemurs, respectively, and there was growing recognition that tarsiers were distinct from all these mammal forms. Storr, in 1780, enumerated the differences between lemurs and tarsiers and argued for the generic separation of these two taxa. Storr coined the genus name *Tarsius* for these unusual primates that possessed exceptionally long tarsal bones. Sulawesian tarsiers were first described as distinct from the Philippine tarsier and given their species name, *Lemur spectrum*, by Pallas in 1778 (thus the origin of the binomial name *Tarsius spectrum*). It was later referred, to as *T. fuscus* (Fischer 1804), *T. fuscomanus* (Geoffroy 1812), and *T. fisheri* (Burmesiter 1846), but according to Hill (1955), *spectrum* has priority over the other species names.

Recently, the validity of *T. spectrum* as a descriptor has been questioned again. According to Hill (1955), Cabrera suggested that Buffon's tarsier was actually an Eastern Tarsier and not a Philippine Tarsier. Despite the loss of Buffon's specimen to study, but based on his written description, Cabrera's opinion has been reaffirmed by Groves (2001b) and Shekelle (2003). The nomenclatural implication of this error is that the name *Lemur tarsier* (Erxleben 1777) has seniority over *Lemur spectrum* (Pallas 1778). Thus, *Tarsius spectrum* would be *Tarsius tarsier*. I continue to use the name *T. spectrum*, but recognize that the correct name *might* be *Tarsius tarsier*.

Ever since tarsiers were finally recognized as primates, and distinct from the lemurs, they have been the focus of numerous controversies. Most notably, there has been considerable debate over tarsiers' classification within the order Primates (Pocock 1918; Wolin & Massoupust 1970; Cave 1973; Luckett 1976; Cartmill & Kay 1978; Rosenberger & Szalay 1980; Aiello 1986). There are two major taxonomies or classifications. The first, cladistic, system is based on the work of Pocock (1918), who believed tarsiers are more similar to the higher primates (monkeys, apes, and humans) than to the lemurs and lorises. To express this relationship, Pocock established two infraorders within the order Primates: the Haplorrhini, which included the suborder Tarsoidea as well as the suborders Ceboidea, Cercopithecoidea, and Hominoidea (monkeys, apes, and humans), and Strepsirhini, which included the lemurs and lorises. Pocock believed tarsiers were more similar to the anthropoid primates because of numerous shared derived characteristics (synapomorphies). Among the characteristics shared by tarsiers and anthropoid primates are haemochorial placentation, absence of a tapetum lucidum, presence of a fovea centralis, reduced olfactory bulbs, lack of a wet rhinarium, well-developed promontory artery, and lack of an attached upper lip (Pocock 1918; Wolin & Massoupust 1970; Cave 1973; Luckett 1976; Cartmill & Kay 1978; Rosenberger & Szalay 1980; Aiello 1986; MacPhee & Cartmill 1986; Fleagle 1988).

The second school of classification is based on the idea that the lemurs, lorises, and tarsiers are more closely related to one another and therefore should be grouped together in the suborder Prosimii, with the higher primates all grouped together in the Anthropoidea (Simpson 1945; Cartmill & Kay 1978; Rosenberger & Szalay 1980; Fleagle 1988). This gradistic classification scheme is based on numerous ancestral characters, such as the tarsier's nocturnal habits, small body size, and parenting strategies (infant parking and oral transport). Anatomical characteristics shared by tarsiers and other prosimian primates include an unfused mandibular symphysis, a grooming claw, multiple pairs of mammae, and a bicornuate uterus (Pocock 1918; Hill 1955; Cartmill & Kay 1978; Rosenberger & Szalay 1980; Aiello 1986; Fleagle 1988).

There has been substantial disagreement not only concerning the taxonomic classification of the tarsiers but also the actual number of tarsier species (Hill 1955; Niemitz 1984; Musser & Dagosto 1987). At present, five species of tarsier are formally recognized: *Tarsius syrichta* (Linnaeus 1758), the Philippine tarsier, *Tarsius bancanus* (Horsfield 1821), the Bornean tarsier; *Tarsius pumilus* (Miller & Hollister 1921; Musser & Dagosto 1987), the pygmy tarsier from central Sulawesi; *Tarsius spectrum* (Pallas 1778), the spectral tarsier from Sulawesi; and *Tarsius dianae* (Niemitz et al. 1991), another lowland tarsier from central Sulawesi (Figure 1–1). These tarsier species differ morphologically from one another in a variety of ways, including their absolute orbit size, their absolute tooth size, the proportion of their tail that is covered by hair, and their limb proportions. In terms of absolute orbit size and absolute tooth size, the Bornean tarsier possesses the largest orbits and largest teeth of any of the species, followed by the Philippine tarsier, the spectral tarsier, and then the pygmy tarsier (Musser & Dagosto 1987; Sussman 1999). There is also a cline in the proportion of the tail that is covered by hair for each species. *T. spectrum* and the other

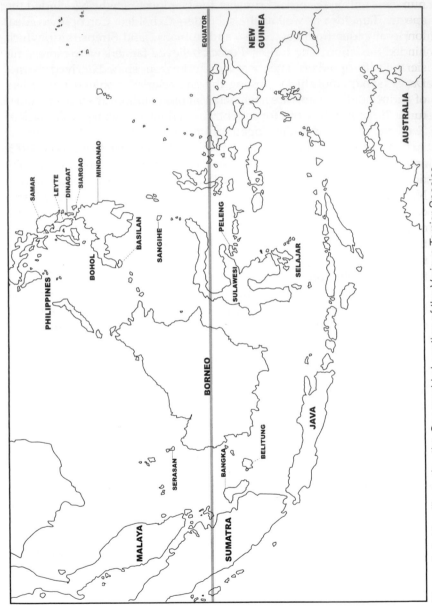

Figure 1–1 Map Illustrating the Geographic Location of the Various Tarsier Species in Indonesia, Malaysia, and the Philippines

4

Sulawesian tarsier species possess the most tail hair, followed by the Bornean tarsier and the Philippine tarsier, whose tail is often described as naked due to the sparse fine hairs that cover it. Niemitz (1984) also recorded numerous differences in limb proportions between the three major tarsier species (*T. spectrum*, *T. bancanus*, and *T. syrichta*). The Bornean tarsier has the longest hindlimb and hand, followed by the Philippine tarsier, whose hindlimbs and hands are intermediate in length, and finally the spectral tarsier, whose hindlimbs and hands are shortest in length. The recent work by Dagosto et al. (2001) has also demonstrated a cline in the locomotor patterns of tarsiers: *T. bancanus* is the most specialized, using vertical clinging postures the most frequently, followed by *T. syrichta*, the Sulawesian tarsiers, *T. spectrum*, and *T. dianae*.

According to Nietsch and Kopp (1998), the Sulawesian tarsiers (*T. spectrum* and *T. dianae*) can be distinguished from one another based on their vocalizations. Using playbacks of the vocal duets sung by tarsiers each morning, Nietsch and Kopp found that each species only recognized the vocalizations of their own species. Neither species responded to the vocalizations of the other Sulawesian tarsier species but responded avidly to the vocalizations of their own species. During their study, Nietsch and Kopp also found that the tarsier population on Togian Island, adjacent to Sulawesi, did not respond to the playback vocalizations of *T. spectrum* or *T. dianae* and so proposed that the Togian tarsier population may also represent a distinct species, *T. togianensis*. Using a discriminant analysis function, Nietsch (1999) found that the degree of separation of the acoustic characteristics of the Togian tarsier population from the *T. spectrum* population was substantial enough to warrant their designation as a distinct species.

Two additional Sulawesian tarsier species, *T. pelengensis* and *T. sangirensis*, have also been tentatively proposed and are awaiting additional studies utilizing larger sample sizes (Shekelle et al. 1997; Groves 1998, 2001; Shekelle 2003). Some scientists naturally question whether there really are so many distinct tarsier species in Sulawesi, or whether they are in fact subspecies. However, Bearder (1999) argues that the continued use of vocalizations is integral for the proper identification of species boundaries when dealing with cryptic primates such as the tarsier.

Another taxonomic argument relating to tarsiers concerns whether the Sulawesian tarsiers are distinct enough to warrant their own genus name. Groves (1998) argues that in his discriminant analyses of the three historically recognized species (*T. bancanus*, *T. syrichta*, and *T. spectrum*), the spectral tarsier is distinct enough from the Bornean and Philippine tarsier species to warrant its own genus name, *Rabienus*. At present, however, even Groves (2001) continues to use the genus name *Tarsius* for the Sulawesian tarsiers.

Interestingly, although there are only minor differences in morphology, there are substantial chromosomal differences between some tarsier species.

The Bornean and Philippine tarsier are each reported to have a karotype of 80 chromosomes (Klinger 1963; Poorman et al. 1985; Dutrillaux & Rumpler 1988), whereas *Tarsius dianae* is reported to have only 46 chromosomes (Niemitz et al. 1991). The karotypes for both *T. spectrum* and *T. pumilus* are still unknown. Duttrillaux and Rumpler (1988) report that none of the chromosomes present in *T. syrichta* or *T. bancanus* are similar to those found in any other primate (100 species) or mammal. It has been suggested therefore that the tarsiers do not have a primitive karotype, but have undergone a large number of chromosomal rearrangements. A large number of fissions have certainly occurred as the diploid chromosome number of 80 is among the highest found in mammals.

Despite plenty of debate regarding the taxonomic classification of the tarsiers and the number of tarsier species, there has been a dearth of studies on the behavioral ecology of wild tarsiers (cf Niemitz 1984; Crompton & Andau 1986, 1987; Nietsch 1999; Dagosto et al. 2001; Neri-Arbodela 2001). This volume will correct that oversight by providing a long-term, in-depth study of one tarsier species, the spectral tarsier, *Tarsius spectrum*. Having been fortunate enough to study the spectral tarsier in its natural environment over the last decade, my primary goal here is to pull together the trajectory of my thoughts and writings on this enigmatic primate. Chapter 2 introduces my field site and the methods that I used while studying this species. Chapter 3 presents data on group size and composition, gregariousness, predation, and moonlight. All of these data focus around the research question, What ecological and social factors select for gregariousness in this species? Chapter 4 presents additional data on habitat usage that I used to answer this research question. Specifically, I address whether spectral tarsiers are territorial (spatially cohesive) as a result of ecological factors (resource defense) or social factors (mate defense). I also evaluate how sociality affects diet, sleeping tree use, site fidelity, and dispersal patterns. Chapter 5 introduces infant care and development, which leads to my research question, Why park? That is, why do spectral tarsiers not transport their infants while foraging as do the majority of primates? Chapter 6 continues to address this research question, but focuses on how it applies to adult males and then to subadult group members. In today's world, it is impossible to study primate behavioral ecology without being concerned about a species' conservation status. Thus, in Chapter 7, I present data on population density and captive conservation. I evaluate how the spectral tarsier's population density and habitat have fared over the last decade. In addition, I provide several suggestions for improving the spectral tarsier's survival probability. Chapter 8 summarizes the results of my studies over the last decade.

2

Field Site and Data Collection Methods

(Photo by the author)

FIELD SITE

Geological History of Sulawesi

The geological history of an area is an important determinant of the fauna and flora that occur there. Sulawesi appears to be composed of two distinct types of geological outcrops that were brought together in the late Cenozoic Era by large-scale plate movements (Audley-Charles 1981). This interpretation is supported by preliminary paleomagnetic studies (Haile 1978). Specifically, it is thought that the Sula Peninsula (a chain of small islands from western Papua New Guinea) collided with an Asian island, Celebes, 15 million years ago (Audley-Charles 1981). Thus, the eastern part of present-day Sulawesi originated in Papua New Guinea, whereas the western part originated in Asia. As a result of these large-scale movements of the earth's crust, Sulawesi comprises two distinct geological provinces: West and East Sulawesi, divided by the north-northwest fault between Palu and the Gulf of Bone. Sulawesi is still a geologically active area, home to eleven active volcanoes (Whitten et al., 1987). The most devastating eruption in recent times was the Colo volcano in July 1983, which covered large parts of the island in ash. More recently, in June 2004, Mt. Awu erupted, requiring the evacuation of more than 7,000 people.

Present-day Sulawesi

Sulawesi is the world's eleventh largest island (Whitten et al., 1987), with a land area of 159,000 kilometers (islands and mainland). The distance between the most northerly island of Miangas (90 kilometer south of the Philippine island of Mindanao, but part of the Sangihe–Talaud Indonesian islands) and the most southerly island of Sattengar is 1,805 kilometer. The island is physically situated between two degrees north of the equator and eight degrees below the equator, with the equator passing through the isthmus separating the northern arm and central part of the island.

Sulawesi is the largest and most central island of the biogeographical region of Wallacea, where the Australian and Asian zoogeographical regions meet. Consequently, Sulawesi shows a blend of Asian and Australian elements in its fauna and flora. Throughout the island's protected area, the marsupials *Phalanger ursinus* and *P. celebensis* occur sympatrically with the primates *Macaca sp.* and *Tarsius sp.*

Sulawesi also exhibits very high levels of endemic species. In his writings about the island, Wallace (1869) noted "that a considerable number of its animals are so remarkable, as to find no close allies in any other part of the world." Sulawesi is the home of more than 260 bird species, 80 of which are endemic. Of the 127 indigenous mammals, 79 (62%) are endemic (Musser 1987). Endemic species include the anoa, macaques, spectral tarsiers, and babirusa. It should be noted that the percentage of endemic mammal species rises to 98% if the volant bats (including the Australian flying foxes) are excluded (Musser 1987; Whitten et al., 1987). In comparison, neighboring Borneo, the largest Indonesian island, has only 29 endemic bird species and 36 endemic mammals (Musser 1987). New species of mammals continue to be recognized throughout Sulawesi (Musser 1987; Musser & Dagosto 1987; Niemitz et al., 1991).

Tangkoko Dua Saudara Nature Reserve, North Sulawesi

Physical Setting. Tangkoko Dua Saudara Nature Reserve lies on the northeastern-most tip of the island of Sulawesi (long. 12514' E and lat. 134') (Figure 2–1). When the reserve was first formed it was comprised of 8,867 hectares with a sea boundary of 12 kilometer (World Wildlife Fund 1980). There is a long black-sand beach for about two kilometers along the edge of the reserve. This is where the research station where I lived while conducting my research is located.

During his travels in the Malay archipelago, Wallace (1869) described the area where the reserve now exists:

> A [S]ituated in the large bay between the islands of Limbe and Banca, [it] consists of a steep beach more than a mile in length, of deep, loose, and coarse black volcanic sand or rather gravel, very fatiguing to walk over. It is bounded at each extremity by a small river, with hilly ground beyond, while the forest behind the beach itself is tolerably level and its growth stunted. (p. 271, with map on p. 254)

This description is still accurate in all respects.

Climate. Throughout my various research projects, I regularly collected rainfall daily, to the nearest millimeter (mm) using a standard rain gauge with a capacity to collect 270 mm of rain. Figure 2–2 illustrates the mean amount of rainfall received each month over the course of my studies. Yearly rainfall averaged between 2,200 and 2,400 mm. According to Whitmore (1987), forested areas that receive less than 100 mm of rainfall during some months, but more than 200 mm during all other months, is characteristic of monsoon forest—not rain forest. Thus, if this pattern of exceptionally low rainfall during July, August, and September is found consistently from year to year, then the forest at Tangkoko may best be described as a monsoon forest, and not a rain forest (Whitmore 1987) as it has been previously described and classified (World Wildlife Fund 1980).

Flora. The reserve exhibits a full range of floral communities from sea-level coastal communities, to lowland forests, to submontane forests and

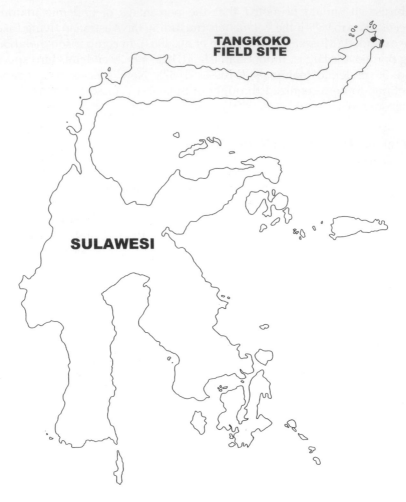

Figure 2–1 Map Illustrating Position of Tangkoko Dua Saudara Nature Reserve on the Northeastern-Most Tip of the Island of Sulawesi, Indonesia

even mossy cloud forests on the summits of Dua Saudara and the Tangkoko Crater (MacKinnon & MacKinnon 1980). The majority of the reserve has been disturbed by human influence (old clearing activities and/or selective harvesting). A vegetation survey of the reserve was conducted by the World Wildlife Fund (1980) and was extended by the Wildlife Conservation Society (Kinnaird & O'Brien 1993). The main vegetation types of the forest within the reserve are: (1) alang-alang grassland (*Imperata cylindrica*), found in open areas that have been cleared by human activity, and as a result of human-induced and natural fire; (2) secondary shrub, found in areas that have been less disturbed, or which have

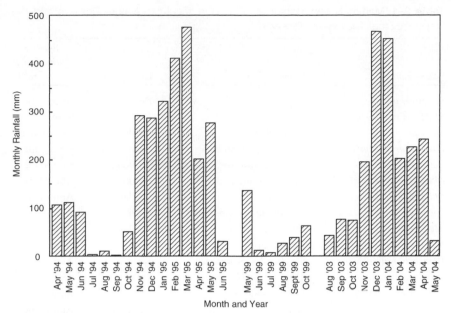

Figure 2–2 The Rainfall (mm) Collected Each Month Between 1994 and 2004

progressed to early secondary forest shrub due to protection from fire; (3) casuarina forest, which occurs in newly exposed sandy and rocky parts of the reserve such as the Tangkoko crater walls; (4) beach formation forest growing along the 12-kilometer coast; (5) lowland forest, which contains a large number of species and stretches from sea level to about 600 meters; (6) submontane forest, which occurs between 600 meters and the crater rim of the volcanoes. Trees generally are smaller than those found at the lower altitudes and are increasingly covered with mosses and ferns. Mean leaf size is also relatively smaller than that found at the lower altitudes, and the undergrowth is denser; (7) Moss forest, which covers the crater rim and the peaks of both Tangkoko and Dua Saudara. Trees are consider-ably shorter in height, have smaller diameters, and are frequently covered with moss. Orchids and ferns are commonly observed, both on the ground and as epiphytes (MacKinnon & MacKinnon 1980).

Fauna. Table 2–1 lists the mammalian fauna that are present in Tangkoko Nature Reserve. The Sulawesi palm civet, *Macrogalidia musschenbrockii*, is thought to occur in the reserve, but over the years I never observed any individuals, or their feces or footprints. *Viverra tangalunga*, the Malaysian palm civet, an introduced species, also occurs in the reserve. Over the course of my research, I have made numerous observations (n>20) of this species—at least one was made in almost all my study group's territory. It

Table 2-1 Mammals and Marsupials Found in Tangkoko Nature Reserve and the Frequency that They Were Observed

Species Name	Common Name	Local Name	Relative Frequency Observed
Phalanger ursinus	Bear cuscus	Kuskus	Abundant
Phalanger celebensis	Cuscus	Tembung	Rare
Pteropus sp.	Flying Fox	Paniki besar	Occasional
Cynopterus brachyotis	Short-nosed fruit bats	Paniki kecil	Abundant
Rouseettus celebensis	Rousette fruit bat	Paniki kecil	Abundant
Macroglossus lagochilus	Long-tongued fruit bat	Paniki kecil	Abundant
Rhinolophus sp.	Horseshoe bats	Kelelawar	Abundant
Hipposideros sp.	Old World leaf-nosed bats	Kelelawar	Abundant
Myotis sp.	Little brown bats	Kelelawar	Abundant
Macaca nigra	Celebes ape	Yaki	Abundant
Prosciurillus murinus	Celebes dwarf squirrel	Tupai	Abundant
Prosciurus leucomus	Celebes dwarf squirrel	Tupai	Abundant
Hyosciurus iheinrichi	Celebes long-nosed squirrel	Tupai	Rare
Rattus sp.	Rats	Tikkus	Abundant
Mus musculus	House mouse	Tikkus	Abundant
Macrogalidia musschenbroeki	Celebes palm civet	Anjing utan	Never
Viverra tangalunga	Oriental civet	Musang	Occasional
Felis catus	Domestic cat	Kuching liar	Occasional
Bubalus depressicornis	Lowland Asian water buffalo	Anoa	Rare
Cervus timorensis	Red deer; Sunda sambar	Rusa	Rare
Babyrousa babirussa	Babirusa	Babirusa	Never
Sus verrucisus	Celebes pig	Babi hutan	Abundant

is unclear whether Malaysian palm civets have very large ranges, or whether each sighting was an independent observation of a new individual. Both civet species are reported to eat small mammals, such as the numerous species of endemic Sulawesian rats (MacKinnon & MacKinnon 1980; Whitten et al., 1987) and, probably, tarsiers. The tarsiers clearly gave a series of alarm calls in response to the presence of a civet. In every case, the tarsier's alert was how I first observed the civet.

The large bear cuscus, *Phalanger ursinus*, was also common in the reserve. It is primarily frugivorous (MacKinnon & MacKinnon 1980; Whitten et al., 1987), is usually observed in pairs, and forages both during the day and at night (pers. observ.), exhibiting a cathemeral activity cycle (Tattersall 1988). *Phalanger celebensis*, by contrast, is much smaller, folivorous, insectivorous, and exhibits a nocturnal activity cycle. This species was also observed to occur in pairs. Both cuscus species are thought to supplement their diet with insects. This is especially true for the smaller, consistently nocturnal species. Thus, to some extent these animals are both foraging competitors of the tarsiers.

Other endemic nocturnal fauna in Sulawesi include rats, bats, owls, and snakes (MacKinnon & MacKinnon 1980; Musser 1987; Whitten et al., 1987). The Sulawesi rats are frugivorous and therefore are not foraging competitors of the tarsiers. Although the tarsiers always gave way to the rats when their paths overlapped, only infants and juveniles gave alarm calls in their presence. I suspect that rats are not predators of the tarsiers, despite MacKinnon and MacKinnon's statements suggesting that the tarsiers seemed afraid of them (1980).

Small insectivorous bats definitely compete with the spectral tarsiers for food and sleeping sites. Several observations (n=8) of a small insectivorous bat swooping down to obtain a large insect just as the tarsier reaches out or leaps toward the same insect, were recorded. This type of competition occurred when the tarsier was foraging auditorally, and not visually. Consequently, competition with the small bats was restricted to noisy insects such as cicadas (n=7) and rhinoceros beetles (n=1). In seven of the eight observations of interspecific competition, the tarsier was the victor.

Numerous species of snakes were occasionally observed including pit vipers, *Trimeresurus wagleri*; pythons, *Python reticulatus*; and the two-headed snake, *Cyclindrophus rufus* (MacKinnon & MacKinnon 1980). Other nonpoisonous snakes occasionally observed by myself, other researchers, or field assistants throughout this study are listed in Table 2–2.

Owls and other birds were occasionally observed, but more frequently were heard. Not all, but some of the larger birds and owls are definitely predators. When specific owls and nocturnal birds were heard vocalizing nearby the focal individual's location, the focal tarsier often froze in place.

Table 2–2 Snakes Observed in Tangkoko Dua Saudara Nature Reserve

Species Name	Common Name
Typhlops sp.	Blind snake
Python reticulatus	Reticulated python
Cyclindrophus rufus	Two-headed snake
Ahaetulla ahaetulla	Painted bronze back
Elaphe erythrurus	Red racer
Elaphe janseni	Black and white racer
Boiga irregularis	Brown cat snake
Psammodynastes pulverulentus	Mountain whip snake
Dryophis prasinus	Green whip snake
Chryosopelea ornata	Flying snakes
Trimeresurus wagleri	Wagler's pit viper

If the tarsier was grooming, its hands and feet remained frozen in position, for as long as several minutes, until the possible threat was over.

Human Population. Minahasa is the most highly populated area in Sulawesi (MacKinnon & MacKinnon 1980; Whitten et al., 1987). As a consequence, the area has been heavily deforested, with less than 1% of north Sulawesi still forested, and less than that undisturbed. The forest that remains is all within nature reserves and, according to MacKinnon and MacKinnon (1980), is the least agriculturally valuable land in the province. MacKinnon and MacKinnon report that the soil in the areas surrounding the reserve is agriculturally very poor. Rice cannot be grown and the staple carbohydrates are taro and cassava. Bananas, coconuts, papayas, and mangoes are the primary fruits grown in the region. Most people depend on coconuts and fish caught at sea for the majority of their food, as well as to supplement their income.

Several villages border directly onto the reserve boundaries and have negatively affected parts of the reserve to varying degrees. The inhabitants of Dua Saudara cleared about 400 hectares of forest in 1959. The villagers at Batuputih also cleared about 400 hectares in 1974. They were forcibly evicted by police, but the damage was already done. This area is now a mosaic of grassland and secondary forest, mostly grassland. According to World Wildlife Fund (1980), another village, Pinganunian, also cleared a large section of the reserve to plant gardens and build homes. All the villages bordering the reserve bring their cows to graze in the grassy areas within the reserve, and their chickens and domestic pigs, too. Park guards who are related to the perpetrators have little desire or ability to enforce the rules and regulations of the reserve.

One of the most damaging things to occur has been the total destruction of the reserve buffer zone. When Tangkoko Nature Reserve was first created in the late 1970s, it encompassed 8,867 hectares and was surrounded by an additional 9,000 hectares, designated as a buffer zone. By the beginning of 1991, all the forest designated as the buffer zone had been depleted by the local populations.

Similarly, in 1995, an additional 1,230 hectares of the reserve's forest was reclassified by the Indonesian government as recreation forest, thereby removing all protection from this section of the forest. The effect of the change in the reserve's status is already noticeable. I suspect that within twenty years a large portion of the recreation forest will no longer exist, except as grassland.

Tourism. Despite the fact that Indonesia has laws stating that nature reserves are for research only and tourism is not permitted, approximately 4,000–5,000 tourists, domestic and foreign, visit Tangkoko Nature Reserve annually. Tangkoko Nature Reserve is very close to a major city, Manado, making tourism simple. The local PHPA (Department of Forestry Park Guards) has a monopoly on guiding tourists into the reserve as well as on providing room and board for them (losmen). It is because of the influx of tourists to the Nature Reserve (and the money that can be made from the tourist business) that a large portion of the reserve was changed to recreation forest.

Occasionally a park guard who was guiding tourists in the reserve would inform me that he had observed a tarsier during the day. I was intrigued that perhaps tarsiers in Tangkoko are not strictly nocturnal and are perhaps cathemeral, as has been observed in *Eulemur mongoz* (Harrington 1978; Tattersall 1988; Engqvist & Richard 1991) and *Eulemur rufus* (Overdorff 1992). Consequently, I conducted several twenty-four-hour focal follows. No observations of the animals leaving their nest or of any activity (except occasional autogrooming) were made. Grooming and play behavior were observed as the tarsiers returned to their sleeping tree and approximately one-half hour before they awoke to begin their nightly foraging. I suspect that observations of the tarsier during the day were the result of individuals being disturbed at their sleeping site and the individuals moving to a new area. This is supported by the fact that park guards frequently locate tarsier sleeping trees for tourists by banging on trees with their machete.

METHODS

Sample Sizes

During my research, I have observed a total of forty-nine adult individuals for various lengths of time, beginning March 1994 through May 2004. From three to eight different individuals were observed during each month. Variation in the number of individuals observed each month was based on my success with mistnetting as well as how long the batteries in the radio collars lasted and my ability to recapture animals to replace dead batteries. All of these factors were highly variable. Tables 2–3a, b, and c illustrate the total number of five-minute scans (Altmann 1974) each individual was observed during each month. The animals trapped and observed each field season were different individuals. Over 55,000 five-minute focal scans were obtained, comprising almost 5,000 hours of data. Although all-night and half-night focal follows were conducted, it was impossible to obtain behavioral data at each and every five-minute interval throughout the night.

In 1994–1995, I conducted the behavioral focal follows with an Indonesian student-assistant, Tigor. Initially, Tigor and I conducted focal follows together until approximately 99% of the data recorded by both of us was the same. At this point, I felt comfortable enough with the consistency in data

Table 2–3a Number of 5-Minutes Scans Each Individual Was Observed During Each Month and the Total Number of 5-Minutes Scans that Each Individual Was Observed Throughout the 1994–1995 Field Season[*]

ID	Month 1994–1995														Tot. # Scans/ Indiv.
	Apr	May	Jun	Jul	Aug	Sep	Oct	Nov	Dec	Jan	Feb	Mar	Apr	May	
226	129	181	275	338	219	431	—	—	—	—	—	—	—	—	1573
325	70	90	188	131	208	128	—	—	—	—	—	—	—	—	815
588	73	28	242	314	109	225	—	—	—	—	—	—	—	—	991
046	93	95	60	170	104	128	—	—	—	—	—	—	—	—	650
128	160	249	83	164	168	128	—	—	—	—	—	—	—	—	988
864	55	169	197	404	50	—	—	—	—	—	—	—	—	—	875
571	—	—	—	—	—	313	270	46	123	118	—	—	—	—	870
763	—	—	—	—	—	—	245	379	303	316	271	—	—	—	1514
914	—	—	—	—	—	—	89	308	230	110	107	—	—	—	844
038	—	—	—	—	—	76	113	46	98	118	—	—	—	—	451
897	—	—	—	—	—	—	—	—	—	—	342	308	305	414	1369
988	—	—	—	—	—	—	—	—	—	270	627	307	300	—	1504
876	—	—	—	—	—	—	—	—	—	—	202	208	222	78	710
Total # 5-min sample/ month	580	812	1045	1521	858	1465	717	779	754	932	1549	823	827	492	13,154

[*] Data represents approximately 1,100 hours of observation.

Table 2–3b Number of 5-Minutes Scans Each Individual Was Observed During Each Month and the Total Number of 5-Minutes Scans that Each Individual Was Observed Throughout the 1999 Field Season*

ID	Month 1999						
	May	Jun	Jul	Aug	Sep	Oct	Tot. # Scans/ Indiv.
686	78	84	157	238	219	231	1007
834	74	99	188	113	208	128	810
103	82	86	242	134	109	225	878
792	97	97	60	107	104	128	593
774	88	74	51	187	99	188	687
732	51	64	81	115	244	167	722
095	133	142	83	146	168	164	836
306	89	132	197	144	50	144	756
008	47	128	78	123	128	213	716
068	68	201	74	78	188	121	730
126	81	215	82	74	167	88	707
627	107	177	97	82	164	76	703
511	91	152	108	231	47	201	830
524	77	132	116	128	68	215	736
543	89	128	105	225	81	177	805
556	67	201	66	54	107	152	647
572	93	68	82	228	94	201	766
580	85	81	97	246	121	215	845
Total # 5-min sample/ month	1,497	2,261	1,964	2,653	2,366	3,033	13,774

* Data represents approximately 1,200 hours of observation.

recording to permit him to conduct independent focal follows. Once each month thereafter, Tigor and I conducted an interobserver reliability test to determine if we were still consistent in our data recording. I found that our data recording was at least 98% during each interobserver reliability test. Tigor only assisted in data collection in 1994–1995, after which, numerous local field assistants helped me collect all behavioral data.

Locating Tarsier Groups

I used the following procedures to locate groups of tarsiers. Prior to dawn, I would stand on the periphery of a one-hectare plot. Plots were chosen randomly (following a random block design) within one square kilometer

Table 2–3c Number of 5-Minutes Scans Each Individual Was Observed During Each Month and the Total Number of 5-Minutes Scans that Each Individual Was Observed Throughout the 2003–2004 Field Season*

ID	Month										Tot. # Scans/ Indiv.
	Aug	Sep	Oct	Nov	Dec	Jan	Feb	Mar	Apr	May	
014	145	116	252	287	193	321	169	197	404	50	2,134
066	43	65	133	164	289	218	233	256	303	79	1,783
191	94	81	76	113	46	98	118	110	187	122	1,045
090	88	178	150	77	135	144	156	167	162	134	1,391
231	97	62	177	145	257	166	160	249	83	164	1,560
110	101	169	83	69	214	288	154	55	138	154	1,425
033	73	28	242	314	109	225	68	226	136	167	1,588
026	31	64	51	87	245	162	178	170	215	267	1,470
146	51	84	81	115	229	312	321	87	124	287	1,691
168	160	249	83	164	168	164	218	115	64	164	1,549
204	55	169	197	404	50	79	98	164	84	113	1,413
050	51	199	225	113	73	313	270	46	123	118	1,531
313	218	133	321	175	93	144	245	379	303	316	2,327
347	41	79	218	47	31	265	89	308	230	110	1,418
394	170	62	177	145	160	43	65	133	164	289	1,408
366	87	198	216	201	55	132	143	169	219	173	1,593
382	115	77	135	144	156	217	62	177	145	270	1,498
403	164	156	149	153	182	99	51	84	81	115	1,234
Total # 5-min sample/ month	1,784	2,169	2,966	2,917	2,685	3,390	2,798	3,092	3,165	3,092	28,058

* Data represents approximately 2,300 hours of observation. Simultaneous focal follows made this large number possible.

of the trail system. As the tarsiers return to their sleeping site, or at their sleeping site, they give loud vocal calls for three to five minutes that can be heard from 300 to 400 meters (MacKinnon & MacKinnon 1980; Niemitz 1984). From these loud vocal calls, I was able to determine the location of all tarsier groups within the one-hectare plot. The trail system at Tangkoko is cut every 100 meters, and marked every 50 meters, making it relatively simple to distinguish whether the animals are within or outside the hectare plot. I followed all groups that I heard vocalizing to their sleeping site.

I then returned to the sleeping site prior to dusk to count the number of individuals leaving each sleeping tree, as well as record their relative age and sex. I determined age by estimating the relative size of all individuals. I considered individuals that were approximately full size (100 grams or more) to be adults whether or not they had already reproduced. Individuals that were three-quarter-size were considered subadults. Individuals that were still very small, approximately half-size or less, but were no longer being transported orally were considered juveniles. I classified individuals that were still being transported orally as infants.

I determined each individual's sex based on the vocal calls given in the early morning on returning to the sleeping site. All group members, including juveniles, join in the family chorus each morning (Niemitz 1984; pers. observ.). MacKinnon and MacKinnon (1980) observed that the vocal calls of the spectral tarsier are sex specific; males give "a series of squeal barks while the female punctuates the calls at diminishing time intervals with a series of squeaks rising in pitch and end in a trill" (p. 376). Thus, determining the sex of all group members was straightforward.

I repeated this procedure for a total of 25 one-hectare plots. The methods I used to locate tarsier groups are analogous to the standard fixed point count and quadrat census methods for estimating population density (Eisenberg & Struhsaker 1981). Thus, groups were located during the population survey.

Additionally, I recorded the type of sleeping tree (species) the group resided in, as well as the diameter at breast height (dbh) (to the nearest centimeter), and the height (estimated with a clinometer) of the tree. I also classified the type of forest the tarsier group resided in, according to the amount of human disturbance, as almost primary, old secondary growth, or young secondary growth.

Mistnetting

Mistnetting is a standard technique for capturing birds. Numerous published studies have used this method on various species of tarsier with a 0% mortality or injury rate (Fogden 1974; MacKinnon & MacKinnon 1980; Crompton & Andau 1986; Gursky 1998a, 2000a). (There was no mortality or injury to any of the birds, bats, or tarsiers captured in this study.) I set up a total of 3 to 14 mist nets (2.5 × 12 m; 1-1/2-inch mesh, 30–50 denier) near the sleeping site of the group approximately one hour before dusk (Bibby et al., 1992). I mistnetted one sleeping site each night with the goal of capturing as many individuals in the group as possible. I continually monitored all the mist nets for captured tarsiers.

Although capture is relatively straightforward, recapture is more difficult and time-consuming. Out of the sixty-two adult individuals I captured and radio-collared, eight individuals removed their radio collars shortly after they were attached, thereby preventing data collection on these individuals. After completion of the research, my recapture rates for the removal of the radio collar was only 76% (41 out of 54 individuals). Each individual that was not recaptured was observed entering and leaving their sleeping site, but they did not reenter the mist nets. In my attempts to recapture my study animals (to remove the collar as well as to insert a new battery), I changed the positions of the mist nets within the individual's territory, changed the time of day (dawn vs. dusk) that I set out the mist nets, and placed the mist nets at different heights. I also attempted to catch these individuals using butterfly nets as well as by hand. However, my recapture rate remained low. Individuals obviously were aware of the presence of the mist nets (and that I was trying to capture them) and gave alarm calls to warn the other group members.

MacKinnon and MacKinnon (1980) report similar results. Initially, they trapped thirteen individuals with mist nets and applied bird bands for later identification. Despite their repeated efforts, no individuals were ever retrapped. "The tarsiers quickly became used to mist nets, learned to avoid them as well as bounce out of them if caught" (p. 364). Similarly, out of nine tarsier individuals initially trapped, Crompton and Andau (1986) only managed to recapture three: five were not recaptured, one individual was lost (died?), one individual was retrapped with the mist net, and two individuals were recaptured by hand.

Radio Tracking

After I removed each tarsier from the mist net, I attached an SM1 radio collar (manufactured by AVM Instrument Co., Livermore, California) weighing either 3.5 or 6.0 grams to its neck by a simple folding of the thermoplastic band. Silver oxide batteries (Hg 41 + Hg 675) were used. This procedure took less than five minutes and did not require immobilization with drugs. After attaching the radio collar, I released the individuals and then followed them to be certain that the radio collar was not adversely affecting their movements.

The basic operation of radio telemetry, or radio tracking, involves a battery-powered transmitter that is attached to the focal individual. The radio transmitter emits low-powered pulsed signals via a transmitting loop antenna that is located within the collar. These signals are received by another, directionally sensitive handheld Yagi antenna connected to the radio receiver. The directional properties of the receiving Yagi antenna permit identification of the focal individual's location (MacDonald & Amlaner 1980; Brooks 1985). For additional information on radio telemetry equipment please refer to White and Garrott (1987) and Kenward (1987).

In this study, an AVM radio receiver powered by twelve rechargeable C batteries was used. The radio receiver was connected to the three-element Yagi antenna via a coaxial cable. The length of the antenna is determined by the frequency that is being used. The radio receivers and collars were tuned to a frequency of 151 MHz. In this study, the radio collars had pulse durations of approximately 40 ms. This is significant because the length of the battery cell life is extended by decreasing the pulse signal duration, but 40 ms was slightly too low for the objectives of this study. As the batteries became older, the pulse duration slowly decreased. For a radio telemetry study that is utilizing triangulation, and is trying to discern the direction only with the strongest signal, a reduction in pulse duration may not affect the study. But in a study involving homing in on the animal's location, when the pulse signal comes at slower intervals, the individual following the animal must wait for the signal to come through. Unfortunately, the focal animal isn't moving any slower. Thus, pulse interval is a critical factor that needs to be looked into more in studies in which the scientist is not triangulating location, but actually determining the animal's exact location.

Justification for Radio Telemetry

Over the last decade an increasing number of primatologists have begun using radio telemetry to study the behavioral ecology of nocturnal prosimian primates (Bearder & Martin 1979; Crompton & Andau 1986, 1987; Harcourt & Nash 1986; Sterling 1992; Corbin & Schmidt 1995; Wright & Martin 1995). Radio telemetry of these nocturnal and cryptic prosimians has enabled the collection of data that was hitherto difficult or impossible to obtain using standard observation methods. Because the type, quantity, and quality of the data are near impossible to obtain without radio telemetry, it is also difficult to test whether the radio transmitters are affecting the behavior of the study animals. That is, there is no control group from which comparable data on animals without radio transmitters can be obtained. Thus, a critical assumption of all studies employing radio telemetry is that the radio transmitters are having no appreciable negative effects on the study animals and are providing unbiased estimates of the variables being studied (Brander & Cochran 1971; Greenwood & Sargaent 1973).

One obvious way that the radio transmitter package may affect the study animal, and its behavior, is through the additional weight that the study animal must now transport. When dealing with small animals, radio transmitter package weight becomes a critical component. All nocturnal prosimian primates are relatively small, with body weights ranging from 40 grams to 8 kilograms (Fleagle 1988; Sterling 1992; Corbin & Schmid 1995). When dealing with very small radio transmitter packages, slight reductions in weight become very costly in terms of both transmitter life and transmission range (Kenward 1987; White & Garrott 1987), because lighter transmission packages utilize smaller and less powerful batteries. Therefore, it is generally recommended that a transmitter package weight be specified that is not significantly below the study animal's "tolerable weight limit." The tolerable weight limit is defined in the literature as the maximum amount of weight an animal can carry in the form of a radio transmitter with no discernable effects on the animal's behavior, survival, and general well-being (Kenward 1987; White & Garrott 1987). In most mammals and birds, less than 5% of body weight is usually suggested as the tolerable weight limit (Amlaner et al., 1979; Garrott et al., 1985; Kenward 1987; White & Garrott 1987). This percentage was based on studies of birds and mammals in which comparable data from non-radio-transmittered individuals was possible to obtain (Kenward 1987; White & Garrott 1987). I was very careful in all my studies that the radio collars were not greater than 5% of the animal's body weight.

To quantify the effect of the radio collars on the tarsiers, I conducted a small study comparing the behavior of the focal animals that were wearing the lighter versus the heavier radio collars. I found that there was no difference in the activity budgets, mobility patterns (nightly path length, distance traveled per fifteen-minute time interval), prey capture rates, or survival of animals wearing the lighter versus the heavier radio collars (Gursky 1998a). I also found that, upon removal of the radio collars, the tarsiers' body weights had not changed significantly since the time they were first captured and fitted with their collars.

Bird-banding

Beginning in 1994, after each tarsier was removed from the mist net, I attached a colored bird band (manufactured by Avinet) around its ankle. This permitted identification of the individual even after the battery in the radio collar died, and when the individual traveled to a new area, such as after dispersing. It also allowed me to follow the movements of the individual from year to year. In addition, each year that I was in the field (1994, 1999, and 2003) I captured and bird-banded ten groups that were not followed regularly using the radio telemetry, but which were surveyed regularly between 1994 and 2004. This methodology enabled me to obtain the first, albeit preliminary, data on the dispersal patterns and site fidelity of a tarsier species.

Habituation

Habituation involved following the recently trapped animals continuously despite their obvious fear. Fear was expressed in terms of continued alarm calls, as well as family groups getting together and alarm calling, trying to scare me off via group efforts. The animals continually traveled high in canopy during the first week or two of focal follow without coming down. During this time, although I continually followed the changes in the location of their signal, I rarely glimpsed the individual. After one to two weeks, the focal individual began traveling lower to the ground, but still spent some time high in the canopy. Individuals quickly became habituated to my presence, stopped giving alarm calls when they observed me, permitted me to observe them from very close distances, and were not afraid to approach me when changing directions.

DATA COLLECTION METHODS

Over the course of my research, I have collected numerous types of data including: (1) activity time budgets, (2) infant and adult weight, (3) locational information, (4) travel rates and distance (daily path length, distance traveled per unit time, and home range), (5) insect abundance, (6) foraging data, (7) height in canopy, (8) substrate size, (9) locomotor style, (10) tree type used, (11) infant development and care, (12) demographic data, (13) copulation data, (14) parenting, and (15) predation. To obtain these various types of data I used the following data collection methods.

Focal Follows and Locational Data

I conducted focal follows and, using focal animal sampling, recorded the focal individual's behavior at five-minute intervals (Altmann 1974). The following behaviors were recorded: foraging, feeding, resting, traveling, and miscellaneous (i.e., scent mark). The definitions of each behavior are presented in Table 2–4.

During the focal follows, I recorded each individual's spatial position at fifteen-minute intervals using a combination of reflective flagging tape, tape measure, and compass locations. I attached reflective flagging tapes noting the individual, the day, and the time to the substrate the focal individual was utilizing during the scan. The following day, two of my assistants were responsible for locating all flagging tapes from the previous night's focal follows. Using a compass and tape measure to determine the location of each reflective flagging tape relative to the trail system in the reserve, they plotted out the movements of each focal individual. Based on these locational data points, the actual home range size was calculated

Table 2–4 Definitions of the Behavioral States Recognized During This Study

Behavior	Definition
Forage	Actively searching the ground or leaves or air for a moving prey item. This also involves ears twitching while trying to locate prey auditorally, but primarily involves active scanning behavior. Head may not be in normal position, turned from 0 degrees (swiveling on the neck). Also included travel movements while foraging.
Feed	The animal is actively eating a prey item. This includes all handling time of prey such as putting the prey into the mouth.
Rest	The animal is motionless. Its ears and head are not moving. Its head is not rotated from the frontal position. Its eyes may be closed and the animal may be sleeping.
Travel	Actively moving from one support to another via various locomotor styles such as vertically clinging and leaping, quadrupedalism, and climbing. Excludes movements while actively foraging.
Social	Involves scent marking (moving the genital region against a substrate from side to side with the tail in a raised position or urinating), grooming others, vocalizing, and play-grappling (running and jumping and tail pulling).
Nurse	Infant's face is located toward mother's chest in pectoral or urogenital region.
Transport	Infant is located within the mouth or on the body of an individual who is traveling.
Miscellaneous:	Grooming self (scratching with the grooming claw and or tooth comb; may include marking own body with scent glands, cleaning body with tongue or hands like a cat and/or tooth comb).

using minimum convex polygons in which all the locational points were connected (Kenward 1987; White & Garrott 1987). To determine the distance each tarsier individual traveled per unit time, I used fifteen-minute step distances (Whitten, 1982; Altmann & Samuels 1992). Thus, I calculated distance traveled as the straight line distance between successive fifteen-minute locations. I calculated nightly path length as the sum of all fifteen-minute step distances each night.

When conducting focal follows, I also recorded the distance and identification of the nearest individuals. Nearby individuals were located through visual and auditory means, but also through searching for their radio signal when the radio receiver's attenuator was placed on high. If a signal was obtained, the distance between the radio receiver and the individual wearing the radio collar was relatively close: generally less than 10 meters, but occasionally as far as 20 meters. After receiving a signal from a nearby transmitter, I then attempted to visually locate the individual without losing from sight the focal individual. This was possible with the assistance of a field assistant. During observations when the nearby individual was visually located, the distance between the focal individual and the nearest individual was recorded using the following distance classes: physical contact; less than or equal to 1 meter; less than or equal to 3 meters; less than or equal to 5 meters; less than or equal to 10 meters; and greater than 10 meters but less than 20 meters.

In 1994–1995 I conducted focal follows with the aid of flashlights with poor-quality batteries because, unfortunately, bringing a third-generation nightscope out of the United States and into a non-NATO country was too difficult. However, during my observations in 1999 and again in 2003–2004 I used an ITT second-generation nightscope.

Physical Measurements and Condition

After the tarsiers were captured in the mist net, they were placed in a cloth bag and weighed with an Ohaus digital scale ($+/-1$g). Individuals were sexed, their reproductive condition assessed through palpation and visual assessment (pregnant, nonpregnant, descended testes). Using digital calipers, I took the following morphological measurements to the nearest millimeter (Glander et al., 1992): (1) full length; (2) body length; (3) tail length; (4) thigh length; (5) leg length; (6) foot length; (7) big toe length; (8) arm length; (9) forearm length; (10) hand length; (11) thumb length; and (12) ear length. In addition, I recorded each individual's ectoparasite load as either low, medium, or high. Definitions of these measurements are described in Table 2–5. Table 2–6 presents morphological measurements taken on all radio-collared adult spectral tarsiers between 1994 and 2004.

Insect Sampling and Identification

The diet of spectral tarsiers is restricted to insects (Gursky, 1997, 2000c), and so to ensure complete data three methods of insect sampling were used to record resource abundance: (1) malaise traps, (2) pitfall traps, and (3) sweep nets (Janzen 1973; Muirhead-Thomson 1991; Southwood 1992). I chose these particular trapping techniques because spectral tarsiers are known to consume insects from the air (malaise traps and sweep nets), from vegetation (sweep nets), and from the ground (pitfall traps).

On nights when insect sampling was conducted, a local PHPA counterpart (Department of Forestry) and Indonesian local assistant were responsible for sweeping the air and vegetation throughout the territory of each focal group with sweep nets one hundred times (sweeps) each hour from dusk until dawn. I also set up two malaise traps, one with coarse netting and one with fine netting in each group's territory. I also set into the ground, near the malaise traps, five to twenty (depending on the year) pitfall traps within each group's territory.

I placed the catch from each trap in plastic Ziploc freezer bags filled with 95% alcohol. The Ziploc was marked with the date and location of the trap.

Table 2–5 Description of the Morphological Measurements Taken on the Living Spectral Tarsier Individuals

Measurement	Definition
Tail-crown length	is measured from the tip of the tail to the most anterior point on the head with the head in its normal position (i.e., chin near the chest).
Body Length	is the tail-crown length minus the tail length.
Tail Length	is measured on the ventral side of the tail from the tip of the tail to the junction of the base of the tail with the peri-anal region.
Hindlimb Length	is measured from the groin to the end of the longest digit.
Thigh Length	is measured from the groin to the center of the knee.
Leg Length	is measured from the center of the knee to the end of the longest digit.
Big Toe Length	is measured from the junction between the big toe and the second toe, to the end of the big toe, excluding the nail.
Forelimb Length	is measured from the axillary region to the tip of the longest digit, excluding the nail.
Arm Length	is measured from the axillary region to the elbow.
Forearm Length	is measured from the elbow to the tip of the longest digit, excluding the nail.
Thumb Length	is measured from the junction between the first and second digits to the tip of the thumb, excluding the nail.
Testicle Width	is measured from the right bottom to the left bottom of both testicles.
Testicle Length	is measured from the right top testicle to the bottom of the right testicle.
Testicular Volume	is calculated by 4/3 pi (.5L) (.5W)2 where L=Length and W=Width.
Ear Length	is measured from the center of the ear at its base near the skull to its longest point.

I counted the specimens and identified them to Order. Specimens that were very small and not easily handled (i.e., smaller than an ant) were not always measured or counted. I dried all specimens, giving a dry weight, or biomass for the sample period. I estimated monthly insect biomass as the dry weight of all insects captured in the traps in a given month.

Demographic Data Collection

Ten tarsier groups were visited two times each month to determine the total group size and record any changes in group composition, including births, immigrations, and disappearances (deaths/emigrations).

Table 2-6 Morphological Measurements of *T. Spectrum* Captured Between 1994 and 2004

Year	ID	Sex	Body Wt (gram)	Total Length (mm)	Body Length (mm)	Tail Length (mm)	Hindlimb Length (mm)	Thigh Length (mm)	Leg Length (mm)	Foot Length (mm)	Big Toe Length (mm)
1994–1995											
	226	F	110	376	259	117	147	44	51	52	15
	864	F	114	394	276	118	152	48	57	47	18
	571	F	94	340	220	120	155	55	52	48	19
	914	F	104	360	240	120	170	60	55	55	17
	897	F	112	370	245	125	185	65	60	60	20
	876	F	104	340	220	120	169	55	57	57	12
	046	F	112	382	268	114	158	47	55	56	16
	325	M	128	385	270	115	165	55	55	55	14
	588	M	126	405	285	120	166	53	60	53	17
	128	M	120	311	216	95	159	50	54	55	14
	763	M	122	382	252	130	190	65	65	60	15
	988	M	132	343	223	120	170	64	48	58	12
	038	M	92	340	220	120	165	55	60	50	15
1999											
	686	F	106	380	265	115	155	45	55	55	15
	834	F	116	401	290	111	162	51	60	51	20
	103	F	86	305	200	105	146	44	52	50	13
	732	F	108	325	105	220	167	47	60	60	13
	095	F	110	340	105	235	168	55	53	60	16
	008	F	114	367	244	123	180	62	59	59	19

(*Continued*)

Table 2-6 Continued

Year	ID	Sex	Body Wt (gram)	Total Length (mm)	Body Length (mm)	Tail Length (mm)	Hindlimb Length (mm)	Thigh Length (mm)	Leg Length (mm)	Foot Length (mm)	Big Toe Length (mm)
	068	F	113	360	239	121	173	58	57	58	17
	126	F	96	335	225	110	147	49	49	49	14
	627	F	101	342	230	112	152	52	50	50	16
	511	M	136	351	227	124	179	66	55	58	18
	524	M	136	344	222	122	174	61	54	59	19
	543	M	129	330	220	110	165	60	55	50	18
	556	M	132	401	275	126	170	60	60	50	17
	572	M	131	360	240	120	168	55	58	55	16
	580	M	130	385	265	120	174	58	58	58	17
	792	M	132	425	295	130	170	60	60	50	15
	774	M	118	325	215	110	165	54	58	53	14
	306	M	121	330	220	110	165	60	55	50	18
2003–2004	014	F	110	376	259	117	147	44	51	52	15
	066	F	116	401	290	111	162	51	60	51	20
	191	F	101	342	230	112	152	52	50	50	17
	090	F	94	340	220	120	155	55	52	48	19
	231	F	86	305	200	105	146	44	52	50	13
	110	F	114	367	244	123	180	62	59	59	19
	033	F	104	360	240	120	170	60	55	55	17
	026	F	94	340	220	120	155	55	52	48	19
	146	F	121	330	220	110	165	60	55	50	18

Year	ID	Sex		Forelimb Length (mm)	Arm Length (mm)	Forearm Length (mm)	Hand Length (mm)	Thumb Length (mm)	Testes Length (mm)	Testes Width (mm)	Ear Length (mm)
	168	M	128	385	265	120	166	53	60	53	17
	204	M	130	385	260	125	174	58	58	58	17
	050	M	122	380	250	130	190	65	65	60	15
	313	M	132	345	220	125	170	64	48	58	12
	347	M	128	375	265	110	165	55	55	55	14
	394	M	136	344	222	122	174	61	54	59	19
	366	M	129	330	220	110	165	60	55	50	18
	382	M	134	350	240	120	168	55	58	55	16
	403	M	133	360	240	120	168	55	58	55	16
1994	226			79	14	32	33	10			
	864			57	19	38	30	10			
	571			90	25	30	30	10			25
	914			87	23	30	34	12			27
	897										
	876			38	24	32	32	10			27
	046			32	17	35	30	11			
	325			99	25	39	35	11	30	19	30
	588			86	23	31	32	13	32	30	

(Continued)

29

Table 2-6 Continued

Year	ID	Forelimb Length (mm)	Arm Length (mm)	Forearm Length (mm)	Hand Length (mm)	Thumb Length (mm)	Testes Length (mm)	Testes Width (mm)	Ear Length (mm)
	128	92	30	34	28	11	25	20	
	763	81	16	34	31	12	21	24	
	988	91	21	40	30	10	32	29	
	038	63	13	24	26	11	18	16	
1999	686	99	25	38	36	12			35
	834	74	20	30	24	10			23
	103	83	25	30	28	10			
	732	82	25	27	30	10			27
	095	90	25	30	35	11			30
	008	82	25	27	30	10			
	068	88	19	37	32	12			
	126	92	25	35	32	10			
	627	90	28	30	32	10			
	511	89	22	34	33	12	27	30	
	524	86	27	33	26	12	28	26	
	543	98	26	38	34	13	25	24	
	556	90	25	30	35	11	26	28	
	572	91	26	34	31	12	27	29	
	580	87	19	38	30	10	32	27	
	792	79	23	29	27	11	16	18	30
	774	82	26	28	28	11	15	10	
	306	79	24	30	25	11	17	16	25

2003

ID							
014	80	25	30	25	11		
066	82	17	35	30	11		
191	79	14	32	33	10		
090	83	21	30	32	12		
231	90	22	33	31	12		
110	84	19	37	32	12		
033	86	21	31	34	13		
026	87	24	31	32	12		
146	81	20	31	30	10		
168	94	26	34	34	12	32	29
204	93	25	32	36	12	31	27
050	96	23	36	34	11	34	31
313	87	22	37	33	12	28	26
347	86	24	27	25	12	27	26
394	99	25	38	36	12	36	33
366	90	25	30	35	11	30	31
382	90	25	30	25	10	31	33
403	82	27	35	30	11	16	18

Vegetation Analyses

I also conducted a study of the trees within two tarsier group's territories (Brower et al., 1990). These two groups were chosen randomly from all the groups in the study area. Within four 1-hectare plots, I counted all the trees that were at least 1 meter in height and had a 1-centimeter dbh. I identified all the trees to the lowest taxonomic unit possible (to at least the level of Family, 95% to the species level). I also recorded the dbh of each tree to the nearest centimeter.

   Based on the tree counts and the dbh measures, I calculated four indexes to quantitatively describe the tarsier's study habitat (Brower et al., 1990). These are: relative species density, relative species frequency, relative species coverage, and the importance value index. Relative species density (RD_i) is the number of individuals of a given species (n_i) as a proportion of the total number of individuals of all species (N): $RD_i = n_i/N$. Relative frequency (Rf) is the frequency of a given species (f_i) as a proportion of the sum of the frequencies for all species (f): $Rf_i = f_i/f$. Coverage is the proportion of the ground occupied by a vertical projection to the ground from the aerial parts of the plant. The relative coverage (RC_i) for species i is the coverage for that species (C_i) expressed as a proportion of the total coverage (TC) for all species: $RC_i = C_i/TC$. The sum of the above three relative measures for each species is an index called the importance value index (IV_i): $IV_i = RD_i + RF_i + RC_i$ (Brower et al., 1990).

Rainfall and Temperature

During each field season, I recorded daily rainfall to the nearest millimeter using a standard rain gauge. I also recorded the minimum and maximum temperature each day.

Moon Phase

Each night that I observed the tarsiers, I categorized moon phase into one of the following five phases: (1) New Moon occurs when the moon's unil-luminated side is facing the earth, and therefore the moon is not visible; (2) Waxing Crescent and Waning Crescent (herein referred to as Crescent), when the moon appears to be partly, but less than one half, illuminated; (3) First Quarter and Last Quarter (herein referred to as Quarter), when one half of the moon appears to be illuminated; (4) Waxing Gibbous and Waning Gibbous (herein referred to as Gibbous), when the moon appears to be more than one half, but not fully illuminated; and (5) Full, when the moon's illuminated side is facing the earth and the moon appears to be completely illuminated.

Predation Experiments

Infant Predation Experiments. In 1999 and again in 2003–2004, I exposed two infants to three different types of simulated predators for the first eight weeks of the infant's life. There were a total of thirty-six experimental nights, nine for each of the four infants. On twelve nights (three nights for each infant), I placed rubber snakes (*Python reticulatus*) near the focal infant. On twelve additional nights, I placed a plastic model of a bird-of-prey within two meters of the focal infant. I utilized two bird-of-prey models: owls (Ochre-Bellied Boobook, *Ninox ochracea*) and falcons (Spotted Kestrel, *Falco moluccensis*). On twelve additional nights, a square piece of wood (as a control) was placed near the location of the focal infant. When conducting these experiments, the PI remained behind a blind of large *Livistonia* leaves. The predator model was attached to a bamboo stick and was exposed to the focal individual from either the top or the side of the blind. I exposed focal animals to the putative predators or the control every four hours, or approximately three times during the night. The predator or control remained present for twenty minutes and was then rehidden behind the blind. While the predator or wood was in view, I observed the behavior of the focal animal using both instantaneous sampling as well as *ad libitum* sampling (Altmann 1974).

On twelve additional nights, I played back the vocalizations of nocturnal birds of prey (Sulawesi serpent eagle, *Spilornis rufipectus*; spot-tailed goshawk, *Accipiter trinotatus*; Sulawesi owl, *Tyto rosenbergii*; speckled boobook, *Ninox punctulata*) near the location of the focal infant. The vocalizations were initially recorded using a Marantz tape player at a local zoo in Bitung, Sulawesi, that houses endemic birds of prey. This enabled me to record the birds' calls without the background noise of the forest. I played the vocalizations from approximately five meters from either the focal female or focal infant every two minutes for approximately twenty minutes at four-hour intervals throughout the night.

Adult Predator Experiments. In 1999 I conducted three types of predator experiments using adult spectral tarsiers. Each experiment was conducted approximately once per week for a total of sixty nights. In the first set of experiments, I scattered twelve rubber snakes (four red-tailed boa constrictors, four green tree snakes, and four coral snakes) throughout the home range of the nine focal groups. The model snakes were lifelike in both size and color. The locations and positions of the poseable predator models were changed nightly. However, because the tarsiers rarely encountered the scattered snakes, I implemented a modification of this experiment in which rubber snakes were placed near the location of the focal individual, as well as distributed around the home range. I attached a predator model to a bamboo stick and exposed it to the focal individual from either the top or the side of the blind. When conducting these experiments, I remained behind a blind of large *Livistonia* leaves. I exposed the focal animals to the predators every four hours, or approximately three times during the night. I kept the predator in view of the focal animal for twenty minutes after which I withdrew the predator. While the predator was exposed, I observed the behavior of the focal animal using both instantaneous and *ad libitum* sampling (Altmann 1974). *Adlibitum* data was collected to record all occurrences of alarm calls for the twenty minutes the predator was present and the twenty minutes directly following the removal of the predator.

The second set of experiments that I conducted were analogous to the first, except instead of exposing the adult tarsiers to rubber snakes, I exposed them to a plastic model of a bird of prey. I positioned the model within five meters of the focal individual. I utilized two bird-of-prey models: owls (ochre-bellied boobook, *Ninox ochracea*) and falcons (spotted kestrel, *Falco moluccensis*). I utilized the same methods for exposing the adult tarsiers to the bird-of-prey models as I used for exposing them to the rubber snakes.

The third set of experiments that I conducted involved playing back the vocalizations of nocturnal birds of prey (Sulawesi serpent eagle, *Spilornis rufipectus*; spot-tailed goshawk, *Accipiter trinotatus*; Sulawesi owl, *Tyto rosenbergii*; speckled boobook, *Ninox punctulata*) near the location of the focal adult individual. I played the vocalizations from approximately five meters from either the focal adult female or focal adult male every two minutes for approximately twenty minutes at four-hour intervals throughout the night. While the vocalizations were being played, I observed the behavior of the focal animal using both instantaneous sampling as well as *ad libitum* sampling (Altmann 1974). *Ad libitum* data was collected to record all occurrences of alarm calls for the twenty minutes the vocalizations were being played and the twenty minutes directly following the cessation of the vocalizations.

In 2003–2004, 18 spectral tarsier adults (9 males and 9 females) were each exposed to simulated predators. I conducted a total of 66 experiments using wooden monitor lizard models, 73 experiments using wooden Malaysian palm civet models, and 75 experiments using rubber and stuffed python models. Focal animals were exposed to the predator for 20 minutes after which it was concealed behind the blind. While the various predators were in view, I observed the behavior of the focal animal using both instantaneous and *ad libitum* sampling (Altmann 1974).

In addition, I also recorded the mobbing vocalizations of each group using a Marantz tape player (PMD 420) and a unidirectional Sennheiser microphone. To determine how the reproductive status of the female affected the mobbing frequency, the mobbing vocalizations were played back 20 meters from the location of the focal female for ten minutes at six-hour intervals. The mobbing vocalizations of neighboring groups and its own group were played back to all eleven adult females while they were gestating and again when they were lactating. The tape player was concealed behind a large palm leaf (*Livistonia rotundifolia*). While the mobbing vocalizations were being played, I observed the behavior of the focal animal using both instantaneous and *ad libitum* sampling (Altmann 1974).

Ad libitum

During focal follows, I collected additional data continuously, or *ad libitum*. This methodology is particularly important for rare events including: all occurrences of insect pursuits and captures; the type of prey; the size of the prey (cm); foraging style (where the insect was captured or pursued: from a leaf, the air, the ground, or a branch/bark); infant transport, parking, nursing, and playing; grooming; scent marking; copulations; predation attempts; food sharing; infanticide; and territorial disputes.

DATA ANALYSIS

Statistical Autocorrelation between Data Points

Janson (1990) noted that, for capuchin monkeys (*Cebus apella*) behaviors sampled at short time intervals are often autocorrelated, that is, successive data points are correlated with one another. As a result, counting each five-minute sample as independent exaggerates sample size and may bias the statistical tests. Therefore, I performed a chi square contingency table analysis (Statview II and Statistica) to determine whether my data collected were autocorrelated. Successive data points were found to be significantly autocorrelated.

According to Janson (1990) the simplest way to deal with the problem of statistical correlation between data points is to "subsample the observed data at increasing intervals until successive observations are no longer significantly correlated." This method is comparable to that espoused by Sussman et al. (1979). Therefore, I subsampled data points until each grouping was no longer autocorrelated at the .05 level of significance. I began subsampling at the first data point and continued until statistical independence was achieved. Subsampling began with the first five-minute observation and a new data point was taken at fifteen-minute intervals. This was performed for the activity budget data. All the data that are discussed in the following chapters have been subsampled to eliminate statistical autocorrelation.

Additional analyses of the data follow Sokal and Rohlf (1981) and Snedcor and Cochran (1987) and were calculated using Statview II and Statistica. The statistical tests utilized will be discussed in the chapters in which they are presented. This will help ensure greater continuity between the way data were treated and the results of the analysis.

CHAPTER SUMMARY

This chapter was broken down into two main parts. Part one described my fieldsite, Tangkoko Nature Reserve, in detail. This section included how Sualwesi was formed, its climate, and its dominant fauna and flora. In particular I discussed the animals that are competitors and predators of the spectral tarsier. The second part of this chapter represents a detailed description of the methods I used to record my data. Specifically, I reviewed how I trapped the animals in mist nets, radio-collared them, and conducted simultaneous focal follows of adult male–female pairs. I also describe the different types of predator experiments on infants and adults of both sexes; and collection of data on insects, moon phase, and basic morphological measurements.

The Ecological and Social Factors Selecting for Gregariousness

Group Size, Composition, Moon Phase, and Predators

(Photo by the author)

Over the last decade, primary question that I have tried to answer is, "What ecological and social factors select for gregariousness?" To address this question, I have collected data on group size and composition, moon-light, and have conducted experiments using model predators. My goal in this chapter is to present these data and to determine which, if any, of them select for gregariousness.

GROUP SIZE AND COMPOSITION

Throughout my research, I have observed a total of thirty-three groups. Figures 3–1a–c illustrate the range of variation in group size in the spectral tarsiers sampled within a one-square kilometer area of Tangkoko Dua Saudara Nature Reserve between 1994 and 2004. I define group size here as the number of individuals sharing a sleeping site. Notice that group size was highly variable, ranging from two to as many as eight individuals per sleeping site. The mean observed group size was three (SD + 1.44), whereas the modal group size was two individuals.

Group composition varied from two adult individuals of the opposite sex to one adult male and three adult females and their numerous offspring. Table 3–1 presents the range of variation in group composition for spectral tarsiers sampled at Tangkoko Dua Saudara Nature Reserve between 1994

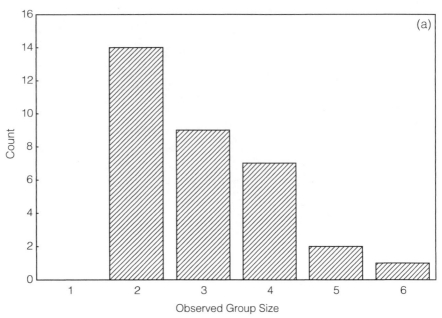

Figure 3–1a The Variation in Group Sizes During 1994–1995 Survey

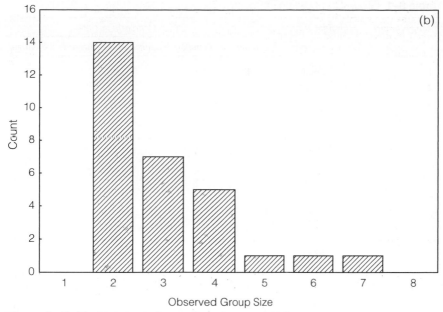

Figure 3–1b The Variation in Group Sizes During 1999 Survey

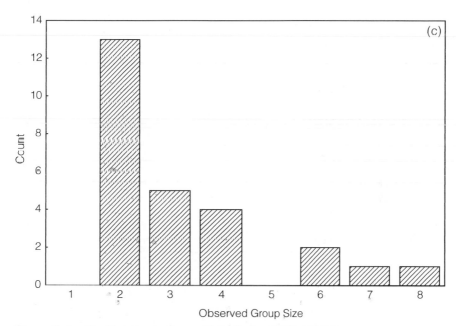

Figure 3–1c The Variation in Group Sizes During 2003–2004 Survey

Table 3–1 Group Composition of Spectral Tarsiersin 1994, 1999, and 2004

Group Number	Group Location	Group Composition 1994				
		Male	Female	Subadult	Juvenile	Infant
1	C600	1	1			
2	E600	1	1			
3	E650	1	1			
4	F600	1	1			
5	J700	1	1			
6	G1000	1	1			
7	G850	1	1			
8	M600	1	1			
9	J800	1	1			
10	L200	1	1			
11	T100	1	1			
12	B400	1	1			
13	S100	1	1			
14	O300	1	1			
15	R900	1	1			1
16	C1000	1	1	1		
17	M200	1	1			1
18	S500	1	1			1
19	P400	1	1			1
20	A200	1	1		1	
21	B300	1	1			1
22	D250	1	1	1		
23	J100	1	1			1
24	H400	1	1	1		1
25	L600	1	1	1	1	
26	M600	1	1		1	1
27	O550	1	1	1		1
28	S400	1	1	1		1
29	T700	1	1	1		1
30	C200	1	2	1	1	
31	L900	1	1		1	1
32	P850	1	2	1	1	1
33	F150	1	1	1	1	1

(*Continued*)

Table 3–1 Continued

Group Number	Group Location	Group Composition 1999				
		Male	Female	Subadult	Juvenile	Infant
1	C600	1	1			
2	P400	1	1			
3	M200	1	1			
4	S100	1	1			
5	T700	1	1			
6	O300	1	1			
7	G200	1	1			
8	T500	1	1			
9	M600	1	1			
10	T100	1	1			
11	S400	1	1			
12	L900	1	1			
13	L750	1	1			
14	S500	1	1			
15	G1000	1	1	1		1
16	A500	1	1			1
17	E600	1	1		1	
18	P850	1	1		1	
19	E650	1	1			1
20	J700	1	1	1		
21	M600	1	1			1
22	J800	1	1	1		1
23	R900	1	1		1	1
24	L200	1	1	1		1
25	C1000	1	1	1	1	
26	M300	1	1		1	1
27	I350	1	1	1	1	1
28	M900	1	2	2	1	
29	D400	1	2	2	1	1

Group Number	Group Location	Group Composition 2004				
		Male	Female	Subadult	Juvenile	Infant
1 C600	1	1				
2 P400	1	1				
3 M200	1	1				
4 S100	1	1				
5 T700	1	1				

(*Continued*)

Table 3–1 Continued

Group Number	Group Location	Group Composition 2004				
		Male	Female	Subadult	Juvenile	Infant
6	O300	1	1			
7	G200	1	1			
8	T500	1	1			
9	M600	1	1			
10	T100	1	1			
11	S400	1	1			
12	L900	1	1			
13	L750	1	1			
14	S500	1	1	1		
15	G1000	1	1			1
16	A500	1	1		1	
17	E600	1	1			1
18	P850	1	1		1	
19	E650	1	1	1		1
20	J700	1	1		1	1
21	M600	1	1	1	1	
22	J800	1	1		1	1
23	R900	1	2	1	1	1
24	L200	1	2		1	2
25	C1000	1	2	2		2
26	M300	1	2	2	1	2

and 2004. Although most groups were comprised of a single adult male and a single adult female, between 6% and 15% of groups contained more than one adult female. Contrary to MacKinnon and MacKinnon's (1980) findings, no groups were observed that contained more than one adult male, although some groups did contain an adult male and a subadult male. Between 1994 and 2004, approximately 23%–30% of groups contained at least one subadult offspring. Similarly, between 21% and 28% of groups contained a juvenile offspring. Approximately 31% to 42% of groups contained an infant. Several groups with more than one adult female also had two young infants, suggesting that there was more than one breeding female per group. This observation also suggests that reproductive suppression, which is observed in many of the small New World monkeys (Tardif et al., 1993), does not play a major role in spectral tarsier reproductive strategies.

What do these data on group size and composition indicate about the mating system of the spectral tarsier? Studies have shown that variability in mating systems is the outcome of adaptive adjustments of males and females to the specifics of their social and ecological environments, as well as to variations in individual capabilities (Clutton-Brock & Harvey 1977; Emlen & Orings 1977; Wrangham 1980; Janson 1988). Mating systems can be classified on many criteria, perhaps the most salient of which are the number of mates an individual takes, either sequentially or concurrently; the duration and exclusivity of the pair bond; and the relative impact of inter- and intrasexual selection in contributing to mating arrangements (Kleiman 1977).

Monogamy is often defined in terms of an adult male and an adult female who mate exclusively with one another for the duration of the breeding season or throughout their lifetime (Kleiman 1977; Wittenberger & Tilson 1980; Barlow 1988; Clutton-Brock 1992). Kleiman (1977) identifies two types of monogamy: facultative and obligate. Facultative monogamy usually occurs when a species exists at such low densities that the home range of a male overlaps only that of a single female. Obligate monogamy occurs when aid from the male is necessary to permit the female to rear her young.

Using either of these definitions, a species is not considered monogamous if one individual is copulating with more than one other individual of the opposite sex. Mating exclusivity is often difficult to discern while in the field. In my research, I defined mating exclusivity in terms of the number of adult individuals of each sex living in the same sleeping site. Using this definition, data on group size and composition suggests that there is considerable variation in the breeding system of the spectral tarsier. Whereas some groups clearly reside in monogamous pairs, a significant percentage of groups contained more than one adult female. Nietsch and Niemitz's (1992) preliminary observations on group size and composition produced similar results. The variation in group size and composition observed in the spectral tarsiers is inconsistent with the traditional interpretation of a strictly monogamous social structure for this species. Instead, facultative monogamy more aptly describes the social structure of this nocturnal primate.

Facultative monogamy may more aptly describe the social structure of *T. bancanus* as well. Niemitz (1984) suggested that *T. bancanus* form male–female bonds, although other researchers (Fogden 1974; Crompton & Andau 1986, 1987) have suggested that this species exhibits a variation on the noyau social system. As the studies mentioned were conducted not only at different field sites, but with different groups, it is possible that this tarsier species exhibits both pair bonds and a noyau social system.

The observation that the spectral tarsier exhibits facultative monogamy and not a strictly monogamous breeding system is also supported by the morphometric data is presented in Chapter 2. Table 2–6 presents the actual morphological measurement for each individual along with their sex and body weight in grams. The arithmetic mean and standard deviation for each adult sex class are presented in Table 3–2 along with the results of a

Table 3-2 Students' t-test of Sex Differences in Numerous Morphological Measurements*

Measurement	Male Mean	Male S.D.	N	Female Mean	Female S.D	N	Mean Difference	T	P
Body Weight	127.38	9.11	24	105.6	9.53	25	21.78	-8.1665	.0000**
Total Length	361.71	28.97	24	355.12	26.59	25	6.59	-0.8299	.4107
Body Length	242.83	24.71	24	230.16	44.79	25	12.67	-1.2192	.2288
Tail Length	118.92	8.16	24	116.9	6.65	25	2.02	-.9218	.3613
Hindlimb Length	170.21	7.47	24	160.72	11.55	25	9.49	-3.398	.0014**
Thigh Length	58.42	4.43	24	52.36	5.97	25	6.06	-4.018	.0002**
Lower Leg Length	56.92	4.13	24	54.70	3.58	25	2.22	-1.9905	.0523*
Foot Length	54.87	4.38	24	53.2	3.54	25	1.67	1.466	.1491
Big Toe Length	16.68	2.44	24	15.96	2.44	25	0.72	-1.131	.2639
Forelimb Length	87.92	7.75	24	85.2	5.44	25	2.72	1.4256	.1605
Arm Length	23.25	4.22	24	21.76	3.21	25	1.49	1.3888	.1716
Forearm Length	32.38	3.50	24	31.28	3.18	25	1.10	1.364	.1788
Hand Length	31.68	4.72	24	30.43	2.93	25	1.25	1.56	.1622
Thumb Length	11.37	0.93	24	10.76	0.92	25	0.61	2.327	.0243*

* An asterisk denotes a statistically significant difference at the .05 level. Using Bonferroni's Correction, P needs to be less than or equal to .003 to achieve statistical significance. Comparisons achieving this level are indicated by two asterisks.

student's t-test for statistical differences between adult males and females (Sokal & Rohlf 1981). These morphometric data indicate that there is dimorphism in body size between males and females, with male spectral tarsiers having significantly larger body sizes than the females. As can be seen from Table 3–2, male spectral tarsiers are statistically larger in body weight than female spectral tarsiers. This pattern of sexual size dimorphism holds for a variety of morphological measurements including hindlimb, thigh, lower leg, and thumb length. The presence of sexual size dimorphism in spectral tarsiers conflicts with previous reports suggesting that there is little to no sexual dimorphism in the Bornean and Philippine tarsiers (Kappeler 1989, 1990, 1991).

There are also some sex differences in limb proportions as calculated by the intermembral index, the humerofemoral index, the brachial index, and the crural index (Jungers 1985; Fleagle 1988). The mean for each of these indices is graphed separately for males and females in Figure 3–2. Specifically, females have slightly larger crural indices, and noticeably larger brachial indices. In contrast, males have slightly larger humerofemoral indices. There was no noticeable difference in the intermembral index of adult males and females. These differences are important to note for

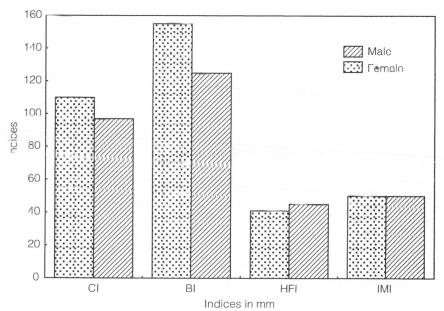

Figure 3–2 The Relative Limb Proportions of Male and Female Spectral Tarsiers Expressed as Mean Indices*

* CI is the crural index, BI is the brachial index, HFI is the humerofemoral index, and IMI is the intermembral index (Jungers 1985).

several reasons. First, limb proportions in living primates are highly correlated with significant differences in positional behavior (Jungers 1985; Fleagle 1999). Thus, these differences might indicate differences in the positional behavior of male and female spectral tarsiers. In particular, the brachial index has been positively associated with an increased amount of animal matter in the diet. It is also possible that the longer radius has evolved in females to provide them with a longer reach so prey can be captured more efficiently (Iwaniuk et al., 1999). Second, as a result of this relationship, limb proportions are often used to reconstruct the locomotor behavior of fossil primates (Plavcan et al., 2002). When identifying species in the fossil record it is necessary to recall that there is intraspecific (sexual) variation in extant species.

Sexual selection theory traditionally has provided the primary explanation for the presence of sexual size dimorphism (Darwin 1871; Trivers 1974; Ralls 1977; Krebs & Davies 1984) although allometric and phylogenetic inertia hypotheses have also been proposed (Leutenegger & Cheverud 1982). Sexual selection theory predicts that males will compete among themselves for access to females, because, in general, they can increase their reproductive success by maximizing the numbers of matings they achieve (Bateman 1948; Trivers 1972). Assuming that physical strength confers an advantage in male–male competition, larger males will be favored by sexual selection, and sexual dimorphism may result. Thus, in monogamous species in which male–male competition for access to females is minimal, sexual dimorphism also will be minimal. It is predicted that sexual dimorphism will be greater in single-male polygynous species and greatest in multi-male groupings (Harcourt et al., 1981; Harvey & Harcourt 1984).

On the basis of the strong relationship between breeding system and sexual size dimorphism that is observed in simians and other mammals (Eisenberg 1981), the presence of sexual size dimorphism in spectral tarsiers suggests that this species is not strictly monogamous and may exhibit either a polygynous or multi-male breeding system.

If spectral tarsiers do not exhibit a monogamous breeding system, but a breeding system with greater male–male competition for access to females (as the presence of dimorphism suggests), then this result has implications for understanding the limited nature of male care in spectral tarsiers discussed in Chapter 6. The lack of a strictly monogamous breeding system may explain, at least in part, the limited nature of male care in this species. Specifically, it may be too risky to expend valuable energy providing paternal care to an offspring that is not guaranteed to carry the male's genes. The synchronous seasonal breeding observed in this species may make it difficult for a male spectral tarsier to simultaneously mate guard all the females in his group, one implication of which is reduced paternity certainty. It is noteworthy that Periera (1991) suggested that mate guarding is possible in

L. catta because of the presence of asynchronous cycling in this seasonal breeder, although this behavior has never been observed (Sussman 1999). This behavioral pattern may exist in spectral tarsiers, but I do not yet have sufficient data to address this topic.

The inability of the group's male to constantly guard the females is demonstrated by the three extra-pair copulations that I have observed during my research. One mating occurred between a focal female and a strange male (i.e., not the group's resident male). He did not have a radio collar so I was unable to discern who he was or which territory he was from. Nonetheless, it was noted that he did not return to the group's sleeping tree. In the two other instances, an unguarded female was observed mating with a radio-collared male from a neighboring group.

It is noteworthy that extra-pair copulations have been observed in numerous species—birds and mammals—that traditionally were thought to be strictly monogamous (Gladstone 1979; Ford 1983; Palombit 1993; Reichard 1995). Monogamous primates in which extra-pair copulations have been observed include gibbons and siamangs (Palombit 1993; Reichard 1995). The presence of extra-pair copulations in the siamang is quite surprising considering that this is the only ape in which extensive direct male care, in the form of infant transport, has been observed. Given that the offspring they are caring for may not be their own, it is unusual that males in this species would provide paternal care. For example, in both tamarins and numerous species of birds, it has been demonstrated that the proportion of care that the male provides to any offspring is based on the frequency that he mated with the female (Goldizen 1987). In other words, males discount the amount of care they provide the young based on the probability that the offspring carries their genes.

The fact that opportunities for extra-pair copulations are available in spectral tarsiers, and do in fact occur, may be one reason why males do not engage in transporting their infants, an energetically expensive activity. That is, time and energy spent transporting an infant that may or may not carry the male's genes could be better spent actively defending the territory against other males who may try to enter mate with the female, or generally patrolling the territory and defending against intruders. This will be discussed more fully in Chapter 4.

In summary, data on group size and composition, as well as morphometric data, indicate that the spectral tarsier exhibits facultative monogamy and is not a strictly monogamous species. The cost to the adult males to provide paternal care to the offspring may be exceptionally high given the nonmonogamous nature of this species' breeding system, the need for males to mate guard females (a difficult task given this species' penchant for seasonal reproduction), and the need to patrol the group's territorial boundaries against other neighboring males.

GREGARIOUSNESS AND GROUP COHESIVENESS

Over the last several decades it has become clear that there is a tremendous amount of variation within the social systems of nocturnal primates. Increasingly, detailed studies have shown that many nocturnal prosimian species reside in groups at their sleeping sites (Martin 1972; Charles-Dominique 1977; Bearder & Martin 1979; Harcourt 1980; MacKinnon & MacKinnon 1980; Clark 1985; Harcourt & Nash 1986; Bearder 1987; Nietsch & Niemitz 1992; Warren 1994). For example, large groups of female galagos have been observed sleeping together in the same nest (Bearder 1987). This pattern has been observed for Demidoff's bush baby (*Galagoides demidof*) and Allen's bush baby (*Galago alleni*) (Charles-Dominique 1977; Bearder 1987). A similar pattern has been observed in the gray mouse lemur (*Microcebus murinus*, Martin 1972) and the slender loris (Nekaris 2003). Milne Edward's sportive lemur (*Lepilemur edwardsi*) has also been reported to sleep in groups, with both males and females present (Warren 1994).

These observations of nocturnal prosimians residing in social groups at their sleeping sites has resulted in a rephrasing or reclassification of nocturnal prosimians as solitary foragers (Harcourt & Nash 1986; Bearder 1987; Janson 1992; Rowe 1996). In other words, although they are gregarious at their sleeping sites (actively interacting), they spend much of their nocturnal activity period foraging alone (Harcourt & Nash 1986; Bearder 1987; Janson 1992; Rowe 1996; Sussman 1999).

However, the classification of all nocturnal prosimians as solitary foragers is dubious given that many of these species have also been observed in pairs or small groups during nightly foraging. For example, during Charles-Dominique's (1977) synecological study of several African nocturnal prosimians, groups of two to five individuals of *Galagoides demidoff* were noted during 25% of his observations (n=263). Mother–infant pairs accounted for only 1% of these observations. Similarly, his observations of *Galago alleni* (n=97) and *Euoticus elegantulus* (n=103) also indicate that these taxa likewise do not remain solitary the entire night, being observed in groups of two or more during 14% and 24% of his nightly observations, respectively. Once again, mother–infant pairs account for only 2% to 4% of these observations. Clark (1985) observed a high frequency of social interactions (e.g., grooming, play, sex, agonism) during nightly forays by *Otolemur crassicaudatus*. She observed 2 to 3 social interactions per hour, or 865 social interactions, during 350 hours of observation. Clark (1985) writes that *Otolemur* were not simply tolerating conspecifics, but were actively seeking affiliative interactions.

A comparable pattern was observed by Sterling and Richard (1995), who noted that among aye-ayes (*Daubentonia madagascarensis*), encounter rates at feeding trees were higher than expected by chance. Similarly, Ganzhorn (cited in Kappeler 1997) found that two to five greater dwarf lemurs (*Cheirogaleus major*) were frequently observed within 10 meters of one another. Warren (1994) observed that among Milne-Edwards Sportive lemur (*Lepilemur edwardsi*), two to five animals regularly travel together at periodic intervals during the night, as well as feed in the same tree without aggression. Together, these observations suggest that these nocturnal prosimians are not completely solitary foragers, that is, they can be gregarious foragers that spend parts of their nightly activity period traveling and foraging together.

Unfortunately, although anecdotal observations of gregarious behavior outside the sleeping site are common, few scientists have explored whether these nightly encounters between group members are merely the result of chance. The lack of quantitative data on patterned social interactions (gregarious behavior) outside the sleeping site results in part from a methodological shortcoming prevalent in many studies. Studies of nocturnal prosimians have often used radio telemetry to record the movements of a single individual during each night (e.g., Bearder & Martin 1979). Further, different individuals are followed on different nights and their individual ranges are recorded. The degree of overlap, or distinctness, of the individual home ranges is then used as one of the major traits for classifying the type of social system exhibited by the species (Type 1–5, Bearder 1987). Given the small size and cryptic nature of many nocturnal prosimians, researchers using these methods are rarely able to observe individuals other than the focal animal, except by *ad libitum* sampling. It is therefore possible that the nonfocal individuals are just not seen or heard by the researcher. Primatologists using these *ad libitum* methods are therefore unable to determine whether or not the association between the group members during the night is a random, chance encounter (Waser 1976; Jolly et al., 1993; Holenweg et al., 1996).

To test whether nocturnal encounters between spectral tarsier group members, outside of the sleeping tree, are the result of chance I utilized Waser's Random Gas Model. According to Waser's model, if group members' movements are random and independent (i.e., solitary foraging), then their territory can be considered a two-dimensional gas of tarsier individuals (Waser 1976; Holenweg et al., 1996; Jolly et al., 1993). Collision (encounter) frequency, Z, or the frequency of approach to within the specified distance, d, is dependent on the mean distance traveled per day (night) in kilometers, v, and home range size in hectares, p, where: $Z = [8 (p) (v) (d)]/3.14$. This model is based on two dimensions, even for arboreal primates that live in a three-dimensional habitat (Waser 1976; Jolly et al., 1993; Holenweg et al., 1996), because the mathematics are not very tractable in three dimensions.

Figure 3–3 illustrates the frequency distribution of distance classes between adults for each simultaneous locational data point. During approximately 28% of the scans outside the sleeping tree, male–female

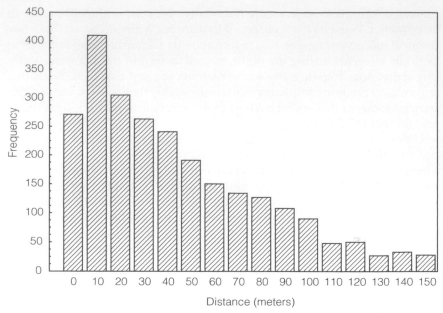

Figure 3–3 The Frequency Distribution of the Observed Distance Between Adults for Each Simultaneous Locational Data Point

pairs were located within distances of less than or equal to 10 meters from one another. During almost 40% of the scans, individuals were less than 20 meters from one another and that includes 11% of the scans during which individuals were in actual physical contact.

The mean number of intragroup encounters per night was 11.3 (SD 5.85), where encounter is defined as distances less than or equal to 10 meters. Nightly encounter frequency ranged from one encounter to more than twenty-four within-group encounters per night. The mean duration of each intragroup encounter was approximately thirteen minutes (SD=18.88). There was substantial variation in the duration of intragroup encounters ranging from less than one minute to more than seventy-three minutes.

There was also considerable variation in encounter frequency according to the hour of the night (Figure 3–4). Most encounters occurred in the early hours of the night as well as during the later hours of the early morning. Encounter frequency ranged from approximately 16% to 25% of all observations according to the month. In June, July, and August there were 113, 124, and 131 encounters, respectively, while in September and October there was a slight increase in encounter frequency to 146 and 167, respectively.

The expected encounter rates (calculated based on the data in Table 3–3), if the male–female pairs' movements were random and independent, (Z), were compared with the observed encounter rates for each interindividual

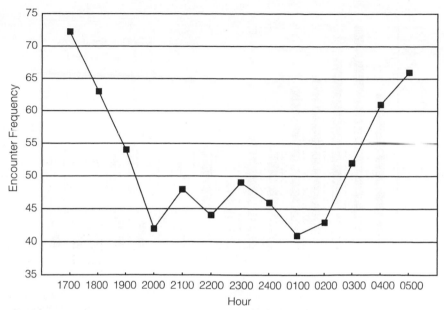

Figure 3–4 The Frequency that Two Adult Spectral Tarsiers Encountered One Another According to the Hour of the Night

Table 3–3 Values Used in Waser's Random Gas Model

	P	V	N
Group	Home Range Size (ha)	Mean NPL (km)	Sample Size
L250	3.16	0.659	40
M300	2.86	0.547	40
M600	3.34	0.747	40

distance class. Figures 3–5a–c presents three examples (Groups: M300, M600, and L250) of the comparisons between the observed and expected encounter rates. I found that at all distance classes less than 50 meters, the tarsiers encountered one another more frequently than expected by chance alone. The increase in encounter frequency is true especially at the closer distance classes. Conversely, at distance classes greater than 100 meters, the tarsiers encountered one another less frequently than expected by chance alone. This pattern held for each individual pair, as well as when all the data were tested overall. These differences are statistically significant for each male–female pair (M600: $X^2=212.8$, p$=$.0001, df$=$15; M300: $X^2=173.1$,

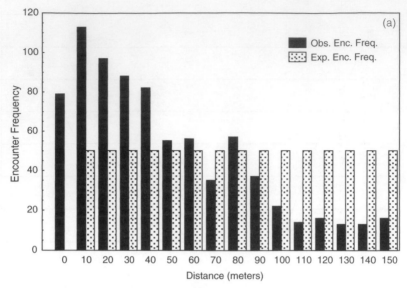

Figure 3–5a The Expected Encounter Rates for Group M300, if the Group Members' Movements Were Random and Independent, Z, Were Compared with the Observed Encounter Rates for Each Inter-individual Distance

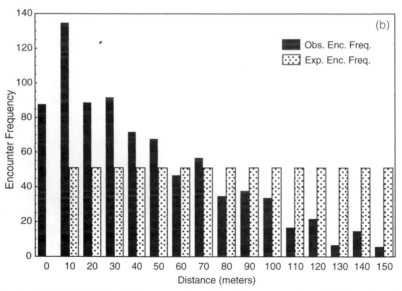

Figure 3–5b The Expected Encounter Rates for Group M600, if the Group Members' Movements Were Random and Independent, Z, Were Compared with the Observed Encounter Rates for Each Inter-individual Distance

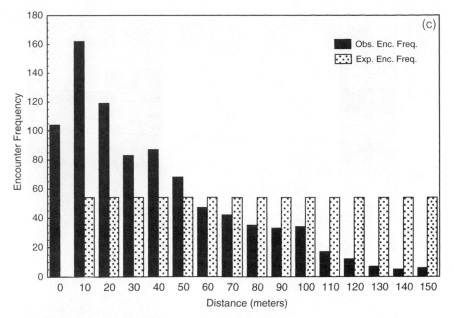

Figure 3–5c The Expected Encounter Rates for Group L250, if the Group Members' Movements Were Random and Independent, Z, Were Compared with the Observed Encounter Rates for Each Inter-individual Distance

p=.0001, df=15; L250: X^2=277.6, p=.0001, df=15) and for the whole data set (X^2=648.18, p=.0001, df=15).

According to Waser's Random Gas Model, the spectral tarsiers spent more scans in proximity to other group members than predicted by chance, given the size of their home range, their nightly travel speed, and their nightly path length. This result, although demonstrating quantitatively that spectral tarsiers are not "solitary" outside of their sleeping site, does not clarify whether they are "solitary foragers."

However, additional analyses do address this issue. First, the tarsiers' activity budget varied substantially with distance from the other adult group member (Figure 3–6). Overall, the spectral tarsiers spent 55% of the scans foraging, 23% traveling, 16% resting, and 6% socializing. However, while at zero meters the tarsiers did not exhibit foraging or traveling, but spent all of their scans resting and socializing. While at a distance of less than of equal to 10 meters, there was a substantial increase in the frequency of foraging scans. Lastly, while at the farther distance classes (50 and 100 meters), there was an increase in the frequency of traveling scans. At the farthest distance classes, there was also an increase in the frequency of socializing scans.

Second, an individual's foraging success varied according to distance from other group members. Throughout my research, I have observed the

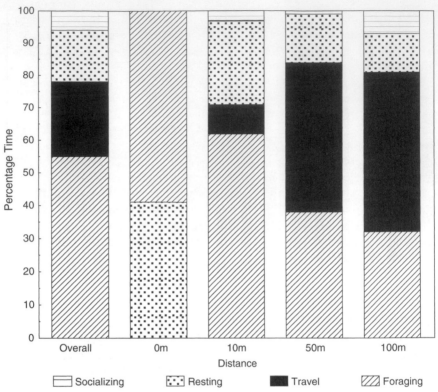

Figure 3–6 The Activity Budget of Spectral Tarsiers Based on Distance from Opposite-sexed Group Member

tarsiers capture and consume a total of 3,528 insects. There was a statistically significant difference in the prey capture rates between males and females (F=2.026; p=.0163; df=53, 479). Adult males captured 1,684 insects during 480 nights for a mean capture rate of 3.51 insects per hour of observation (SD 6.51). Adult females captured 1,844 insects during 480 nights for a mean capture rate of 3.84 insects per hour of observation (SD 7.61).

During approximately 312 and 297 hours, respectively, the male and female spectral tarsiers were foraging solitarily (more than 10 meters from another adult group member). The adult female captured 1,365 insects while the adult male captured 1,229 insects. Thus, the mean insect capture rate while foraging solitarily was 4.59 insects per hour for the female (SD 7.52) and 3.94 insects per hour for the male (SD 8.57). In contrast, during the 168 and 183 hours during which the male and female spectral tarsiers was foraging gregariously (less than 10 meters from another adult group member), the adult female captured 479 insects while the adult male captured 455 insects. Thus, the mean insect capture rate while foraging gregariously was 2.62 insects per hour for the female (SD 6.01) and 2.48 insects per hour for the adult male (SD 7.30). Adult females foraging solitarily had a significantly greater mean insect capture rate than adult females foraging gregariously (F=1.783, df=25, 476, p=.0405). Adult males foraging solitarily also had a statistically greater mean insect capture rate than adult males foraging gregariously (F=1.853, df=23, 476, p=.0313). The statistical decrease in foraging efficiency when foraging nearby another group member may be one reason why these tarsiers increase the proportion of scans allocated to foraging when in proximity to other adults.

This result naturally begs the question, if the tarsiers are experiencing substantial intragroup competition over food resources when foraging in close proximity to another adult, then why do they continue this behavior? Group living is predicted to occur only when the benefits of living in a group outweigh the costs incurred (Krebs & Davies 1984; Dunbar 1988; Kappeler & Ganzhorn 1993). So, if living in a group is costly to tarsiers, then why don't they actively avoid one another while traveling throughout their territory? One possibility is that they are foraging only in proximity when the benefits of being in proximity outweigh the costs of intraspecific food competition (in the form of lower insect capture rates).

One situation in which it might benefit tarsiers to be gregarious is when there is a young infant in the group. Gregariousness might help to minimize infanticide by males as well as to maximize the number of eyes and ears able to detect potential predators. My data provide some preliminary support for this hypothesis. I have found that the mean distance between the adult male and the adult female varied significantly based on female reproductive condition (F=21.586; P=.0001; df=2474). Females that were pregnant or nonreproductive were found at significantly greater distances from the group's adult male than the females that were lactating. The mean distance between adult group members when females were pregnant was 40.31 meter (SD=34.67, n=314). The mean distance between the male–female pair when the female was nonreproductive (cycling) was 41.78 meter (SD=35.86, n=1266). The mean distance between adult group members when females were lactating was 26.34 meter (SD=18.14, n=896). Thus, females were closer to the male when lactating, relative to other reproductive conditions. These results suggest that spectral tarsiers adult pairs are more cohesive when there are young infants in the group than when there are no infants in the group.

This raises the question concerning who is responsible for the change in distance between the male and the female. Observations suggest that the change in distance was not a coordinated effort by the male and female, at least not initially. During the first week or two of lactation, the female resides at a sleeping site of the group, but not at her normal sleeping site. The male then actively tries to enter the female's new sleeping site, emitting a series of vocalizations that state his intentions. The adult male is always chased away, as are all group members, including previous offspring. Thus, the female is actively trying to increase distance between herself and the new baby and the rest of the group. The adult male and other group members are all trying to decrease distance. Part of this may be the group members' initial curiosity about the new infant. However, there is more to this decreased distance than simple curiosity, because the curiosity and decreased distance do not end as soon as the group members become acquainted with the new infant, but continue throughout the infant's entire dependency.

Another situation in which it might benefit tarsiers to be gregarious is when females are sexually receptive. However, it is difficult to untangle this hypothesis from the preceding one (infant in group selects for group cohesiveness) because the months when females are sexually receptive are also the months when infants are nursing. This is the result of the postpartum estrus exhibited by this species.

PREDATORS/PREDATION

Another situation in which it might benefit tarsiers to be gregarious is when they are exposed to predators. Whereas most animals make considerable effort to avoid their predators, numerous species are known for their tendency to approach and confront their predators as a group in certain circumstances. This behavior is known as mobbing and has been observed in fish, birds, mammals, and primates (Owings & Coss 1977; Shields 1984; Bartecki & Heymann 1987; Kobayashi 1987, 1994, 1996; Loughry 1988; Tamura 1989; Heymann 1990; Srivastava 1991). Boesch and Boesch-Achermann (2000) studying chimpanzees in Tai National Park reported seeing a party of chimpanzees mob a leopard. In the chase, the leopard fell into a hole; the chimpanzees stood around the hole, screaming and throwing sticks and debris at the leopard before losing interest and leaving. Similarly, when Siberian chimpunks find snakes, they approach and stay by the snake, exhibiting tail shaking, foot thumping, and similar stress-related behaviors (Kobayashi 1987). Ground squirrels approached snakes very closely (sometimes nose to nose), kick sand, hit them with their paws, pounce, and bite them (Owings & Coss 1977).

Among the types of predators that elicit group mobbing, snakes seem to be the most consistent recipients of this type of predator-directed behavior (Owings & Coss 1977; Curio 1978; Shields 1984; Bartecki & Heymann 1987; Loughry 1988; Tamura 1989; Isbell 1994; Kobayashi 1994, 1996; Gursky 2002a). In several recent studies, snake mobbing has been observed in numerous primate species including hanuman langurs (*Presbytis entellus*), saddle-back tamarins (*Saguinus fuscicollis*), Geoffroy's marmosets (*Callithrix geoffroyi*); white-faced capuchins (*Cebus capucinus*), and *Galago sp.* (Chapman 1986; Bartecki & Heymann 1987; Heymann 1990; Srivastava 1991; Ross 1993; Passamani 1995; Bearder et al., 2002; Gursky 2002b, 2003b).

Throughout my research, I have found that spectral tarsiers mob their predators and that there are individual differences (age, sex, reproductive condition) in mobbing behavior. Between 1994 and 2004, I observed a total of nineteen live snakes being mobbed. The number of tarsiers assembled at a mobbing site for a live snake varied from 3 to 10, the average being 5.1 (SD±1.1). The duration of a mobbing bout (i.e., the time from the first mobbing call to the last one) ranged from 15 to 49 minutes with a mean of 33.7 minutes (SD=11.8). The duration of mobbing bouts toward live snakes increased as the number of assembled mobbers increased (r=0.723; p=0.0000) (Figure 3–7).

Because my sample size of actual mobbing events is so small, I decided to experimentally elicit mobbing behavior. Snakes were presented to a focal tarsier on 90 occasions. Mobbing behavior was exhibited on 40 occasions (9 in 1999 and 31 in 2003). The average number of tarsiers assembled at a mobbing site for the rubber snake was 4.7 (SD±1.4, n=40), with a range from 3 to 9. The difference between this figure and that obtained from natural mobbings was not statistically significant (t=−0.84, P=.41, df=58). The duration of mobbing bouts using the rubber snakes was 35.3 minutes (SD=4.2, n=40) and ranged from 14 to 51 minutes. This did not differ statistically from the natural mobbings (t=−0.65, P=.52, df=58). The duration of mobbing bouts toward rubber snakes also increased with

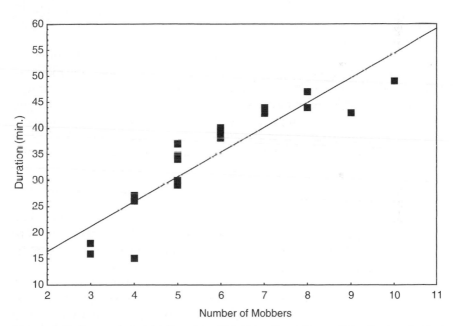

Figure 3–7 Regression of the Duration of Mobbing Bouts Toward Live Snakes Against the Number of Assembled Mobbers

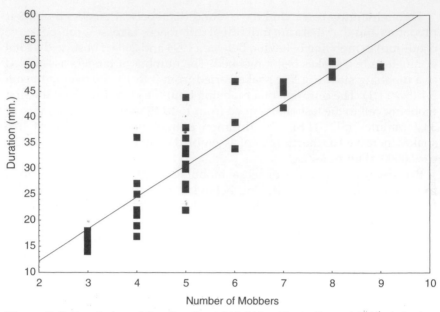

Figure 3–8 Regression of the Duration of Mobbing Bouts Toward Rubber Snakes Against the Number of Assembled Mobbers

the increase in number of assembled mobbers ($r=0.83$; $n=40$; $p=0.0000$) (Figure 3–8).

In fifteen of the nineteen natural (unsolicited) mobbings, the mobbed snake retreated into a tree hole or bush. In nine of these cases, the mobbers left one by one, but in six mobbing events the spectral tarsiers continued to attack even after the snake retreated. This is similar to the results of the artificially elicited mobbing events (19/40) in which the spectral tarsiers continued to attack even after the snake was removed. In twenty-one of the artificially elicited mobbing events, the spectral tarsiers slowly left the mobbing site before the snake was removed.

The variation in whether the snake or tarsier retreated first can be explained in terms of the number of mobbers. The tarsiers were more likely to leave before the snake when there were four or fewer mobbers. However, when there were five or more mobbers, the snake was more likely to retreat before the tarsier. This difference was statistically significant (Median Test $X^2=8.432$, $df=58$, $P=.0379$).

Table 3–4 shows the members of the mobbing groups that occurred either naturally or were obtained experimentally. Approximately two-thirds of all mobbing groups (both natural and experimentally induced) contained only one adult female. The other 30% of the mobbing groups contained two adult females. However, in only two groups (one natural

Table 3-4 Number, Sex, and Relative Age of Mobbers Observed in 59 Mobbing Episodes, Including Naturally Occurring and Experimentally Induced Events

Experiment Type / Group	Number of Individuals at Mobbing Site	Adult Females	Adult Males	Subadult Females	Subadult Males	Juveniles	Infants	From Neighboring Group
Natural								
O350	5	2	2*	0	0	0	1	S350
E650	4	1	1	0	1	1	0	
J700	5	1	1	1	0	1	1	
G850	9	2	4**	0	1	1	1	
G1000	10	2	3**	1	1	1	2	
F600	5	1	1	0	1	1	1	
C600	4	1	1	1	0	1	0	
K350	5	1	1	1	1	1	0	
K50	8	2*	2*	0	2	1	1	M50; F100
F850	7	2	2*	0	1	1	1	F1000
E50	6	1	1	1	0	2	1	
I50	4	1	2	0	0	1	1	
I450	8	2	3	0	1	1	1	
I550	9	1	1	1	0	1	2	
G350	3	1	1	0	1	1	1	
M300	5	1	2	1	1	1	0	
M600	9	2	2	0	1	1	0	
L300	8	1	1	1	0	1	1	
G50	7	1	1	1	1	1	1	
J750	6	2	3	0	2	2	1	

(Continued)

Table 3–4 Continued

Experiment Type	Group	Number of Individuals at Mobbing Site	Adult Females	Adult Males	Subadult Females	Subadult Males	Juveniles	Infants	From Neighboring Group
Experimental									
	G350	5	2	2**	0	1	0	0	
	I600	5	1	1	1	1	1	0	
	I450	7	1	3**	0	1	1	1	
	I50	4	1	1	1	0	0	1	
	M300	5	1	1	1	0	1	1	
	M600	9	2**	3*	1	1	1	1	M900
	L300	3	1	1	0	0	0	1	
	S200	5	1	1	0	1	1	1	
	J750	9	2	3*	1	1	1	1	I750
	I50	8	1	1	0	1	0	1	
	I50	7	1	1	1	1	1	1	
	I50	6	1	1	0	1	1	2	
	I50	5	1	1	1	0	0	1	
	I450	4	2	2	1	0	1	0	
	I450	5	2	2	1	1	1	0	
	I450	9	2	2	0	1	0	1	
	I450	5	2	1	0	1	1	1	
	I450	6	2	1	1	0	1	1	
	I550	6	1	1	0	0	0	1	
	I550	9	1	1	0	0	1	1	
	I550	3	1	1	1	0	1	2	
	G350	5	1	2	0	1	0	1	

G350	4	1	2	1	0	1	0
G350	5	1	2	1	1	1	0
G350	3	1	1	1	1	0	1
G350	7	1	1	0	1	1	1
M300	3	1	1	0	1	1	1
M300	5	1	1	1	0	0	1
M300	4	1	1	0	0	1	1
M300	8	1	1	0	0	1	2
M600	7	2	2	1	0	1	1
M600	6	2	2	0	1	1	1
L300	5	1	1	1	0	1	1
L300	5	1	1	1	1	0	2
L300	5	1	1	1	1	1	1
K50	2	1	1	0	1	1	0
K50	8	1	1	0	0	0	0
K50	7	1	1	1	0	1	1
K50	3	1	1	0	0	1	1
J750	4	2	2	1	0	0	1

* includes individuals from neighboring groups that participated in the mobbing event. These are individuals who were identifiable due to the presence of radio collars or bird bands.

** includes individuals from neighboring groups who participated in the mobbing event but whom were not identifiable.

and one experimental) was a female from another group present. That is, when there was more than one adult female present both females resided in the territory and were not from another group. In contrast, although nearly 40% of all mobbing groups contained more than one adult male, the additional males were always from another territory.

The number of males assembled per mobbing varied from one to four in natural and experimental mobbings. Two or more males were present in 52.6% of natural and 32.5% of experimental mobbing groups. Initiation of the mobbing events was primarily by adult males (60%). Adult females (25%) and subadult males (15%) were responsible for initiating the other mobbing events.

There was a significant difference in mobbing duration between the sexes (Natural: $t=2.878$, $P=.0069$, $df=61$; Experimental: $t=3.37$, $p=.0026$; $df=105$). Adult males mobbed significantly longer than did adult females during both natural and experimental mobbing events. The mean duration for mobbing by females during natural mobbing events was 23 minutes (SD 7.11) compared to 37 minutes (SD 10.26) for males. Similarly, the mean duration for mobbing by females during experimental mobbing events was 22 minutes (SD 8.6) compared to 33.4 minutes (SD 13.5) for males.

For the convenience of description, I divided mobbing behavior into two categories according to their intensity. The first category is intensive mobbing, including close approach, touching, sniffing, and pouncing on the snake. The second category is the mere attending of a mobbing event at a distant point from the snake (about 1 meter or more apart). Table 3–5 shows a comparison of the mobbing intensity among adults and immatures of both sexes observed in the 19 natural and 40 experimental mobbings. In the 19 natural mobbings, 35 adult males were observed, 74% of which mobbed intensively and 26% mobbed passively. Although a similar number of adult females were observed at these natural mobbing events ($n=28$), only 44% of adult females intensively mobbed and 56% mobbed passively. A similar pattern was found during exposure to rubber snakes. At the 40 experimental mobbings, 81% of adult males mobbed intensively whereas 19% of adult males mobbed passively. Fifty-eight percent of adult females at the experimental mobbings mobbed intensely while 42% mobbed passively. Subadult males also tended to actively mob (100% natural vs. 81% artificial), whereas subadult females did not (33% natural vs. 40% artificial). Although juveniles and infants were regularly present at mobbings, they were never observed participating in either natural or artificial mobbings.

In addition to age and sex differences in mobbing behavior, I also observed statistically significant differences in mobbing behavior according to female reproductive state (Wilcoxon matched-pairs test $T=0.0$, $P=.0000$, $N=25$). When mobbing calls of the group were played back near a lactating female, the female usually moved toward the source. Prior to

Table 3–5 Mobbing Intensity in Adult and Immatures of Both Sexes Observed in Natural and Experimental Mobbings

	Number of Intense Mobbings	Number of Passive Mobbings
Natural		
Adult Male*	26	9
Adult Female*	12	16
Subadult Male	15	0
Subadult Female	3	6
Juvenile	0	2
Infant	0	17
Experimental		
Adult Male*	45	11
Adult Female*	30	21
Subadult Male	17	4
Subadult Female	8	13
Juvenile	0	26
Infant	0	36

* Mobbing intensity was characterized as intense or passive (see text). The number of adult males and adult females includes individuals from neighboring groups who joined in to mob the snake.

beginning the playbacks, the lactating female was 20 meter from the tape player. Following the playbacks of the mobbing calls, lactating females averaged only 2 meter (SD 1) from the tape player. In contrast, when mobbing calls of the group was played back near a heavily gestating female (fifth and sixth month of pregnancy), the female usually moved away from the vocal playbacks. Prior to the playbacks the gestating female was approximately 20 meter from the tape player. Following the playbacks of the mobbing calls, the gestating female averaged 32 meter (SD 8.8) from the tape player.

This research clearly indicates that mobbing behavior in spectral tarsiers varies according to an individual's age, sex, and reproductive state. Adult spectral tarsiers were more likely to mob snakes than were subadults or juveniles. Similarly, males were more likely to initiate mobbing events and to mob snakes for longer periods of time than were females. The total mobbing time increased with the number of mobbers. The majority of mobbing groups also contained numerous adult males. Given that all spectral tarsier groups contain only one adult male, this implies that adult males from other groups also participated in the mobbing events. In a few cases, some of the additional males were radio-collared and/or bird-banded, allowing me to determine the group to which they belonged. They were usually from neighboring groups, although once a male from three territories over was observed at a mobbing event. Unfortunately, a lack of genetic data prevents me from knowing the relationship between individuals at these mobbing events. In contrast, the majority of females attended only mobbings that occurred within their home range and rarely trespassed onto a neighbor's home range to mob. This pattern of sex differences in mobbing is not unique to spectral tarsiers, but has also been observed in numerous other animals. For example, in the great tit, males mob more intensely than females (Regelmann & Curio 1986). Similarly, in black-tailed prairie dogs, living in coteries containing several female kin defended by one dominant male, males spent more time driving away snakes than did females (Loughry 1988).

Using playbacks of mobbing calls, I found that the reproductive state of females significantly affected whether they moved toward or away from the site of mobbing. Gestating females seldom congregated to mob whereas females that were rearing young—specifically, lactating females—mobbed frequently. Once again, this pattern has been observed in numerous other species. For example, in prairie dogs, lactating females attack snakes more intensely than do nonbreeding females (Loughry 1988).

INFANTS AND PREDATORS

In addition to exploring how adult spectral tarsiers modify their behavior in response to potential predators, I have also explored how infant spectral tarsiers behave in the presence of potential predators. As noted earlier, most nocturnal prosimians, including spectral tarsiers, do not continually transport their infants on their bodies throughout the night, but instead park them and leave them alone for long periods (Charles-Dominique 1977; Klopfer & Boskoff 1979; Bearder 1987). This strategy of infant parking (which varies tremendously in how it is expressed) is believed to increase an infant's susceptibility to predation while waiting for its mother to return (Klopfer & Boskoff 1979; Morland 1990; Gursky 1997; Nekaris 2003). When an infant is parked alone, it must first recognize the predator as a predator, and then it must respond appropriately (call mother, move out of range of the predator) to avoid being preyed upon. In contrast, when a primate mother transports her infant on her body and spots a predator, she can immediately carry herself and her infant to safety (Clutton-Brock 1992).

The most obvious result from this experimental study was that infants moved from their parked location following exposure to potential predators. The mean distance infants moved from their parked location on nights when they were not exposed to any potential predators (control nights) was only 0.25 meter. However, as might be expected, the distance infants moved from their parked location varied significantly according to infant age (F=132.53; p=0.0001; df=574). In particular, infants moved more during their second month (x=0.37; SD=0.17) than during their first month (x=0.12; SD=0.08). Thus, all additional analyses of infant movement from their parked location were broken down into month one and month two.

The mean distance infants moved from their parked location when exposed to a model predator or model vocalization during month one was approximately 0.57 meter (SD=0.69), and during month two was 2.08 meter (SD=1.59). These values are statistically different than the distance infants moved from their parked locations on nights when no potential predator was presented to them (F=41.07; p=0.0001; df=574).

Breaking down this movement according to the type of potential predator, as well as infant age, illustrates that the infants responded very strongly to the snake models, followed by the vocalizations of birds of prey, and lastly the bird-of-prey models (Table 3–6). The distance one-month-old infants moved in response to the snake models and birds-of-prey vocalizations was substantially greater than the distances moved by the same-aged infants when there were no potential predators evident (Table 3–7). In contrast, one-month-old infants moved slightly less, but not significantly, from their parked location on nights when they were exposed to a bird-of-prey model.

The distances two-month-old infants moved in response to the snake models and birds-of-prey vocalizations was significantly greater than the distance moved by these infants when there were no predators (Table 3–7). In contrast, two-month-old infants moved significantly less from their parked location on nights when they were exposed to a bird of prey model.

Following all predator experiments, when an infant left the location where it was parked, it was never observed to return to the original location. However, if an infant left its parked location so it could explore its environment (not because of a potential predator), it was then observed returning to its original parked location. The infant's movements away from its parked

Table 3–6 Mean Distance (m) the Infants (n=4) Moved from the Parked Location Following Presentation of the Possible Predator

Experiment	Mean Distance 1-month-old Infants Moved (m)	SD	Mean Distance 2-month-old Infants Moved (m)	SD	Total Number of Nights
Snake	0.93	0.84	3.617	0.62	12
Birds of Prey	0.06	0.09	0.03	0.06	12
Vocalization	0.72	0.56	2.54	0.64	12
Control	0.12	0.08	0.37	0.17	12

Table 3–7 F-Statistics Comparing the Distance Infants Moved Following Exposure to Three Different Predator Types Relative to Nights Without Predator Exposure

Predator Type	Infant Age					
	1-month-infant			2-month-infant		
	F	P	df	F	P	df
Snake	89.29	0.0001	1,135	173.87	0.0001	1,574
Bird of Prey	2.60	0.1163	1,60	43.09	0.0001	1,574
Vocalization	109.72	0.0001	1,120	127.41	0.0001	1,574

site were always in directions that increased the distance to the potential predator and never decreased the distance to the predator. Often, the infant moved closer to its mom, but not always as the infant's movements were dependent on the location of branches that the infant could traverse.

In addition to moving away from their parked location on encountering a predator, spectral tarsier infants also repeatedly gave a series of alarm calls in response to the predator models. Infants emitted an alarm call in response to all presentations of the model predators, regardless of their age. However, the type of alarm call they emitted varied depending on the type of potential predator. The infants consistently emitted a twittering alarm call in response to both the bird-of-prey models and vocalizations, whereas they emitted a harsh loud call three times in rapid succession in response to the model snakes. Even when the infants were less than one-week old, they emitted these specific types of alarm calls in response to each potential predator type. Given that such young infants were capable of making the distinction between a snake and a bird of prey may suggest that the alarm calls are not predator-specific. Instead, following Hauser (1993), it is possible that these acoustic differences represent the infant's assessment of individual risk from a particular predator's attack. Twittering may be given in response to low-risk predator events whereas harsh loud calls are given to high-risk predator attempts. This behavioral pattern has been noted in ground squirrels (Owings & Hennessy 1984) and also suggested for vervet monkeys by Hauser (1993).

When not exposed to a potential predator, the mean number of alarm calls given, per 40-minute time interval, by one-month-old infants was 13.2 (SD=3.38). Similarly, the mean number of alarm calls given by two-month-old infants, on nights when not exposed to a potential predator, was 14.1 (SD=2.03). There was no statistically significant difference in the mean number of alarm calls infants gave during nights when birds-of-prey vocalizations were played back near the focal infant (F=0.77; p=0.3875; df=1,120) nor when they were presented with a bird-of-prey model (F=2.57; p=0.1163; df=1,120). In contrast, infants increased tremendously

Table 3–8 The Mean Number of Alarm Calls that Infants Produced During the 20-Minutes of Exposure to a Potential Predator and the 20-Minutes After the Predator Is Removed

Experiment	Mean # Alarm Calls per 40-min Interval by 1-month-old Infants	SD	Mean # Alarm Calls per 40-min Interval by 2-month-old Infants	SD	Total Number of Nights
Snake	21.00	2.74	25.33	2.00	12
Birds of Prey	17.89	3.76	13.00	1.73	12
Vocalization	13.44	1.33	15.33	2.50	12
Control	13.20	3.38	14.1	2.03	12

the mean number of alarm calls they emitted when exposed to the rubber snake models (Table 3–8) ($F=90.70$; $p=0.0001$; $df=1,135$).

The alarm calls given by the two infants were not only in response to the potential predators, infants occasionally responded to nonthreatening aspects of their environment, including rats, couscous, falling leaves, the control wooden blocks, and odd-shaped branches. Over the course of the study, the infants emitted inappropriate alarm calls fifty-four times. Breaking down the inappropriate alarm calls (for both infants) according to infant age, I found that they were all made within the first four weeks of life, with the majority of them during the infant's first two weeks (Figure 3–9).

There are two possible interpretations for the "inappropriate" alarm calls made by spectral tarsier infants. Seyfarth and Cheney (1990) argue that infants make classification mistakes when producing alarm calls to inappropriate objects. Hauser (1993) argues that, instead of making mistakes, infants use alarm calls to ask questions about the things they encounter in their environment. Supporting the latter interpretation is the observation that mothers often follow with the same type of alarm call, especially when a potential predator may be present. In contrast, when an infant makes an inappropriate alarm call, it is much rarer for the mother to respond with an alarm call.

MOTHER'S RESPONSE

When mothers with very young infants were exposed to potential predators, their response depended on the type of potential predator. The mother's response generally involved two behavioral components: alarm calling and traveling to or away from the infant or predator. Newly parturient mothers always produced alarm calls in response to the model predators. However, the type of alarm call varied depending on the predator. Like

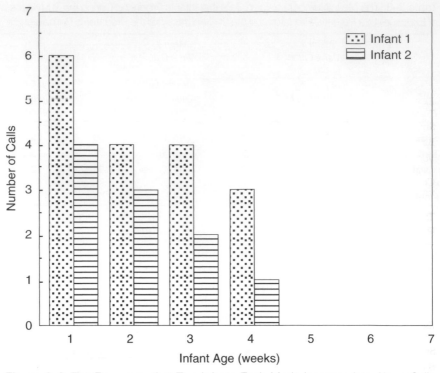

Figure 3–9 The Frequency that Two Infants Each Made Inappropriate Alarm Calls, Broken Down Based on Infant Age

the infants, newly parturient mothers consistently emitted a twittering call in response to the bird of prey whereas they emitted a harsh loud call three times in rapid succession in response to the snake.

The mean number of alarm calls emitted by mothers (per 40-minute time interval) on nights when they were exposed to potential predators and nights when they were not exposed to potential predators was statistically different (F=5.36; p=0.0001; df=1,48) (Table 3–9). When large rubber snakes were placed near the mother, the mother's response always involved giving a series of alarm calls. The number of alarm calls that recent mothers gave on nights when they were exposed to snakes was nearly three times greater than the mean number of alarm calls given (per 40-minute time interval) on nights when no predators were presented (F=28.02; p=0.0001; df=1,12). On two nights, the mother's alarm calls escalated to mobbing behavior. Mobbing involved lunging and retreating at the snake. The mean number of alarm calls (per 40-minute time interval) that new mothers gave on nights when they were exposed to birds-of-prey was significantly greater than the mean number of alarm calls (per 40-minute time interval) given on nights when no predators were presented (F=23.24; p=0.0001; df=1,12). In contrast, the mean

Table 3–9 The Mean Number of Alarm Calls Per 40-Minutes Interval that New Mothers Emitted on Nights when They Were Exposed to Potential Predator Models of Vocalizations

Experiment	Mean # Alarm Calls per 40-min Interval	SD	Number of Nights
Snake	8.74	2.57	12
Birds of Prey	6.19	1.24	12
Vocalization	4.03	1.31	12
Control	3.21	1.85	12

Table 3–10 Mean Distance Between Mothers and Parked Infants Following Presentation of the Possible Predator

Experiment	Mean Distance (m) Btwn Mom and 1-month-old Infants	SD	Mean Distance (m) Btwn Mom and 2-month-old Infants	SD	Total Number of Nights
Snake	0.36	0.55	0.64	0.87	12
Birds of Prey	4.53	2.60	7.47	1.94	12
Vocalization	7.03	2.62	7.74	1.44	12
All Predators	3.97	3.49	5.20	3.63	36
Control	2.98	2.12	5.03	1.95	12

number of alarm calls (per 40-minute time interval) that new mothers gave on nights when they were exposed to birds-of-prey vocalizations was no different than the mean number of alarm calls (per 40-minute time interval) given on nights when no predators were presented ($F=1.69$; $p=0.2012$; $df=1,12$).

The mean nightly distance between mothers and infants is known to vary according to infant age (Table 3–10). When no predators were displayed, the mean distance between mothers and their parked one-month-old infants was 2.98 meter (SD=2.12) and the mean distance between mothers and their two-month-old infants was 5.03 meter (SD=1.95). In comparison, when any type of predator model or vocalization was presented, the mean distance between mothers and their one-month-old infants was 3.97 meter (SD=3.49) and 5.20 meter (SD=3.63) for their two-month-old infants. These values are statistically significant for one month ($F=4.81$; $p=0.0291$; $df=1,287$), but not for two months ($F=0.14$; $p=0.7048$; $df=1, 287$).

Breaking this down according to the type of predator experiment conducted yields some interesting findings. Overall, the mean distance between moms and infants when the mom was exposed to a rubber snake was 0.50 meter (SD=0.74). When infants were one month old the mean distance was only 0.36 meter (SD=0.55) compared to when infants were two months old and the mean distance was 0.64 meter (SD=0.87). When large plastic models of birds of prey were placed near the mother, mothers did not move toward their infant. Instead, they moved farther away from the infant or remained in their present location. The mean nightly distance between mothers and infants on nights plastic birds of prey were distributed throughout the group's territory was 6.0 meter (SD=2.72). The mean distance between mothers and infants varied with infant age, with one-month-old infants parked approximately 4.53 meter (SD=2.60) from their mother's foraging location and two-month-old infants parked approximately 7.47 meter (SD=1.94) from their mother's foraging location.

The mother's response to the playback vocalizations of large nocturnal birds of prey also involved moving farther away from the infant or remaining in her present location. The mean distance between mothers and infants on nights when the birds-of-prey vocalizations were played was 7.25 meter (SD=4.69). The mean distance between mothers and infants varied with infant age, with one-month-old infants parked approximately 7.03 meter (SD=2.621) from the mother's foraging location and two-month-old infants parked approximately 7.74 meter (SD=1.44) from the mother's foraging location.

The fact that the spectral tarsier mothers behave so differently (moving closer vs. farther away) in response to two different predators is interesting and deserving of a short discussion. In regards to the mother moving closer to the infant following exposure to the rubber snake, it could be hypothesized that the mother returned to the infant to protect it from the snake and help it evade the snake predator. By returning to the infant, the mother might be distracting the snake from the infant and increasing her own risk of predation. In regards to the bird-of-prey models, the data indicate that mothers move farther away from the infant on exposure to a bird of prey or remain where they are. Several explanations for this behavioral pattern come to mind. First, by moving farther away from the bird of prey, the mother might be decreasing her own risk of predation. This hypothesis could also account for the lack of movement regularly exhibited by mothers following exposure to a bird of prey.

Birds of prey and snakes are known to hunt differently from one another even though, to some extent, they are both sit-and-wait predators that ambush their prey (Pavey & Smith 1998). However, a bird of prey can ambush a tarsier at a shorter distance (due to their more rapid speed) than can a snake. Thus, tarsiers might realize the greater risk of threat by nearby birds than by snakes. Also, birds of prey hunt by sensing movement; moving away from the infant might be a parental strategy to distract the bird of prey from the infant. In contrast, snakes do not hunt by detecting motion as much as by sensing body heat and smell. Thus, it is imperative that parked infants be moved away from snakes and not encouraged to move on. The parents' strategy of moving farther from the infant might be the equivalent of the "broken wing display" exhibited in several bird species to chase predators away from their infants' nests.

In addition to giving alarm calls when exposed to predators, mothers also were known to respond to their infants' alarm call. On nights when infants were exposed to model predators, and produced an alarm call, mothers often responded with their own alarm calls (Figure 3–10). In contrast, when an infant emitted alarm calls for inappropriate objects, the mother was less likely to emit a responding alarm call.

Clearly, additional research is needed to further tease apart how spectral tarsier infants identify and categorize different predators, as well as how mothers modify their parental care in response to potential predators. One avenue that needs to be explored is the role of nonmaternal family members in warning parked infants of nearby potential predators. Given previous studies that have shown that nonmaternal group members often remain near parked infants, their presence may confound the results (Gursky 2000b). Another avenue for future research involves quantifying the acoustic characteristics of the two alarm calls given by the spectral tarsier infants and mothers.

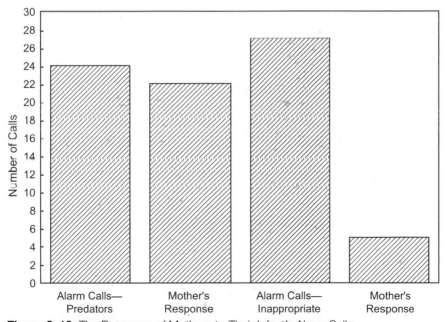

Figure 3–10 The Response of Mothers to Their Infant's Alarm Calls

MOONLIGHT

An ecological variable that is often ignored by primatologists, but can severely affect a species' predation risk, is moonlight. The influence of moonlight on behavior has been well documented for many nocturnal mammals including rodents, lagomorphs, badgers, and bats (Jahoda 1973; Lockard & Owings 1974; Morrison 1978; Butynski 1984; Kotler 1984; Price et al., 1984; Bowers 1988, 1990; Cresswell & Harris 1988; Wolfe & Summerlin 1989; Gilbert & Boutin 1991). The results of these studies have consistently shown that nocturnal mammals respond to bright moonlight by reducing their use of open space, restricting their foraging activity, restricting their movement, reducing their vocalizations, reducing the duration of the activity period, or by switching their activity to darker periods of the night. For example, the old field mouse and the snowshoe hare are both reported to decrease the amount of time they spend in open areas during full moonlight (Wolfe & Summerlin 1989; Gilbert & Boutin 1991). Similarly, Allenby's gerbil, the greater Egyptian sand gerbil, and Merriam's kangaroo rat all have been observed decreasing their total activity during full moons (Daly et al., 1992; Kotler et al., 1993). Exceptions to this lunar phobic behavioral response are known to occur among less than a handful of bat and bird species, but do not involve lunar philia as much as lunar neutrality (Brigham & Barclay 1992; Negraeff & Brigham 1995).

It might be assumed that nocturnal primates, as mammals, would also be lunar phobic. However, the majority of studies of the effect of moonlight on the behavior of nocturnal primates have shown that nocturnal primates are lunar philic. For example, the night monkey, *Aotus trivirgatus*, increased its activity levels during the full moon (Erkert 1976, 1989; Wright 1981, 1985, 1989, 1997; Erkert & Grober 1986). The increase in activity levels during bright moonlight also occurred during artificial stimulation in captivity (Erkert 1974, 1976; Erkert & Grober 1986). Similarly, Nash (1986) reports that both *Otolemur crassicaudatus* and *Galago zanzibaricus* travel substantially more during full moons compared to nights when moonlight is less available. *G. zanzibaricus* also vocalizes more during moonlight nights compared to moonless nights.

In a recent comparison, Bearder et al. (2002) found similar behavioral responses to moonlight exhibited by two additional primates, *Galago moholi* and the Mysore slender loris (*Loris tardigradus*). They noted that slender lorises call more frequently when there is more moonlight (full moon) compared to moonless nights (new moon). Bearder et al. (2002) noted that slender lorises increased foraging and travel during the full moon and decreased their behavior during the new moon.

Bearder et al. (2002) noted that South African *G. moholi* traveled more during moonlight. Interestingly, they only observed this pattern for adult males and not subadults or females. *Lepilemur mustelinus* has been observed to call more frequently during nights with bright moon relative to nights with little or no moon (Hladik & Charles-Dominique 1976).

A similar behavioral pattern has also been observed in a cathemeral prosimian primate. Colquhoun (1998) has shown that when *Eulemur macaco* is nocturnal, they increase their activity during full moons relative to other moon phases. Specifically, black lemurs increased their calling, as well as increased the frequency of group progressions during full moons relative to nights with little or no moon.

I explored whether the spectral tarsier, *T. spectrum*, exhibits the lunar phobic behavioral response observed in almost all other nocturnal mammals and a few nocturnal primates (slow loris, *Nycticebus coucang*; mouse lemur, *Microcebus murinus* (Trent et al., 1977; Erkert 1989)), or whether they are lunar philic, increasing their activity levels during moonlight (Gursky 2003a).

The amount of time adult males and females spent foraging varied significantly according to moon phase. Males and females both increased the amount of time they allocated to foraging during full, gibbous, and quarter moons while decreasing the time they spent foraging during the other moon phases (F=68.348, P=.0001, df=4, 298, females; F=106.589, P=.0001, df=4,298 males (Figure 3–11). In contrast to the increase in time spent foraging, spectral tarsiers decreased the amount of time they spent resting during full moons relative to new crescent, quarter, and gibbous

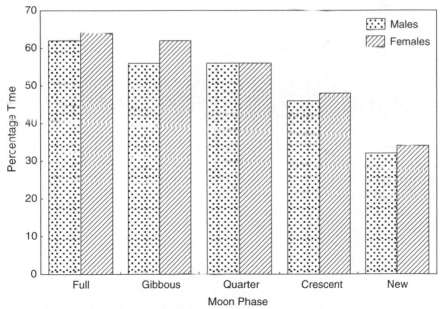

Figure 3–11 The Amount of Time Male and Female Spectral Tarsiers Spent Foraging, Broken Down According to Moon Phase

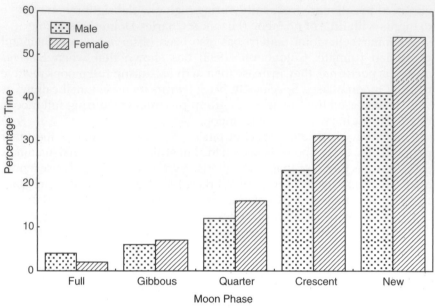

Figure 3–12 The Amount of Time Male and Female Spectral Tarsiers Spent Resting, Broken Down According to Moon Phase

moons (F=269.546, P=.0001, df=4,298 females; F=296.626, P=.0001, df=4,133 males) (Figure 3–12).

The ranging behavior of both the adult male and adult female spectral tarsiers also varied significantly according to moon phase. Overall, the mean distance traveled per 15-minute interval was 29.2 meter and 26.6 meter for males and females, respectively. During full moons, the mean distance traveled per 15-minute interval by male and female spectral tarsiers was substantially greater than the mean distance traveled per 15-minute interval during other moon phases (Figure 3–13) (F=13.555, P =.0001, df=137 males; F=18.123, P=.0001, df=303 females).

The mean nightly path length for spectral tarsiers was 790.6 meter for males and 447.7 meter for females. During full moons, the mean nightly path length was substantially greater than the mean nightly path length used by males and females during other moon phases (Figure 3–14) (F=17.928, P=.0001, df=137 males; F=17.538, P=.0001, df=303 females).

Overall, the average home range size (ha) for males and females throughout this study was 2.32 hectares for females and 3.07 hectares for males. During full moons, the home range used by male and female spectral tarsiers was substantially greater than that used during other moon phases (F=29.318, P=.0001, df=137 males; F=43.762, P=.0001, df=304 females) (Figure 3–15).

The frequency that spectral tarsiers gave loud calls also varied signifi-cantly according to moon phase (F=84.605, P=.0001, df=959). A total

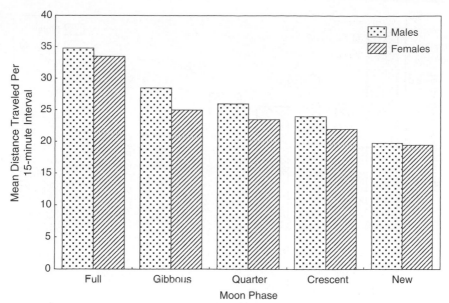

Figure 3–13 The Mean Distance (m) Male and Female Spectral Tarsiers Traveled Per 15-Minutes Interval, Broken Down According to Moon Phase

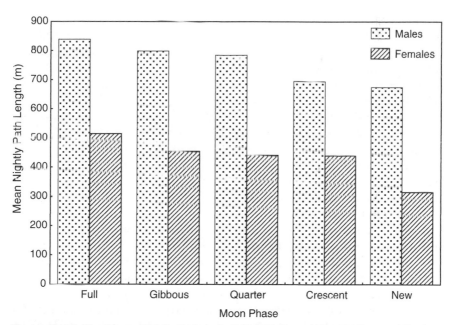

Figure 3–14 The Mean Nightly Path Length (m) Male and Female Spectral Tarsiers Traveled, Broken Down According to Moon Phase

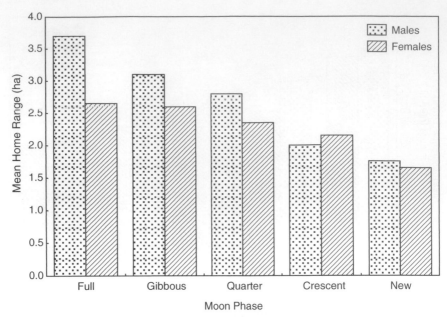

Figure 3–15 The Mean Home Range Size (ha) Male and Female Spectral Tarsiers Traversed, Broken Down According to Moon Phase

number of 621 loud calls were made by spectral tarsiers over a period of 960 nights. During this study, the mean number of loud calls made was 0.65 loud calls per night (±0.06). During nights when there was a full moon, the mean number of loud calls made per night was 2.32. This is substantially greater than the mean number of loud calls given during other moon phases (Figure 3–16).

Not only did vocal communication vary according to moon phase, but olfactory communication was also affected by moon phase (F=6.639, P=.0001, df=441). A total number of 448 scent marks were made by spectral tarsiers during scan samples (excludes *ad libitum* data) over a period of 960 nights. During this study, the mean number of scent marks made was 0.69 per night. During nights when there was a full moon, the mean number of scent-marking episodes per night of observation was 0.32 (±0.48). This is substantially less than the mean number of scent-marking episodes during other moon phases (Figure 3–17). Given the increase in the amount of light during full moons, it is not surprising that spectral tarsiers decrease their reliance on their olfactory senses and increase their reliance on the visual senses during this lunar phase.

A total number of 531 territorial disputes were observed throughout this study. The mean number of territorial disputes was 0.55 disputes per night. The frequency of territorial disputes varied significantly according to

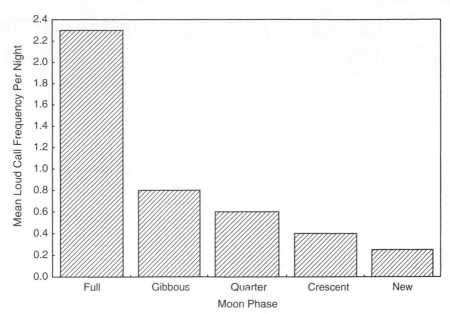

Figure 3–16 The Mean Frequency that Male and Female Spectral Tarsiers Gave Loud Calls, Broken Down According to Moon Phase

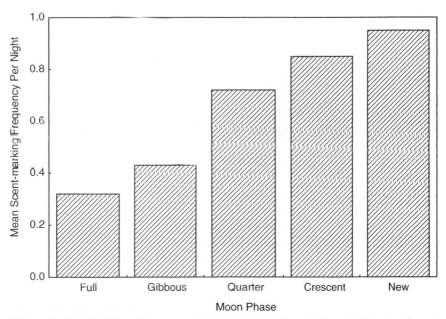

Figure 3–17 The Mean Frequency that Male and Female Spectral Tarsiers Scent-marked, Broken Down According to Moon Phase

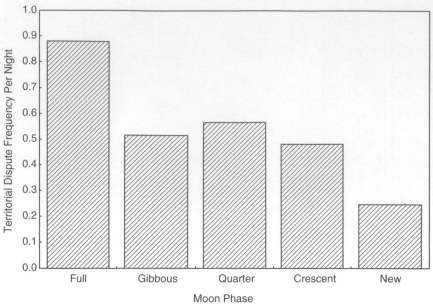

Figure 3–18 The Mean Frequency that Spectral Tarsiers Engaged in Territorial Disputes, Broken Down According to Moon Phase

moon phase (F=12.136, P=.0001, df=441). During nights when there was a full moon, the mean number of territorial disputes per night was 0.89 (± .32). This is substantially greater than the mean number of territorial disputes per night of observation during other moon phases (Figure 3–18).

A total number of 1,072 within-group encounters were observed over a period of 442 nights. The mean number of intragroup encounters during this study was 2.42 encounters per night. The frequency encounters between group members during focal follows varied significantly according to moon phase (F=19.358, P=.0001, df=441). During nights when there was a full moon, the mean number of intragroup encounters per night of observation was 3.36 (± 2.71). This is substantially greater than the mean number of intragroup encounters per night of observation during other moon phases (Figure 3–19).

The spectral tarsier's behavioral response to moonlight is intriguing because lunar phobia is generally believed to be a form of predator avoidance (Lockard & Ownings 1974; Fenton et al., 1977; Morrison 1978; Watanuki 1986; Nelson 1989; Bowers 1990; Daly et al., 1992; Kotler et al., 1993; Kramer & Birney 2001). Specifically, it has been argued that during full moons nocturnal animals are more easily seen and preyed on by nocturnal and diurnal predators, thereby increasing the risk of predation. For example, according to Watanuki (1986), Leach's storm petrels avoid moonlight to prevent getting

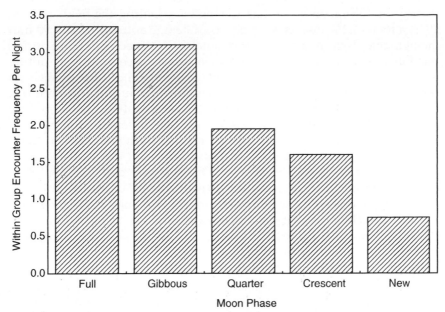

Figure 3–19 The Mean Frequency that Spectral Tarsiers Encountered One Another per Night

preyed on by slaty-backed gulls. His data indicate that Leach's storm petrels are primarily preyed on during moonlit nights and not new-moon nights. Similarly, Nelson (1989) demonstrated that for Cassin's auklet, predation risk is correlated with the lunar cycle. He found that the birds suffer heavier predation by western gulls (*Larus occidentalis*) on moonlit nights than on dark nights.

It thus hypothesis is accurate (nocturnal mammals are lunar phobic because of increased predation risk during full moons), and numerous studies suggest that it is, then by extension it implies that tarsiers and other nocturnal primates are increasing their exposure to predators when they increase their activity during full moons. This hypothesis raises two equally intriguing questions. First, are the benefits of foraging during the full moon so high that they outweigh the costs of increased predation pressure? Second, how do spectral tarsiers deal with the increasing predator pressure during full moons? As the goal of this study was only to determine the tarsiers' response to moonlight, only limited data are available to address these questions.

In regard to the first question, a comparison of foraging efficiency (defined as the number of insects captured per unit time) during full moon relative to the other moon phases suggests that the benefits of foraging during the full moon are in fact tremendous. During the field study in 1999, a total of 286 insects were observed being captured during 90 full-moon nights. This amounts to approximately 3.2 insects per night during the full moon. In comparison, only 36 insects were captured during 31 nights when there was no moonlight (a new moon). These numbers do not just reflect a bias in observation conditions because this pattern was also observed in terms of the numbers of insects captured in the malaise and pitfall traps and sweep nets during the different moon phases (Gursky 1997, 2000c). That is, the number of Orthopterans and Lepidopterans captured in the malaise traps during full moons was significantly greater than the number of Orthopterans and Lepidopterans captured during the other moon phases (Gursky 1997). Thus, for the spectral tarsiers the benefits of foraging during full moons are tremendous. Another possibility is that the tarsiers are only increasing their activity during full moons because their prey (Orthopterans and Leipidopterans) increase their activity on brightly lit nights.

On the other hand, the increase in foraging efficiency during full moons may have to do with improved visual acuity. Although spectral tarsiers are presently nocturnal, it has been suggested that historically they were diurnal. Unlike the majority of nocturnal mammals, including primates, tarsiers do not possess a *tapetum lucidum*, a reflective layer behind the eye that enhances all available light. The lack of this anatomical structure, in conjunction with the presence of a *fovea*, an anatomical feature found only in the eyes of diurnal mammals, supports this hypothesis (Woolard 1925; Hill 1955; Castenholz 1984). If tarsiers are secondarily nocturnal, then the spectral tarsier's improved vision during full-moon nights might account for the modified activity patterns and the tremendous improvement in foraging efficiency during these times of the month.

As to the second question, to deal with the increase in predation during full moons (when diurnal and nocturnal predators can take advantage of the additional light), spectral tarsiers modified other aspects of their behavioral repertoire. Most interestingly, they increased the frequency that group members traveled together. In particular, the frequency that any two group members were observed together increased substantially during full moons. It is believed that the more individuals that are in the group to scan for predators, the less time each individual will have to spend in vigilance (Krebs & Davies 1984). Living in a group, though, is costly in terms of intragroup foraging competition. The spectral tarsiers overcome this costly behavior by consuming insects that are abundant in moonlight.

Another possible explanation for the lack of lunar phobia exhibited by the spectral tarsiers is that full moons do not increase predation pressure for nocturnal primates. Nash (1986) has suggested that the nocturnal primates are actually safer from predators during full moons than they are during new moons. Although the tarsiers (and other nocturnal primates) would be more easily seen during full moon, they would also be more likely to see their predators before the attack. It is well-known that the probability of a successful hunt is tremendously decreased if the prey becomes aware of the predator prior to the attack. A major distinction between primates and other mammals is their highly developed visual system and sociality (Martin 1990; Fleagle 1999). This emphasis on visual systems, even in primates that still rely on olfaction, makes increased moonlight attractive. Additional support for this paradoxical hypothesis comes from Bearder et al.'s (2002) observation that genets are more likely to capture *G. moholi* when there is no moon than when there is full moon. That is, the genets take advantage of the darkness and the inability of the galagos to see them during new moons, and thus, are more successful in capturing their prey. This hypothesis is much more parsimonious in accounting for the unusual behavior of nocturnal primates including spectral tarsiers during full moons.

CHAPTER SUMMARY

The primary goal of this chapter was to explore the social and ecological factors selecting for gregariousness in spectral tarsiers. First, using group size and composition data, I found that spectral tarsiers are facultatively monogamous. That is, approximately 10% of groups contained two breeding females. Similarly, I also observed several extra-pair copulations. Second, I found that gregariousness and group cohesion caused decreases in foraging efficiency. Yet, spectral tarsiers spent more time together than expected based on the size of their home range and their nightly path length. My observations suggest that predation pressure is the primary ecological force selecting for gregariousness in this primate. Additional support for the importance of predation pressure comes from data on moonlight. Most nocturnal mammals are lunar phobic. Spectral tarsiers are lunar philic. This unusual behavior pattern might be in response to their strong visual sense whereby they can see better at night during full moons than new moons. Thus, on moonless nights there is increased predation pressure. At present, data support this hypothesis.

4

Ecological and Social Factors Selecting for Gregariousness

Territoriality, Diet, Site Fidelity, and Dispersal Patterns

(Photo by the author)

In the previous chapter I showed that the most important factors selecting for sociality in spectral tarsiers are ecological pressures. In particular, I found that predation pressure significantly increased group cohesion. In this chapter I explore how additional ecological factors—specifically, diet, sleeping tree use, site fidelity, and dispersal patterns—affect gregariousness in this species.

TERRITORIALITY

In virtually all primate species, groups range over a relatively fixed area, and members of a group can be found consistently in a particular area over time. The majority of these ranges, commonly called home ranges, represent an undefended living space. However, some primate species maintain exclusive access to fixed areas. For territorial primates, the boundaries of the territory are essentially the same as for their home range, and territories do not overlap. The defense of a territory has been observed in several primate species including *Hapalemur griseus* (Nievergelt et al., 1998), *Indri indri* (Pollock 1979), *Hylobates lar* (Tenaza 1975; Palombit 1993), *Colobus guereza* (Stanford 1992), and *Leontopithecus rosalia* (Peres 1989). Throughout my research, I have consistently observed territorial behavior by the spectral tarsiers (Gursky 2003c).

Numerous hypotheses have been proposed to explain the presence of territoriality in animal species (Hinde 1956; Brown 1964; Kaufmann 1983; Cheney 1987; Krebs & Davies 1984). A primary hypothesis is defense of resources (Brown 1964; Kodric-Brown & Brown 1978; Ostfeld 1985; Kinnaird 1992). First advanced by Brown (1964), the concept of economic defensibility posits that individuals will establish exclusive ranges that are defended when it is cost-efficient to protect those areas' resources, that is, when the exclusion of other individuals from the territory has higher payoffs than ignoring the intruders. For example, when food resources are ephemeral, individuals may have to roam over a large area to obtain sufficient nutrients; here, it would not pay to be territorial. Mitani and Rodman's (1979) work extended Brown's concept of economic defensibility with the development of an index of range of defensibility. The index of defendability (D) is the ratio of observed daily path length (d) to an area equal to the diameter (d') of a circle equal to the home range area of the animal and is mathematically illustrated as:

$$d' = \frac{(4A)^{.05}}{pi}$$

Mitani and Rodman's (1979) comparative study indicated that territoriality was observed only in populations whose ranges were economically defendable (i.e., having an index of 1.0 or greater), a conclusion supporting the resource defense function of territoriality in primates.

In spectral tarsiers, d equals 0.783 meter and 0.476 meter for males and females, respectively; d' equals $3.98^{.05}$ and $2.95^{.05}$ for males and females, respectively. It is clear that the spectral tarsiers also have an index of defendability greater than 1.0, providing some support for the resource defense function of territoriality for this primate species.

Other researchers have suggested that the function of territoriality is the defense of mates (Stanford 1991; van Schaik et al., 1992; Slagsvold et al., 1994). This hypothesis is based on sexual selection theory (Bateman 1948; Trivers 1972), which suggests that the factors that limit the reproductive success of males and females tend to be different. Specifically, female reproductive success is limited by access to resources, whereas male reproductive success is limited by access to fertile mates. Females are expected to compete among one another primarily for access to resources whereas males will compete mainly for matings. For example, Stanford (1991) showed that territorial behavior in the capped langur, *Presbytis pileata*, supports the predictions of mate defense better than resource defense. In intergroup encounters, male capped langurs directed their aggression toward their group females, thus controlling access by extra-group males to the females. Similarly, van Schaik et al. (1992) found that in six *Presbytis* species, not only were loud calls produced solely in males, but antagonism between groups was restricted to males.

In my attempts to understand the function of territoriality in spectral tarsiers, I predict that if they exhibit territoriality to defend their mates, then (1) males will be hostile toward nonresident males but not toward nonresident females. Similarly, females will be hostile toward nonresident females but not toward other males. (2) The number of intergroup confrontations will increase during the mating seasons as individuals attempt to locate potential mates outside their ranges. (3) There will be an increase in the number of intragroup encounters during the mating season as males will be mate guarding the female.

On the other hand, if spectral tarsiers exhibit territoriality to defend resources from nongroup members, then (1) confrontations between neighboring groups will involve both males and females. Similarly, (2) confrontations between groups will increase during the dry season when resources are less abundant relative to the wet season. (3) There will be a decrease in the number of intragroup encounters during the dry season to minimize within-group competition.

DESCRIPTION OF TERRITORIAL BEHAVIOR

The exact distance an animal travels per unit time is difficult to determine (Altmann & Samuels 1992). The amount of time spent traveling usually inadequately represents the actual distance traveled, as speed is not incorporated into the measure (Taylor 1970, 1980). Nonetheless, to obtain a preliminary estimate of the distance each individual tarsier traveled per unit time, I used fifteen-minute step distances (Whitten 1982; Kinnaird 1992). Thus, distance traveled was calculated as the straight-line distance between successive fifteen-minute locations. Table 4–1 shows the mean distance traveled per fifteen-minute time interval for each individual summed for all nights. Another measure that is frequently used in calculations of the distance individuals travel per unit time is the daily path length. Because tarsiers are nocturnal this measure represents the total distance individuals traveled per night, as measured by the fifteen-minute step distances

Table 4–1 The Mean Distance Traveled Per 15-Minutes Interval by Male and Female Spectral Tarsiers

Female		*Male*	
Individual	*Mean Distance Traveled (m)*	*Individual*	*Mean Distance Traveled (m)*
226	28.5	325	35.4
864	28.8	588	34.2
571	17.5	128	28.2
914	20.8	763	27.6
897	19.1	988	36.8
876	40.3	038	28.5
046	35.7		
686	27.6	511	28.4
834	29.3	524	37.5
103	28.4	543	28.8
732	30.2	556	28.2
095	34.4	572	29.5
008	36.9	580	32.1
068	24.7	792	27.1
126	27.1	774	30.6
627	28.5	306	33.3
014	26.8	168	27.3
066	27.9	204	28.9
191	28.1	050	33.7
090	25.8	313	27.4
231	26.3	347	26.6
110	28.8	394	29.2
033	26.4	366	34.8
026	32.5	382	27.6
146	33.7	403	29.0
Mean Distance Traveled (m)	28.56 m		30.45 m

throughout the night. I refer to this as the nightly path length, and occasionally NPL. Table 4–2 shows the mean nightly path length for each individual tarsier. A third measure that is frequently used in calculations of the distance individuals travel is the home range (Whitten 1982; Kinnaird

Table 4–2 The Mean Nightly Path Length (m) of Male and Female Spectral Tarsiers

	Female			Male	
Individual	Mean Nightly Path Length (m)	N*	Individual	Mean Nightly Path Length (m)	N*
226	465.7	51	325	792.7	23
864	461.5	43	588	743.5	28
571	302.1	54	128	661.2	27
914	384.3	35	763	851.0	24
897	311.6	42	988	904.7	36
876	704.2	30	038	862.1	25
046	548.9	25			
686	511.3	18	511	727.4	18
834	539.2	11	524	753.7	11
103	565.5	16	543	621.6	16
732	588.4	12	556	815.6	12
095	623.8	17	572	947.6	17
008	657.6	13	580	621.8	13
068	699.4	19	792	721.1	19
126	625.7	16	774	633.8	16
627	322.2	14	306	799.9	14
014	442.4	12	168	884.2	12
066	469.2	11	204	865.7	11
191	376.3	14	050	922.4	14
090	348.8	17	313	784.5	17
231	356.7	13	047	729.3	13
110	415.6	18	394	754.6	18
033	343.8	15	366	612.2	15
026	334.5	19	382	801.8	19
146	366.1	16	403	977.6	16
Mean Nightly Path Length (m)	475.99 m	551		782.91 m	434

* N represents the number of nights locational data points were obtained to contribute to the home range estimate.

1992). Home range is determined by actual observations of the animal in specific locations. From these observations, lines are drawn around the out-ermost points in a convex fashion, or in the creation of a concave range. Whereas the former estimate frequently overestimates the individual's home range, the concave range frequently underestimates the individual's range (White & Garrott 1987). Table 4–3 shows the convex nightly home range size for each individual. Home range varied between 1.6 and 4.1 hectares, with an average size of 2.3 hectares for females and 3.1 hectares for males.

Table 4–3 The Home Range (ha) of Male and Female Spectral Tarsiers

	Female			Male	
Individual	Home Range (ha)	N*	Individual	Home Range (ha)	N*
226	1.89	1573	325	2.12	815
864	1.64	875	588	2.91	991
571	2.68	870	128	2.83	988
914	3.16	844	763	4.05	1514
897	2.66	1369	988	3.45	1504
876	2.28	710	038	3.27	451
046	1.72	650			
686	1.94	1007	511	4.27	830
834	2.49	810	524	3.76	736
103	1.94	878	543	2.67	805
732	2.31	593	556	3.52	647
095	1.83	687	572	4.06	766
008	1.58	716	580	2.89	845
068	2.74	730	792	3.71	593
126	1.98	707	774	3.38	687
627	2.32	703	306	3.49	756
014	1.67	2134	168	2.96	1549
066	2.24	1783	204	2.77	1413
191	1.79	1045	050	3.28	1531
090	2.12	1391	313	3.45	2327
231	3.28	1560	347	2.93	1418
110	1.46	1425	394	2.54	1408
033	2.39	1588	366	2.12	1593
026	3.36	1470	382	3.47	1498
146	1.64	1691	403	3.38	1234
Home Range (ha)	2.20 ha	27809 (2317 hr)		3.22 ha	26899 (2242 hr)

* N represents the number of 5-minute locational data points that were obtained to contribute to the home range estimate.

Using CALHOME software (Kie et al., 1996), I calculated the degree of home range overlap between groups. Overlapping areas between neighboring groups constituted, on average, approximately 15% (Gursky 2003c). Thus, the majority of each group's range was used exclusively by the resident group and only occasionally occupied by neighboring individuals. Both successive and simultaneous use of overlap areas occurred, the latter of which represent the basis for encounters.

Throughout my research, 493 agonistic intergroup encounters were observed over a period of 960 nights. This amounts to approximately 0.51 territorial disputes each night, or approximately one territorial conflict every other night. When a group member observed a stranger in its territory, it immediately gave a loud call. All the resident group members responded by congregating around the initial caller to vocalize their defense of the territory, as well as lunging at and retreating from the intruder, until the intruder departed. The location of the territorial disputes was often at territory boundaries (n=414). The boundary constituted the 10 meter radius around the edge of an individual's territory. Sometimes, though, the dispute occurred closer to the center of the group's territory (n=79). The average overall duration of intergroup encounters was eight minutes. Intergroup encounters occurred throughout the entire night, but were unevenly distributed (Figure 4–1). Encounter rates peaked between 1800 and 2000 hours and then again shortly between 0400 and 0600 hours (Gursky 1997).

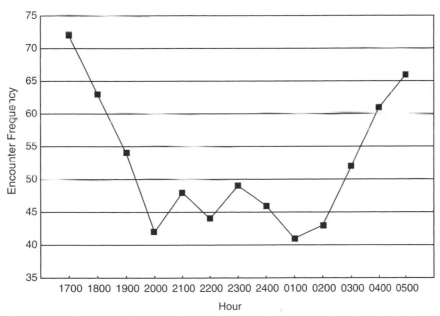

Figure 4–1 The Frequency that Spectral Tarsiers Encountered Another Adult Group Member Each Hour of the Night

MATE DEFENSE

During intergroup encounters, when the observed intruder was a male and was encountered by the resident male (n=177), the resident male always (100%) immediately responded harshly by vocalizing (alarm calling) and lunging at the intruder. Often, other group members would come to the area where the resident male was vocalizing. Subadult males would often contribute calls. When an intruding male was encountered by the resident female (n=128), she varied in her response. Frequently, she emitted a loud call (63%), but sometimes (37%) the female emitted another softer call that could not be heard by other group members, only by the intruder. When the intruder was a female (n=89), then the resident male occasionally (26%) emitted a loud call, but more often gave another softer call (74%). This led to several extra-pair copulations. However, when a female intruder was encountered by the resident female (n=99), the resident female immediately responded harshly by vocalizing, emitting a loud call and lunging at the intruder (100%).

The mean number of territorial disputes in the nonmating season (June to October and January to March) was 12.3 per month (SD=6.7, n=148 disputes, n=16 months) compared to the mean number of territorial disputes in the mating season (April to May and November to December) which was 19.8 per month (SD=11.4, n=345, n=11 months). Territorial disputes were significantly more frequent in the mating seasons than they were during other times of the year (t=6.65, p=.0001, df=1).

While conducting focal follows on a single adult, interactions between the focal individual and another adult group member were observed on 2,324 occasions. The mean number of intragroup encounters during this study was 2.42 encounters per night (SD=2.7). They ranged from zero encounters to as many as 18 within-group encounters per night. The frequency of encounters was not normally distributed (Shapiro Wilk W test, W=0.728, P=0.000), nor did it represent a Poisson distribution (Kolmogorov-Smirnov, d=0.241, P < .01; X^2=401.93, df=6, P=.00000). The modal duration of each intragroup encounter was approximately four minutes, and the mean duration was 48 minutes. There was substantial variation in the duration of intragroup encounters ranging from less than one minute to as long as 3 hour, 12 minute.

The mean number of intragroup encounters per night of observation during the mating season was 3.97 (SD=3.8, n=1396 encounters, n=383 nights) compared to 1.41 (SD=1.14, n=748 encounters, n=577 nights) intragroup encounters per night of observation during the nonmating season. That is, group members encountered one another significantly more frequently during nightly forays in the mating season than during the nonmating season (X^2=86.96, p=.0001, df=1).

Together, these results on territorial and within-group encounters suggest that spectral tarsiers spend quite a bit of time each night in social interactions (both agonistic and passive). This is especially true during the mating season. Obviously, both the increase in territorial encounters and in within-group encounters can be attributed to a form of mate guarding. Males are traveling outside their own territory to try and mate with strange females, thus accounting for the high frequency of territorial encounters. The high rate of within-group encounters represents the other way adult males are guarding females as well as mating with her when she is sexually receptive.

RESOURCE DEFENSE

Of the 493 intergroup territorial encounters observed throughout this study, only 63% (n=311) of them involved joint defense of the resources by the resident male and female. When the resident male encountered an intruder (n=149 male intruders, n=109 female intruders) and began emitting a loud call to elicit support from his mate, the female returned her mate's call on only ninety occasions (35%). Despite how infrequently the female responded to her mate's alarm calls, she was equally likely to return her mate's call for both male and female intruders. However, when the resident female encountered an intruder (n=143 male intruders, n=92 female intruders) and began emitting a loud call to elicit support from her mate, the male always returned her call and immediately traveled to her location.

Resource availability, as measured according to insect biomass, is illustrated in Figure 4–2. Two distinct periods of resource abundance at Tangkoko Nature Reserve can be distinguished: a period of high insect biomass (November–April) and a period of low insect biomass (May–October). These two periods are also observed if one compares the number of insects captured during each month (Gursky 2000a) and roughly correspond to the rainy season and the dry season, respectively (Figure 4–3). Consequently, it seems appropriate to use the terms *dry season* and *period of low resource abundance* interchangeably and *rainy* or *wet season* and *period of high resource abundance* interchangeably when discussing how spectral tarsiers modify their behavior in response to seasonal resource bases.

There is a significant correlation between monthly rainfall and the number of insects captured in the traps each month (Spearman rank order Z=3.05, p=.0023), between monthly rainfall and insect biomass each month (Spearman rank order Z=3.42, p=.0006), and between monthly insect biomass and the number of insects captured by the tarsiers each month (Spearman rank order Z=3.33, p=.0009).

During months of high resource abundance (December–May), only 164 territorial disputes were observed over a period of 557 nights. In contrast, during months of low resource abundance a total number of 329 territorial

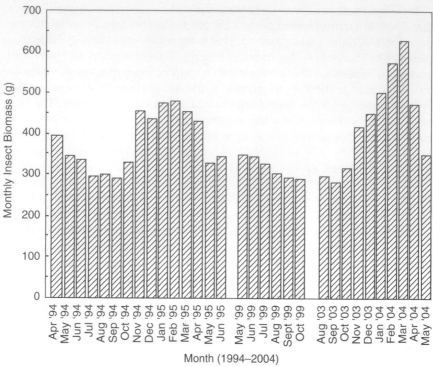

Figure 4–2 The Monthly Insect Biomass (gm) Each Month of Study Between 1994–2004

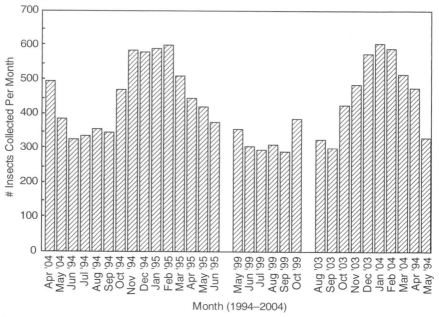

Figure 4–3 The Total Number of Insects Captured Each Month of Study Between 1994–2004

disputes were observed over a 403-night period. The mean number of territorial disputes per night of observation during the wet season was only 0.29. In contrast, the mean number of territorial disputes per night of observations during the dry season was 0.71. Territorial disputes were significantly more common during the dry season than during the wet season (t=−13.83, p=.0001, df=958 nights). The increase in the number of forays that individuals made into a neighboring territory during the dry season may represent an attempt by individuals to minimize intragroup feeding competition by trying to feed elsewhere. The result of this strategy is that by feeding elsewhere and expanding the group's range, they are increasing intergroup feeding competition.

Intragroup encounters involve interactions between two adult group members, which I observed while conducting a focal follow on one of the adult group members. According to this measure of the effect of seasonality on sociality, group members encountered others much less frequently during nightly forays in the dry season than during the wet season (t=6.32, p=.0001, df=958) (Figure 4–4). The mean number of intragroup encounters per night of observation during the dry season was 1.09 (SD=0.83, n=408 encounters, n=403 nights) compared to 3.39 (SD=2.15, n=1,736 encounters, n=557 nights) within-group encounters per night of observation during the wet season. That is, intragroup encounters decreased in frequency in the dry season relative to encounters during the wet season. This suggests that

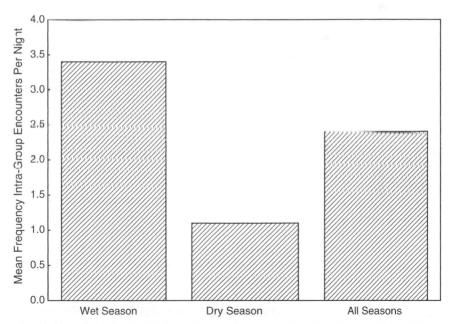

Figure 4–4 The Mean Number of Intragroup Encounters Per Night of Observation in the Wet and Dry Seasons

group members may have been avoiding one another, which may be another strategy to minimize intragroup feeding competition during times when resources are scarce.

These results do provide substantial support for the mate defense function of territoriality in spectral tarsiers. Predictions number two and three of the mate defense hypothesis were supported. There was an increase in the number of territorial encounters, as well as intragroup encounters, during the mating season compared to the nonmating season. However, the results of prediction number one do not provide complete support for the mate defense hypothesis. Spectral tarsiers were not consistent in their behavioral response toward strange members of the opposite sex. Sometimes resident individuals were friendly and responded with a friendly soft call; other times they responded harshly with a loud territorial defense call. Both males and females exhibited this variability in response to members of the opposite sex. This may reflect the fact that spectral tarsiers are facultatively polygynous (Nietsch & Niemitz 1992).

The results of this study also provide mixed support for the resource defense function of territoriality in spectral tarsiers. Both prediction one and prediction three were not supported. Male and female spectral tarsiers did not jointly encourage the removal of nonresident individuals that were encountered in the territory. Similarly, in contrast to prediction number three, there was also a substantial decrease in the number of intragroup encounters during the dry season. Interestingly, although predictions number one and three were not supported, prediction number two of the resource defense model was supported: The number of intergroup encounters (territorial disputes) increased during the dry season.

Overall, these results indicate that the primary function of territoriality in spectral tarsiers may be mate defense and not resource defense. Nonetheless, there is some minor support that some territorial behavior stems from the defense of resources. It is interesting that territorial behavior increases so substantially during the mating season. The mating system is also concurrent with the biannual birth season (Gursky 1997, 2002a). The high rate of within-group encounters during the birth season may indicate that the function of territoriality is perhaps infanticide avoidance whereby potential intruders are kept away from vulnerable infants (Reichard & Sommer 1997). This model has been invoked to explain female territoriality among rodents (Ebensperger 1998), the intensity of which increases during pregnancy and decreases after the weaning of infants. Unfortunately, because the periods of time with low insect abundance were also the months when the females were pregnant and the periods of time with high insect abundance were also the months when the females were lactating, it was not possible to distinguish between these two hypotheses. Both pregnancy and lower insect abundance were predicted and found to be associated with more distance between pairs, as lactation and high insect abundance were predicted and found to be associated with less distance between pairs. The best way to untangle the confounding effects would be to observe the spectral tarsiers during (1) times of low abundance and pregnant, (2) high abundance and pregnant (during the population's second annual birth peak), (3) low abundance and lactating, and (4) high abundance and lactating. Future studies with more specific predictions distinguishing between these two hypotheses will be necessary to fully tease apart these conflicting results.

DIET

As indicated above, one reason spectral tarsiers may be territorial is to maintain access to food resources. Spectral tarsiers are unusual among primates in that they do not eat leaves or fruit, only insects and other arthropods (MacKinnon & MacKinnon 1980; Niemitz 1984, Gursky 1995, 1997, 1998a, 2000c, 2002c). Unlike the Bornean tarsier, the spectral tarsier does not consume small mammals, birds, or snakes. Table 4–4 lists the total number of insects that were observed captured by the tarsiers, the number that were identified to a taxonomic group, and their taxonomic group.

The distribution and quality of food resources is generally recognized as the preeminent factor explaining much interspecific and intraspecific variation in the behavior of nonhuman primates (Clutton-Brock & Harvey 1977; Wrangham 1980; Crompton 1984; Harcourt 1986; Robinson 1986; Boinski

Table 4–4 Dietary Profile of Spectral Tarsiers in Tangkoko Dua Saudara Nature Reserve, Sulawesi, Indonesia

Taxonomic Composition of Prey Consumed	Common Name for Insects	N	Number (and Percentage) of Identified Prey Consumed	Number (and Percentage) of Identified Prey Consumed
Order Aranae	Spiders		58 (2.39)	58 (2.39)
Order Coleoptera	Beetles		276 (11.32)	276 (11.32)
Order Isoptera	Termites		318 (13.08)	318 (13.08)
Order Homoptera	Cicadas		117 (4.79)	117 (4.79)
Order Hymenoptera	Ants		322 (13.24)	322 (13.24)
Order Lepidoptera	Moths		353 (14.51)	
	Caterpillars		415 (17.07)	768 (31.58)
Order Orthoptera	Katydids and Crickets		120 (4.94)	
	Grasshoppers		260 (10.69)	
	Cockroaches		148 (6.06)	
	Walkingsticks		47 (1.91)	575 (23.60)

1987; Remis 1997). Primates that live in seasonal environments often show predictable responses to fluctuating resources (MacArthur & Pianka 1966; Charnov 1976). To compensate for the reduction in resource availability, primates may switch to alternative, poorer quality food sources and incorporate them into their diet in greater than usual quantities (Hladik 1977; Crompton 1984; Richard 1985; Harcourt 1986). For example, Hladik (1977) found that during the nonfruiting season, frugivorous hanuman langurs must consume leaves and often suffer an energy deficit. Similarly, Kavanagh (1978) found that vervets consume a large proportion of invertebrates only during the dry season, when other food resources are limited.

Moreover, when resources are limited, primates often increase the amount of time they spend foraging (Dunbar 1988; Overdorff 1992). Some primates increase their daily path length (DPL) in order to find sufficient food resources when resource abundance is low; other species decrease the amount of time allocated to travel to reduce their daily energy needs (Boinski 1987; Dunbar 1988). For example, daily path length is reported to increase during the dry season in baboons (Anderson 1981), vervets (Struhsaker 1967), gibbons (Raemakers 1980), and sifaka (Richard 1978). Similarly, home range itself may increase during the dry season for rufous lemurs, baboons, and colobus (Clutton-Brock 1975; Anderson 1981; Overdorff 1992).

Finally, many primate species reduce their group size or maximize their group dispersion during the dry season (Caldecott 1986; Boinski 1987; Doran 1997). Caldecott (1986) observed that the paucity of fruit forces pig-tailed macaque groups to disperse while foraging. Doran (1997) found similar dispersion patterns in response to seasonality among chimpanzees of Tai Forest.

Although changes in food type, distance traveled, and group dispersion in response to seasonal resources have been reported for many frugivorous and folivorous primates, very few researchers have attempted to assess quantitatively the effects of seasonality on the behavior of insectivorous primates (Harcourt 1986). Although Harcourt (1986) compared the effect of seasonality on the behavior of two galago species, she did not measure resource abundance, but instead assumed that it would decrease in the dry season. Although this assumption is probably correct, it is still imperative that resource abundance be measured to understand precisely how seasonal changes affect the behavior of insectivorous primates. Thus, the question is, do spectral tarsiers modify their behavior in response to seasonal resources in the same ways as do frugivorous and folivorous primates?

Male and female spectral tarsiers each modified their activity budgets in response to seasonal resources (males $X^2=254.14$, p$=.0001$, df$=3$; females $X^2=178.47$, p$=.0001$, df$=3$). Qualitatively, during periods of low resource availability versus high resource availability, male and female spectral tarsiers increased time spent both traveling and foraging, while decreasing the time allocated to resting and social behavior (Figure 4–5).

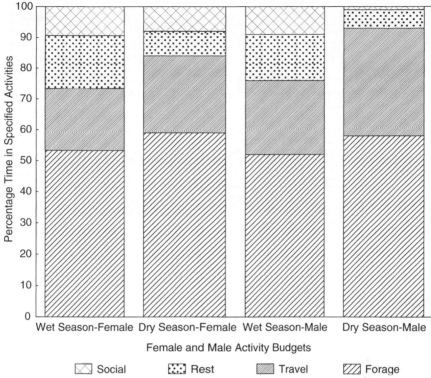

Figure 4–5 Stacked Column Illustrating the Activity Budgets of Male and Female Spectral Tarsiers in the Wet Season Compared to the Dry season

Males and females not only increased the amount of time spent foraging during times of low resource abundance but also modified their foraging behavior. I was able to identify approximately 69% of the insects captured in the traps and sweep nets to the ordinal level. The tarsiers consumed seven different Orders of insects with statistically different frequencies during months of high resource abundance and low resource abundance (X^2=59.022, p=.0030, df=6).

During the wet season, when resource abundance was higher, tarsiers ate Orthopterans and Lepidopterans with greater frequency and Coleoptera, Isoptera, and Hymenoptera with reduced frequency (Figure 4–6). These changes in insect consumption do not correspond directly to changes in insect availability (Figure 4–7). For example, whereas Orthopteran consumption increased 84%, the availability of Orthopterans only increased 31%. Similarly, Lepidopteran consumption increased 64% while their availability only increased 19%. Homopteran consumption increased 31%, which is much less than the 56% increase in its availability. During the wet season,

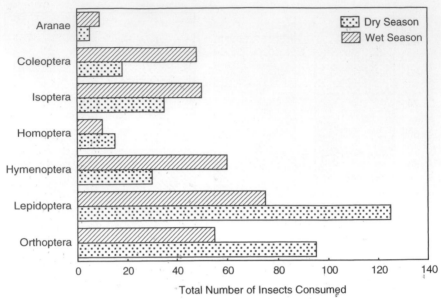

Figure 4–6 The Number of Insects from Each Order that the Spectral Tarsiers Consumed in the Wet and Dry Seasons

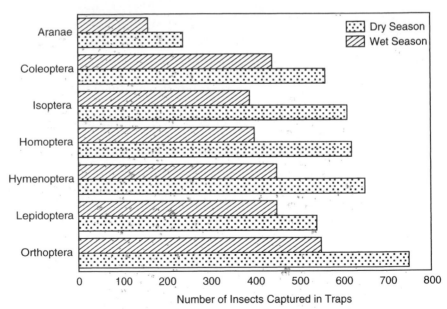

Figure 4–7 The Numbers of Insects from Each Order that Were Collected from Traps During the Wet and Dry Seasons

the frequencies that they consumed Hymenoptera, Isoptera, Coleoptera, and Aranae all decreased while their availability increased. For example, Hymenoptera consumption decreased 132% relative to the dry season whereas its availability increased.

Spectral tarsiers also modified the locations where they foraged for insects during the dry season versus the wet season (Figure 4–8). In general, they obtained insects in four different locales: from the air (34.8%), from the ground (7.8%), from a leaf (46.3%), or from a branch (11.1%). They captured 41.1% of their prey from the air (Isoptera, cicadas, moths, katydids, crickets) during the wet season compared to 27.9% during the dry season. Similarly, they also captured 50.5% of their prey from a leaf (walking sticks, grasshoppers, crickets, caterpillars, cicadas) during the wet season, but leaf captures decreased to 41.6% during the dry season. In contrast, the number of insects consumed off the ground (spiders, beetles,

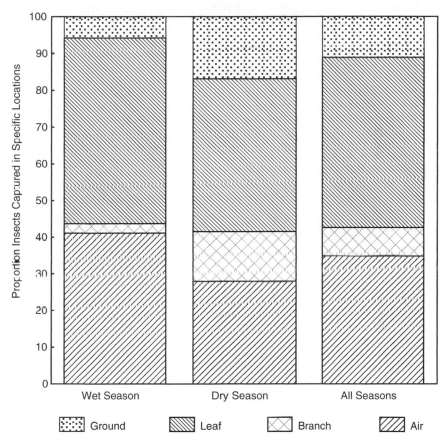

Figure 4–8 The Proportion of Insects that Were Captured in Different Locations During the Wet and Dry Seasons

cockroaches) increased from 2.6% during the wet season to 13.6% during the dry season. Similarly, the number of insects captured off a branch (cockroaches, ants, termites) increased from 5.8% during the wet season to 16.9% in the dry season. Overall, the frequency that spectral tarsiers captured insects between seasons, from various localities, is statistically significant (X^2=73.309, p=.0001, df=3).

The shift in foraging behavior between the wet versus dry seasons probably has several causes. First, there may be more insects on leaves during the wet season relative to the dry season. However, it might just be a reflection that during the dry season, there are a lot fewer leaves in the trees for insects to hide under as Tangkoko is a deciduous rainforest. This hypothesis could easily be tested by searching all the leaves on trees and bushes within a cubic area. Similarly, there may be more insects on the ground during the dry season relative to the wet season, so that is where the tarsiers preferentially forage. Once again, it would be relatively simple to test this hypothesis by comparing the number and types of each insect captured in each locale during the wet and dry seasons.

A second potential cause of the shift in foraging behavior might be predation risk. During the dry season, when many of the leaves have fallen off the trees and bushes, foraging on the ground litter might reduce risk because of increased camouflaging, compared to foraging in the trees.

Both males and females modified their locomotor behavior in response to seasonality of resources (Figures 4–9a–f). Spectral tarsier males and females traveled longer distances per unit time (females: t=−2.898, p=.0231, df=24; males: t=−3.179, p=.0336, df=23), traveled longer nightly path lengths (females: t=−4.8762, p=.0310, df=24; males: t=−6.477, p=.0003, df=23), and had larger home ranges (females: t=−5.902, p=.0006, df=24; males: t=−3.205, p=.0327, df=23), during the dry season than during the wet season.

The pattern of seasonal changes in foraging behavior and habitat use exhibited by spectral tarsiers is consistent with the predicted responses to fluctuating food abundance (MacArthur & Pianka 1966; Charnov 1976). The lower the abundance of food, the greater the amount of time and effort that must be expended to procure it. Numerous studies show that foraging takes precedence over nonforaging activities during periods of limited food availability (Altmann 1980; Post 1981; Iwamoto & Dunbar 1983). Spectral tarsier males and females increased their foraging and travel time in response to low resource availability and decreased the time allocated to social behavior. The increase in time they allocated to insectivorous foraging behavior and their decrease in social behavior is in accord with studies of the effect of seasonality on the behavior of some New World insectivorous primates. For example, Garber (1991) noted that tamarins spend more time foraging during the dry season months than at other times of the year. Similarly, Boinski (1987) observed that squirrel monkeys allocate varying amounts of time to foraging depending on

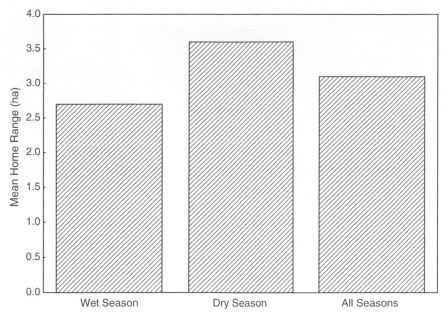

Figure 4–9 The Mean Number of Territorial Disputes per Night of Observation in the Wet and Dry Seasons

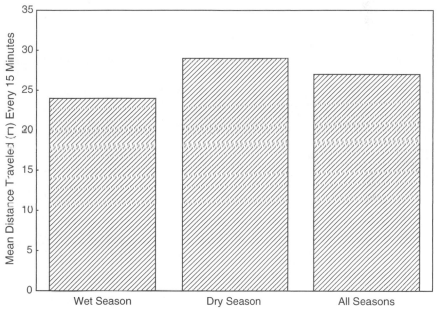

Figure 4–9a The Mean Distance Traveled Per 15-Minutes by Female Spectral Tarsiers During the Wet and Dry Seasons

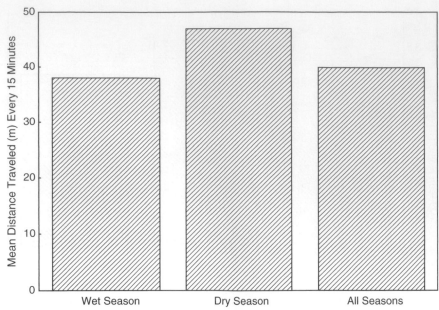

Figure 4–9b The Mean Distance Traveled Per 15-Minutes by Male Spectral Tarsiers During the Wet and Dry Seasons

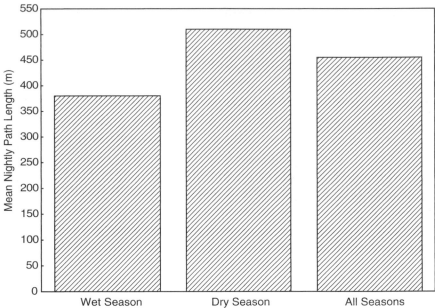

Figure 4–9c The Mean Nightly Path Length (m) Female Spectral Tarsiers Traveled During the Wet and Dry Seasons

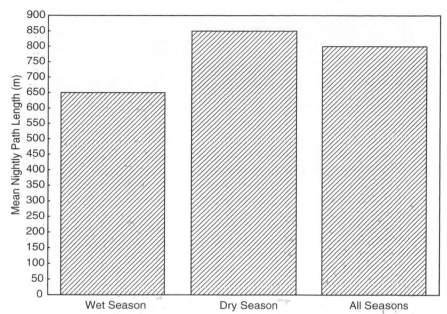

Figure 4–9d The Mean Nightly Path Length (m) Male Spectral Tarsiers Traveled During the Wet and Dry Seasons

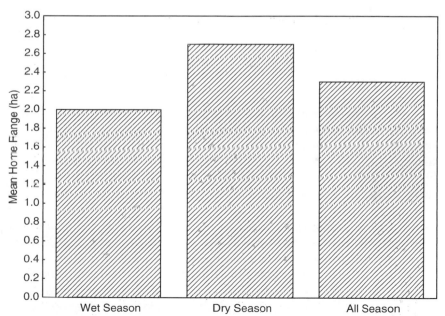

Figure 4–9e The Mean Home Range Size (ha) Female Spectral Tarsiers Traveled During the Wet and Dry Seasons

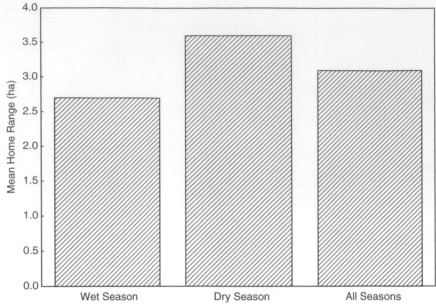

Figure 4–9f The Mean Home Range Size (ha) Male Spectral Tarsiers Traveled During the Wet and Dry Seasons

resource availability. Accordingly, the faunivorous spectral tarsiers modify their behavior in ways similar to Neotropical insectivores in response to seasonal resources.

SLEEPING TREES

There is a large amount of variation among tarsier species with regard to sleeping site preferences. This has important implications for determination of social groups and mating systems, because tarsier groups are often identified by which animals sleep together. The majority of sleeping trees utilized by spectral tarsiers were *Ficus sp.*, with *Ficus caulocarpa* being used much more frequently than all other species. Spectral tarsiers primarily utilized one major sleeping site although most groups had one alternate sleeping site as well. A few groups had three sleeping sites. The mean circumference of these strangler fig sleeping trees was 287 centimeter, ranging from 30 to 700 centimeter. The mean height of the sleeping trees was 20.17 meters, ranging from 6 to 38 meters. There was no significant difference in the number of sleeping sites used by monogamous groups and polygynous groups (Mann Whitney U test U=50.5; Z=0.979; P=.327). The names of all sleeping sites for the tarsier groups are listed in Table 4–5, along with the diameter at breast height (dbh) and the approximate height of the tree.

Table 4–5 Characteristics of the Sleeping Trees Utilized by Spectral Tarsier Groups Between 1994 and 2004

Tree Number	Latin Name of Sleeping Tree With the Name of the Original Host Tree in Parentheses	DBH (in cm)	Height of Sleeping Tree (in m)
1	Ficus caulocarpa (Alstonia ramvolfia)	300	37.75
2	Ficus benjamina (Barringtonia acuteangula)	167	25.37
3	Ficus akutania (Chisochetin kingii)	236	21.61
4	Ficus caulocarpa	263	10.35
5	Ficus caulocarpa	384	30.77
6	Ficus caulocarpa (Alstonia ramvolfia)	411	17.78
7	Ficus caulocarpa (Garuga floribunda)	430	21.25
8	Ficus cordulata	700	20.70
9	Vitex quinata	215	19.65
10	Ficus altissima (Dracontomelum dao)	403	13.23
11	Ficus caulocarpa	363	26.26
12	Ficus caulocarpa	560	26.80
13	Ficus virens	515	26.70
14	Ficus caulocarpa (Alstonia ramvolfia)	367	28.56
15	Melia azedarach	97	21.23
16	Ficus benjamina	249	24.10
17	Eugenia densiflora	47	10.24
18	Ficus akutania	398	20.02
19	Ficus chrysolepis (Alstonia ramvolfia)	278	26.11
20	Eugenia densiflora	30	9.99
21	Ficus chrysolepis (Alstonia ramvolfia)	105	13.31
22	Ficus caulocarpa	303	32.10
23	Ficus spp. (Alstonia sumatrana)	66	6.15
24	Ficus altissima	377	19.81
25	Ficus spp. (Homalium celebicum)	81	17.39
26	Ficus chrysolepsis (Vitex quinata)	127	14.29
27	Ficus benjamina	181	12.89
28	Ficus caulocarpa (Alstonia ramvolfia)	380	19.10
29	Ficus benjamina (Alstonia ramvolfia)	317	22.24
30	Ficus caulocarpa	514	22.46
31	Ficus spp.	218	17.25
32	Ficus benjamina	–	–
33	Ficus spp.	129	9.94

Fig trees are relatively common within Tangkoko as evidenced by their high cumulative Importance Value (IV) of .12429; thus, it is not surprising that the spectral tarsiers use these trees for their sleeping sites (Table 4–6). However, trees of such large diameter are relatively uncommon. Within a 4-hectare study area, there were 33,898 trees greater than 1 meter in height, accounting for 127 different species. The total number of trees with a dbh greater than or equal to 5 centimeter was 3,164. The total number of trees with a dbh greater than or equal to 10 centimeter was 1,727. The total number of trees in the 4-hectare with a dbh greater than or equal to the mean size of sleeping trees used by tarsiers in this study (287 centimeter) was approximately 4.5. Thus, each hectare averages only one tree large enough to house a group of tarsiers. Its size does not necessarily imply that the tree is hollowed, allowing for tarsiers to live inside. Thus, it is certainly possible that the territoriality exhibited by the spectral tarsiers reflects their need to defend their sleeping trees. This is supported by the observation that the sleeping tree is usually in the tarsier's core area.

MacKinnon and MacKinnon (1980) also observed several spectral tarsier groups utilizing vine tangles and grass platforms when groups were found in secondary forest and grassland areas. In comparison, data from Crompton and Andau (1986) on *T. bancanus* indicate that vine tangles and naturally formed platforms of creepers were the most common sleeping sites.

Table 4–6 The Relative Density, Frequency, Coverage, and Importance Value Index (Brower et al., 1990) for the Fig Trees Within the Four-Hectare Vegetation Plot at Tangkoko Nature Reserve

Tree Species	Relative Species Density	Relative Frequency	Relative Coverage	Importance Value (IV)
Ficus ampelas	.00012	.00083	.00000	.00095
Ficus annulata	.00004	.00042	.00016	.00062
Ficus benjamina	.00004	.00083	.00016	.00103
Ficus bracheata	.00004	.00042	.00000	.00096
Ficus caulocarpa	.00004	.00042	.00042	.00466
Ficus chrysolepsis	.00031	.01666	.00004	.01701
Ficus cordulata	.00004	.00042	.00001	.00047
Ficus drupacea	.00004	.00042	.00000	.00046
Ficus pubinervis	.00035	.00250	.00001	.00286
Ficus septica	.00059	.00458	.00002	.00519
Ficus tinctoria	.00098	.00500	.00011	.00609
Ficus variegata	.01295	.01583	.02491	.05369
Ficus virens	.00012	.00083	.00020	.00115
Ficus spp.	.00098	.00416	.00138	.00236
Total	**.01664**	**.05332**	**.02742**	**.09750**

Niemitz et al. (1991) in their description of *T. dianae* state that this species does not return to the same nest each night. This description agrees with MacKinnon and MacKinnon's (1980) observation that tarsiers in central Sulawesi do not use the same sleeping site each night. Tremble et al. (1993), however, found that Dian's tarsier did return to the same nest tree each night. At two sites (Kamarora and Posangke), I also found that *T. dianae* also returned to the same nest each morning (Gursky 1997, 1998b). Nest sites for *T. dianae* include vine tangles, tree cavities, and fallen logs (Tremble et al., 1993). The type of sleeping site used might account for this variation in whether groups return to their sleeping site.

Western tarsiers sleep singly unless it is a mother and her infant (Niemitz 1984; Crompton & Andau 1987). Niemitz found that his tarsiers sleep clinging to vertical branches at 2 meters or lower. Crompton and Andau (1987) found that *T. bancanus* sleep in vine tangles 4–5.5 meters above the ground and on 50–90 degree supports. Thus, the sleeping sites utilized by *T. bancanus* were much lower in the forest canopy and more open compared to those used by *T. spectrum*. They also noted that the sleeping sites tend to cluster at the edge of a tarsier's home range, in areas of overlap with neighbors of the opposite sex. This contrasts with spectral tarsiers, whose sleeping sites tend to be located near the center of the group's home range.

Dagosto and Gebo (1998) report that *T. syrichta* in Leyte always sleep singly, never in groups, and this result has been replicated by Neri-Arboleda (2001) with another population. Philippine tarsiers in Leyte utilized three or four different sleeping sites. They were primarily *Arctocarpus, Pterocarpus,* and *Ficus*, were low to the ground, and were surrounded by very dense vegetation. Philippine tarsiers in Bohol generally utilized one sleeping site, but had several alternate sleeping sites. Males tended to move from one sleeping site to another on a more frequent basis than the females. Males utilized seven to eight sleeping sites whereas females tended to limit their sleeping sites to three or four different locations over the entire duration of the study. Five of the fourteen tree species used as sleeping sites were *Ficus sp.* The average tree height of sleeping sites was 7.53 meters. The sleeping sites of the Bohol Philippine tarsier were highly variable. They ranged from rock crevices near the ground (3%), vine tangles (10%), dense thickets of *Pandanus* palms (15%), tree trunks (45%) and fork branches of trees (27%).

SITE FIDELITY

Of the thirty-three sleeping trees that were used in 1994 within the 100-hectare area, twenty of them were still being used in 1999. Five of the thirteen sleeping trees not used in 1999 had fallen, while the others were left vacant. Extending the duration from 1994 to 2004, sixteen of the same sleeping trees continued to be used. Of the twenty-nine sleeping trees that were first used in 1999, twenty continued to be occupied throughout 2004. Five of the trees not used in 2004 were the result of tree falls, while the other four trees were left vacant. Unfortunately, because not all individuals within the 100-hectare study areas were bird-banded I was unable to determine if the same groups were occupying these trees or if they were new ones.

Site fidelity for the bird-banded groups was relatively high over the duration of this study. For five of the ten groups bird-banded in 1994, both the adult male and the adult female continued to occupy the same sleeping tree in 1999. In the sixth and seventh group, only the adult female partner was still present at the original sleeping tree in 1999. The eighth sleeping tree had fallen down and the adult group members could not be relocated in 1999. The ninth and tenth sleeping trees were still standing, but were unoccupied in 1999.

For the ten groups bird-banded in 1999, six groups continued to use their original sleeping tree in 2004. The seventh group now occupied a nearby sleeping tree as a result of their original tree falling down. The eighth, ninth, and tenth sleeping trees were still standing, but were unoccupied in 2004. Members of these groups could not be relocated.

Concerning site fidelity, the spectral tarsiers remained at their sleeping sites over long periods of time. Two of the trees that were left vacant were in fact my old study groups. After I completed my research at Tangkoko, park guards started bringing tourists to my old study groups. The park guards often banged on the trees using their machetes or climbed up the tree to see if the tarsiers were still there, and brought groups of thirty or more tourists to the sleeping tree. After having thirty or more flashlights aimed at their eyes and being continually disturbed (day and night), the tarsiers at these sleeping trees were noted by the park guards to have disappeared. In fact, they had just changed to a new tree as the old one was no longer desirable because of the level of disturbance by the tourists.

Not only did the spectral tarsiers remain at their sleeping sites for multiple years, but males and females maintained the same partners for multiple years as well. This study provides the first evidence of the long-assumed, long-term relationships observed in spectral tarsiers. Fifty percent of the groups that were bird-banded in 1994 were still together five years later whereas 60% of the groups bird-banded in 1999 were still together five years later (2004).

DISPERSAL PATTERNS

During 1994, five subadults and eleven infants/juveniles were bird-banded, enabling individual identification. In 1999, I was only able to re-locate eight of these sixteen individuals. The fate of the other individuals is unknown. Both males and females were found to disperse from their natal sleeping site. Of the eight individuals re-located in 1999, five were females and three were males (Table 4–7). Male spectral tarsiers dispersed significantly farther

Table 4–7 The Mean Dispersal Distance of Subadult, Juvenile, and Infant Spectral Tarsiers Captured in 1994 and Relocated in 1999

Individual	Sex	Location of Original Sleeping Site 1994	Age Class at First Capture	Location of New Sleeping Site 1999	Distance Between Sleeping Sites
Blue/Black	F	A300	Subadult	A500	200
Red/Red	F	M600	Infant	F600	400
Yellow/Red	F	J800	Infant	M600	300
Red/Black	F	R900	Subadult	N200	700
Green/Blue	F	C1000	Juvenile	A900	200
Green/Yellow	M	E600	Infant	M900	700
Blue/Orange	M	S100	Infant	P800	800
White/Black	M	0300	Juvenile	A900	700

Table 4–8 The Mean Dispersal Distance of Subadult, Juvenile, and Infant Spectral Tarsiers Captured in 1999 and Relocated in 2004

Individual	Sex	Location of Original Sleeping Site 1999	Age Class at First Capture	Location of New Sleeping Site 2004	Distance Between Sleeping Sites (m)
Black/yellow	M	M200	Juvenile	X500	300
Blue/White	M	P400	Subadult	A500	800
Red/Orange	F	S500	Infant	0300	200
Silver/White	F	U100	Juvenile	S100	100
Yellow/White	F	B400	Juvenile	E200	200
Green/Orange	F	L200	Subadult	M300	100

than did females. The mean dispersal distance for males was 733 meter whereas the mean dispersal distance for females was only 360 meter. There was no difference in dispersal distance based on age at first capture.

During 1999, six subadults and eight infants/juveniles were bird-banded, enabling individual identification. In 2004, I was only able to re-locate six of these fourteen individuals. The fate of the other individuals is unknown. Of the six individuals re-located, four were females and two were males (Table 4–8). Once again, the male spectral tarsiers dispersed significantly farther than did females. The mean dispersal distance for males was 550 meter whereas the mean dispersal distance for females was only 150 meter. There was no difference in dispersal distance based on age at first capture.

Partly as a result of the differences in dispersal distances, males and females formed groups differently. Females were likely to form groups adjacent to their parents' range. In 1999, three of the five females were located in territories adjacent to the parents' territory. None of the males that were re-located were in territories adjacent to the parents' territory. In 2004, the four females were located in a territory adjacent to the parents' territory, whereas one male was in a territory adjacent to the parents' territory.

CHAPTER SUMMARY

The primary goal of this chapter was to explore some additional ecological factors selecting for gregariousness in spectral tarsiers. In the first section, I outlined theories as to why some species are territorial, described the territorial behavior exhibited by spectral tarsiers, and explicitly tested whether they display mate or resource defense territoriality. Although the results were mixed, there was substantially more support for the mate defense hypothesis than the resource defense hypothesis. Next, I explored how spectral tarsiers modify their behavior in response to seasonal resource abundance, in particular, how changing amounts of resources affected interactions with group members as well as with neighboring groups. I found that while interactions with group members decrease when resource abundance is low, interactions with other groups increase. In the third section of this chapter I explored how the abundance of sleeping trees affects gregariousness and group cohesion in this species. There was no significant result. Finally, I demonstrated that spectral tarsiers exhibit substantial amounts of site fidelity and sex-biased dispersal patterns. Although both males and females disperse, males disperse much farther than do females.

5

Infant Care and the Cost of Infant Transport

(Photo by the author)

The primary goal of this volume is to address the question of why spectral tarsiers park (do not continually transport) their young; however, it is also informative to look at the types of care given to infants, who their principal caretakers are, and the length of time that care is given to infants. Specifically, how long are infants parked? What is the average size of substrates where infants are parked? What percentage of time are infants alone? How frequently are infants nursed, groomed, and transported? Is there any noticeable weaning conflict for either nursing or transport? Which group member is most frequently the infant's nearest neighbor? What is the mean distance of the infant from other group members? How does the infant's behavior and the behavior of other group members change with the infant's age? At what age does the spectral tarsier achieve its major developmental markers such as its first successful leap, its first successful prey capture, its last nursing bout, and the last time it is transported?

Throughout this chapter, I attempt to draw comparisons of the strategies observed during my research with spectral tarsiers with those of other prosimians and New World monkeys. I emphasize the differences and similarities of prosimian species that park their infants with prosimian species that continually transport their young. In addition, I clarify how the mother–infant bond develops in a primate that parks its young. Continuous contact has been assumed to be critical for the proper development of the mother–infant bond (Harlow 1958; Maestripieri 2001; Dettling et al., 2002). Therefore, the presence of this bond in the spectral tarsier, and how it develops in a species in which mother and infant are not in continual physical contact, is addressed.

GESTATION LENGTH

I observed copulation for six females. In 1994, one female was observed mating on November 8 and gave birth some time between May 21 and 23. Assuming that the observed mating resulted in the conception of the infant, gestation length can be estimated as 195 days ($+/-$ 3 days). A second female was observed copulating three times, with the same male, on November 27. This female was also observed copulating once on November 16 with an unknown male. This female gave birth some time between May 26 and 29, providing a gestation length of either 193 ($+/-4$ days) or 182 ($+/-4$ days) days, depending on whether conception resulted from the mating with the first or second male. In 1999, one female was seen copulating on June 21 and gave birth on approximately December 28, providing a gestation length of 190 days. In the 2003–2004 field season, I observed three additional copulations on October 8, October 16, and April 24, respectively. The first two females gave birth on April 24 and 28. The sixth female had not given birth before the end of the study. These dates provide gestation lengths of 199 days and 195 days, respectively.

These estimates suggest the mean gestation period for this species is approximately 193 days (n=5). It is noteworthy that this estimate is comparable to the estimate of 178 days observed in captive *Tarsius sp.* (Izard et al., 1985; Wright et al., 1986; Roberts 1994; Sussman 1999). The gestation period of spectral tarsiers is nearly the longest among all prosimian primates. *Microcebus murinus*, the mouse lemur, has one of the shortest gestation periods of 62 days, compared to 163 days in *Loris lydekkerianus* and 193 days in *Nycticebus coucang* and *Perodicticus potto* (Harvey et al., 1987; Nekaris 2003). The variation in gestation length has important implications for the parental investment provided to each offspring. Assuming that a fetus requires a set amount of energy, by either increasing or decreasing the length of the gestation period, a mother can reduce or increase the amount of energy she provides her developing offspring each day.

LITTER SIZE

All female spectral tarsiers observed gave birth to a single infant. There was no variation in litter size. All additional reports of litter size in spectral tarsiers have indicated a litter size of one with no variation (i.e., no occasional occurrences of twins) (Catchpole & Fulton 1943; Ulmer 1963; Niemitz 1984). The lack of variation in litter size in spectral tarsiers is surprising for two reasons. First, tarsiers are morphologically capable of producing twins, that is, they possess a bicornuate uterus enabling two offspring to be produced (Luckett 1976; Fleagle 1988). Second, all tarsier species have two to three pairs of mammary glands (Schultz 1948; Niemitz 1984) such that they could nurse more than one infant without any difficulty. Yet, tarsiers exhibit a life history strategy that minimizes the number of offspring produced each year, while at the same time producing a single large infant (22% of adult weight at birth) over an exceptionally long gestation period (6 months) (Izard et al., 1985), with rapid postnatal growth (Wright 1990).

BIRTH SEASONALITY

Although *T. bancanus* and *T. syrichta* are not reported to be seasonal breeders (Ulmer 1963; Niemitz 1984; Crompton & Andau 1986, 1987; Wright et al., 1988; Roberts & Kohn 1993), the spectral tarsiers do reproduce seasonally. All the observed matings occurred during the months of April–June and October–November. Based on the focal individuals followed throughout this study as well as the groups on which I collected demographic data, births are very seasonal. A total of forty-six births were noted, all occurring during five of the twelve months (Figure 5–1). It is important to note that the births occurred primarily during two peaks: (1) April to May and (2) November to December. This result is comparable to data collected by MacKinnon and

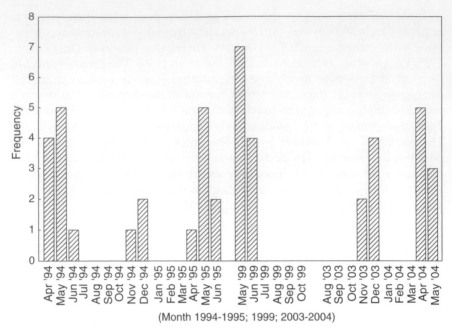

(Month 1994-1995; 1999; 2003-2004)

Figure 5–1 The Months that Infants Were Born Covering the Periods 1994–1995, 1999, and 2003–2004

MacKinnon (1980) who also found two breeding seasons at about six-month intervals (n=4).

None of the females observed in this study reproduced twice in one year. This is interesting as tarsiers are reported to have a postpartum estrus (Wright et al., 1986). There are also no reports in the literature of captive tarsiers reproducing twice in one year although Myron Shekelle's captive population in Indonesia has had several spectral tarsiers reproducing twice per year (Shekelle, pers. comm.). I suspect that the high energetic cost of infant care makes it difficult for these primates to reproduce twice in a given year. The rarity of biannual reproduction in these primates also would be observed if the postpartum estrus exists only to enable the rapid replacement of offspring that were lost earlier in the year. On the other hand, throughout my research a total of eleven females reproduced twice. For these latter females, it was possible to calculate their interbirth intervals. The mean interbirth interval was 13.45 months, and ranged between 12 and 19 months.

LACTATION LENGTH AND FREQUENCY

Infant spectral tarsiers nursed until they were between 2 and 3 months of age, with a mean lactation length of 80 days (n=18) (Table 5–1). Infants were nursing during 15.32% of all infant observations. There were no statistically

Table 5–1 The Age (in Days) at Which Infant Spectral Tarsiers Were Weaned and When They Were Last Observed Being Transported*

Infant ID	Age in Days Infant Nursing Stopped	Age in Days Infant Transport Stopped
C600-226	85	64
F600-046	72	52
F600-864	77	57
M600-571	78	46
M300-686	83	55
J750-110	79	59
I450-050	94	60
K50-231	84	49
G350-627	71	56
J700-914	78	61
E950-897	76	48
L200	83	68
S100	83	65
I50	69	68
I550	77	59
O300	90	59
A500	84	58
G200	72	59
Mean	79.72	57.94

* All data are plus or minus 4 days, the maximum amount of time that passed between consecutive focal follows for each study individual.

significant differences in the frequency male and female offspring nursed overall ($X^2=.6049$; $p=.4367$; $df=1$). When the male and female data were pooled, there was a significant negative relationship between infant age and the frequency infants nursed ($r^2=.8439$). On the other hand, although the proportion of time that infants spent nursing changed between weeks one and ten, there were no statistically significant differences between adjacent weeks. In other words, the decline in the proportion of time that infants spent nursing was relatively gradual. There was no dramatic change between adjacent weeks of life. Nonetheless, as infants grew older, the frequency they were observed nursing decreased (Figure 5–2).

Considering that the infant is growing, the decline in the proportion of time spent nursing is somewhat surprising. There are at least three possible explanations for the decline in the time the infants spent nursing at each age. First, the infant may be more efficient in obtaining milk from the mother, that is, the infant is taking shorter bouts to drain the female. The difficulty of ascertaining when an infant is in fact nursing or just holding

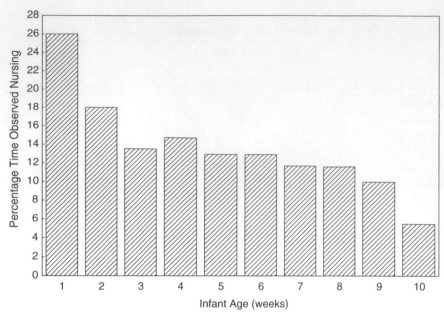

Figure 5–2 The Percentage of Time that Infants Were Observed Nursing at One-Week Age Intervals

the mother's nipple in its mouth is well known (Tilden 1993). Thus, it is hard to determine if the first explanation holds for this study. Second, as the infant matures, the mother's milk improves in quality, thereby requiring less time to obtain higher quality milk. Studies of the change in milk composition over the course of the lactation period indicate that milk quality does improve over time, thereby decreasing the length of time an infant needs to nurse (Tilden 1993). The third possible explanation for the decline in the amount of time that the infant is spending nursing, despite its increasing size, is that the infant is supplementing its diet with solid foods. As I will show in later sections, spectral tarsier infants begin consuming solid foods at a relatively early age (by three weeks).

Data from captive populations on lactation length in *Tarsius* are comparable to my observations of a wild population. According to Wright et al. (1987) and Haring and Wright (1989), captive *Tarsius spp.* (*bancanus* and *syrichta*) are weaned by 60 days. Data from Roberts (1994) on lactation length in captive *T. bancanus* suggests that this species is weaned between 68 and 82 days of age, a little over 2 months. Similarly, Niemitz (1984) reports that a young captive Bornean tarsier was completely self-reliant by the age of 7 weeks (49 days). He also noted that the infants were preferentially using the inguinal mammae over the pectoral. Further studies by Niemitz (1984) indicated that in tarsiers the pectoral mammae are significantly smaller than the inguinal mammae. Although Niemitz was able to distinguish whether the infants were utilizing pectoral or inguinal nipples during his captive observations, my observation abilities under natural conditions were not as good. Thus, I cannot say for certain whether the wild spectral tarsiers used the inguinal mammae more frequently than the pectoral.

In comparison with other primate species, the lactation length of *T. spetrum* is relatively short (Table 5–2). *Lemur mongoz* nurses for four months (Harvey

Table 5–2 The Life History Strategy of Prosimian Primates*

Species	Adult Weight (g)	Birth Weight (g)	Gestation Length (days)	Litter Size	Weaning Age (days)	+Mode of Infant Transport
Lemur catta	2197	86	135	1.20	135	T
Eulemur fulvus	2201	74	119	1.00	135	T
Eulemur macaco	2046	88	127	1.00	135	T
Eulemur mongoz	1799	53	128	1.10	166	T
Varecia variegata	3100	97	102	1.80	90	P
Hapalemur griseus	2000	48	140	1.00	46	P/T
Lepilemur mustelinus	594	27	135	1.00	75	P
Cheirogaleus major	356	18	70	2.50	46	P
Cheirogaleus medius	300	19	60	1.00	46	P
Mirza coquereli	302	12	89	1.50		P
Microcebus murinus	109	6	62	1.93		P
Microcebus rufus	43	6		2.00		P
Indri indri	8000	300	160	1.00	365	T
Propithecus verreauxi	3480	107	151	1.00	180	T
Loris tardigradus	193	12	167	1.00	180	T/P
Nycticebus coucang	1195	51	192	1.00	180	T/P
Arctocebus calabarensis	298	37	134	1.00	131	P
Perodicticus potto	989	47	193	1.06	150	P/T
Otolemur crassicaudatus	1242	44	136	1.64	134	P/T
Galagoides demidovii	69	8	114	1.34	45	P
Galago moholi	266	12	124	1.55	101	P
Galagoides zanzabaricus	136			1.00		P
Tarsius syrichta	117	26	180	1.00	82	P
Tasius bancanus	117	23	178	1.00	80	P

* Most data are taken from Ross 1994 and Harvey et al., 1987. Additional references include: Wright & Martin 1995; Schmid & Ganzhorn 1996; Schmid & Kappeler 1994; Roberts 1994; Wright 1995; Bearder & Martin 1979; Rasmussen & Izard 1988; Izard & Nash 1988; Nash 1983; Harcourt & Nash 1986; Izard & Rasmussen 1988; Ehrlich & MacBride 1990; Jewell & Oates 1969; Bearder 1986; Kappeler 1995.

+ P represents infant parking; T represents continual infant transport; P/T represents a combination of both strategies.

et al., 1987). *Callicebus* and *Aotus* nurse their infants for seven months (Wright 1990). Comparing lactation length in prosimian species that park their infants and those that continually transport them yields some interesting differences. Comparing prosimians of relatively equal body weight such as *Propithecus verreauxi* and *Varecia variegata* (3,000–3,500 g) and *Loris tardigradus* and *Arctocebus calabarensis* (260–310 g) suggests that prosimians that park their infants may have shorter lactation lengths than do prosimians that transport their infants. This difference can be more clearly seen in Table 5–2. Why primates that park have shorter lactation lengths than species that transport their young clearly deserves additional attention.

INFANT TRANSPORT

Mode of Transport: Oral versus Fur

During all but one observation, infant spectral tarsiers were transported orally. Infants are transported in the mother's mouth, similar to domestic cats, and are not transported ventrally or dorsally (often referred to as "on the fur") as is observed in most primate species. During one unusual observation of transport, a four-week-old infant was transported on the mother's ventrum. During this particular observation, the mother was sitting on a horizontal substrate approximately one meter from the ground. The five-week-old infant was cuddled in her ventrum and was nursing. An adult male in a different tree less than 10 meters away gave an alarm call. The mother scanned the ground, noted the presence of a civet, and then quickly and quietly climbed upward into the canopy without rearranging the position of her infant. Thus, the infant was clinging to her ventrum as she climbed up in the canopy. The civet was less than five meters away. This observation indicates that the mother can at least climb while transporting an infant and that the infant is capable of clinging to its mother.

The presence of this one contrasting observation is interesting because there have been several contrary reports in the literature concerning the mode in which *T. bancanus* and *T. syrichta* mothers transport their young. It has been suggested that infant *T. bancanus* are carried on the fur, whereas *T. spectrum* and *T. syrichta* are carried orally. For example, Niemitz (1984) reports that his Bornean tarsiers in captivity were never observed transporting their infants in their mouths. LeGros Clark (1924) watched seven Bornean tarsier mothers and never saw one carrying her baby in her mouth. On the other hand, additional observations of *T. bancanus* in captivity indicate that the Bornean tarsiers do transport their infants orally (Roberts 1984; Haring & Wright 1989). Among the Philippine tarsier, reports in the literature indicate that mothers carry infants in their mouths (Ulmer 1963) as do *T. spectrum* (MacKinnon & MacKinnon 1980). Although it is still unclear as to which mode of transport these two species of tarsier prefer, I feel comfortable stating that *T. spectrum* seems to preferentially transport its infants orally, but can, and occasionally will, transport infants ventrally, if necessary.

There has been only one hypothesis proposed, to date, regarding why some prosimians choose to transport their infants orally versus on their fur. Doyle (1979) suggests that galagos exhibit this behavior because of the infant's inability to grip onto the mother's fur. Roberts (1994) also proposed this explanation for captive *T. bancanus* infants as he observed infants having difficulty holding onto their mother's fur, but then he also noted that infants do not have any difficulty grasping a branch. MacKinnon and MacKinnon (1980) noted that the infant spectral tarsier was able to cling to the mother's chest without aid. In this study of the spectral tarsier, only one observation was made of ventral transport. In this instance, the infant had no difficulty holding onto the mother while being transported ventrally, nor did the mother have to assist the infant. Similarly, while the infant was nursing it did not have any difficulty holding onto its mother's chest.

In my opinion, this hypothesis is unsatisfactory for explaining why some primates transport their infants orally versus on their fur. This hypothesis predicts that nonprosimian primates that produce altricial young, incapable of grasping at birth, should also transport their infants orally. Instead, what we observe is that baboon and chimpanzee mothers often provide assistance to the infant while carrying the infant on their ventrum (Goodall 1986; Dunbar 1988). Similarly, the hypothesis also predicts that prosimians that produce precocial young, capable of grasping onto the mother's fur, should transport their infants on their fur. Yet these species still transport their infants orally (i.e., *Hapalemur;* Wright 1990). The spectral tarsier falls into the latter category. Directly after birth, spectral tarsiers can grasp onto small-diameter branches, yet they are still transported orally. In fact, spectral tarsier infants are transported orally even after they are capable of independent locomotion. Clearly, if the infant is capable of vertically clinging and leaping then it can also cling to its mother's fur.

Transport Frequency

Infants were transported on average 19.36% of all observations. There were no statistically significant differences in the overall frequency that male and female offspring were transported ($X^2=3.6192$, $p=.0671$, $df=1$) or in the frequency with which male and female infants were transported when viewed according to infant age. This lack of sex differences in the amount of time infants are transported seems to be consistent across numerous primate species (Altmann 1980; Berman 1980; Dunbar 1988; Altmann & Samuels 1992).

Figure 5–3 illustrates the relatively gradual decline in infant transport as a function of increasing infant age. There were no statistically significant

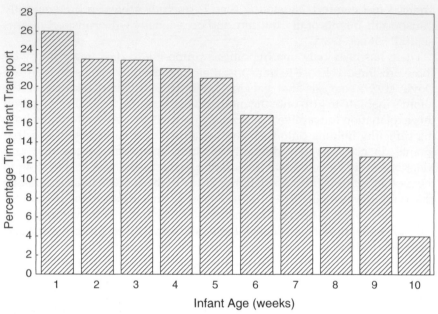

Figure 5–3 The Percentage of Time that Infants Were Observed being Transported Orally, for Each One-week Age Interval

differences in the frequency of transport when comparing infants in adjacent age classes. By three months of age infants were no longer being transported. In Table 5–1, I list the approximate age at which each individual infant was last observed transported. The decline in the amount of time infants are transported with increasing infant age is a pattern observed among numerous primate species. Interestingly enough, Altmann and Samuels (1992) found that while the amount of time infant baboons were transported decreased with infant age, the distance infants were transported remained constant over the first few months. This was because the infant was still being transported when the group was moving over long distances rapidly. Consequently, the baboon infant was transported for the majority of the distance that its mother moved. This has also been observed in *Aotus, Callicebus* and *Propithecus* (Wright 1984, 1985).

In spectral tarsiers, the mean distance that infants were transported between parked locations did not remain constant with time, but varied significantly with infant age. This is probably the result of the rapid postnatal growth observed in this species. The change in the distance infants were transported between parked locations is presented in Table 5–3. Initially, the distance infants were transported were quite small, whereas with time

Table 5–3 The Mean Distance Infants Were Transported Between Parked Locations at
Different Age Intervals (In 2–week Intervals)

Age Interval	Mean Distance (m)	N	Standard Deviation	Standard Error
1–2 weeks	10.23	13	4.55	1.26
3–4 weeks	42.79	24	25.59	5.22
5–6 weeks	48.90	10	10.24	3.24
7–8 weeks	34.53	19	8.37	1.92
9–10 weeks	33.20	10	2.94	.93

the distance increased. After several weeks, the distance infants were transported began to decrease again.

During travel, female spectral tarsiers utilized several different modes
of locomotion. The dominant mode of locomotion, used during 56.12% of
observations, was vertical clinging and leaping (VCL; Napier 1967). Vertical clinging and leaping is characterized by an animal clinging to a branch
in a vertical position, even when at rest, and the use of its hindlimbs to
push off (leap) from one vertical substrate to another. Quadrupedal locomotion, during which animals use their feet in the same manner as their
hands, was observed in 36.33% of observations and climbing was
observed in 7.55% of all observations (Figure 5–4). In contrast, while transporting an infant the amount of time that the female utilized each of the
three locomotor types (vertical clinging and leaping, quadrupedal, and
climbing) changed drastically to the following percentages: 37.82%,
58.88%, and 3.30%, respectively. Thus, quadrupedalism was the preferred
locomotor style while transporting the infant, not vertical clinging and
leaping. The frequency of both climbing and vertical clinging and leaping
decreased significantly (Climbing: $X^2=9.7540$, p=.0018, df=1; VCL:
$X^2=11.4787$, p=.0001, df=1), whereas the frequency of quadrupedalism
increased significantly during infant transport ($X^2=65.2900$, p=.0001,
df=1). The decrease in vertical clinging and leaping in females that are
transporting their young may be attributable to the fact that VCL may not
always be a feasible locomotor strategy when females have their infants in
their mouths. That is, it may not be biomechanically possible to utilize vertical clinging and leaping when transporting a large load anteriorly. The
weight and size of the infant, at birth, and postnatally, may make vertical
clinging and leaping too expensive for a female to handle. Thus, she is
forced to change her locomotor style when transporting her infant.
Crompton et al. (1993) discuss the fact that jumping/leaping is an
extremely expensive locomotor mode because it is a noncyclical activity
and consequently there is no way to conserve either potential or kinetic

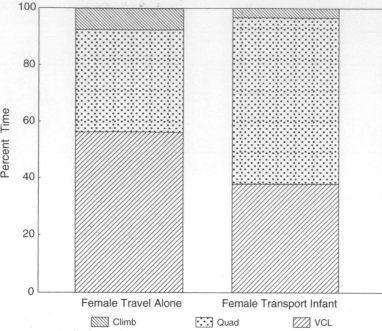

Figure 5–4 Stacked Columns Illustrating the Frequency that Females Used Three Different Locomotor Styles (Vertical Clinging and Leaping, Quadrupedalism, and Climbing) When Traveling Alone Compared with When Transporting an Infant

energy (Taylor 1980). This supports the need for females to change their locomotor style while transporting their infants.

PARENT–OFFSPRING CONFLICT

While there is considerable overlap between the reproductive interests of parents and offspring, there is a point at which they diverge. Although off-spring will want to minimize the cost they inflict on their parents (to ensure future siblings), they are ultimately more heedful of their own reproductive success. Trivers (1974) argued that the difference in the reproductive interests of parents and offspring can best be understood in terms of Hamilton's concept of inclusive fitness. Trivers noted that the coefficient of relatedness between offspring and their future full siblings, and between parents and their offspring, is only $r=0.5$, whereas the off-spring is related to itself by $r=1.0$. Consequently, parents and offspring disagree over when the benefits of the care to the infant outweigh the costs of the care to the parent.

According to Trivers (1974), parents should stop investing in an offspring when a greater benefit can be obtained by investing in another offspring. By contrast, the offspring will only stop asking for investment when the cost it inflicts on the parent is more than two times the benefit it receives from the parent's care. As a result, the offspring always favors longer periods of parental investment than parents are selected to provide. Thus, conflict is a result of the different ways that parents and their offspring maximize their own inclusive fitness.

Conflict over the amount of parental care given is a major process in the offspring's development. Conflict occurs over access to maternal milk as well as to infant transport. When conflict over access to maternal milk is observed in a mammalian species, more is involved than simple maternal rejection. The mother may reject some attempts to nurse while permitting others. At a proximate level, weaning of the infant may be in response to the need to slowly change the female's hormonal levels, instead of a drastic change in them (Carter & Cushing 2004). For example, oxytocin, which is produced during lactation, is known to influence parental behavior. Thus, if a female stopped lactating then her body would all of a sudden stop producing oxytocin. However, if she slowly decreases the frequency of lactation, then her body slowly decreases the amount of oxytocin it produces. Similarly, elevated levels of the hormone prolactin, usually associated with lactation, has been implicated in predisposing individuals to providing nonmaternal care (Sussman in press). Prolactin levels are also known to fluctuate based on the quality of the male's relationship with his mate.

According to Nicholson (1987), "weaning is not accomplished by an absolute denial of milk, but by a gradual shifting of the conditions under which the infant is granted the nipple." Mothers begin to restrict suckling to times when it will not interfere with their own activities (Altmann 1980; Nicholson 1982; Whitten 1982). In other words, nursing conflict is generally not only a dispute between the mother and her infant over the amount of milk that the mother should provide, but it is also a conflict over the timing of the infant's access to milk (Nicholson 1982; Dunbar 1988). In other words, although conflict arises in part because of the energetic cost of nursing the infant, it also arises because the infant's presence on the mother's nipple interferes with the mother's ability to do anything else.

This latter problem is easily observed in ground-feeding primates, such as baboons, where the mother sits to feed. Dunbar (1988) observed that once the infant is more than a few months old, the mother cannot see over its head or get her arms comfortably around her baby to reach food on the ground immediately in front of her if the infant is on the nipple. Dunbar suggests that females therefore encourage their infants to go onto their laps, or on the ground nearby if they are not involved in active nursing.

Parent–offspring conflict, although present, is relatively mild in the spectral tarsier. No excessive tantrums and fighting were observed during nursing conflicts. Nursing conflict primarily involved the mother swiping at the infant's head and trying to distract the infant by quickly grooming it. The

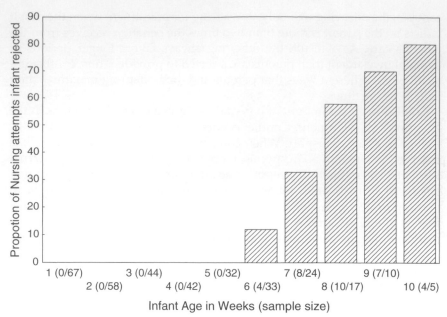

Figure 5–5 The Proportion of Time that Infants Attempted to Nurse and Were Denied Access to the Nipple from 1 to 10 Weeks of Age*

* The number in parentheses represents the number of nursing attempts rejected over the total number of nursing attempts.

mother began to occasionally reject the infant's demand to nurse as early as the sixth week. However, as can be seen in Figure 5–2, nursing was observed in some infants well into the tenth week of life. Conflict over the infant's ability to nurse peaked during the eight and ninth week (Figure 5–5), but dropped significantly thereafter.

Parent–offspring conflict in spectral tarsiers also occurred when the infant wanted to be carried by its mother when she moved them to a new location, whereas the mother attempted to solicit the infant to follow her through a series of vocalizations and movements to and from the infant. Conflict over transportation was much more pronounced in the spectral tarsier than over nursing (Figure 5–6), and involved the infant calling its mother to return to retrieve it, giving soft alarm calls, and not following the mother as she solicited the infant to follow. Basically, it comprised a game of chicken, or wait and see who gives in first.

The observation that spectral tarsier mothers and infants exhibit more pronounced conflict over transportation than nursing is somewhat surprising. Given the low conversion coefficient of lactation, it has been argued that females will expend less energy carrying their infants than providing them with additional milk (Nicolson 1987). The spectral tarsier

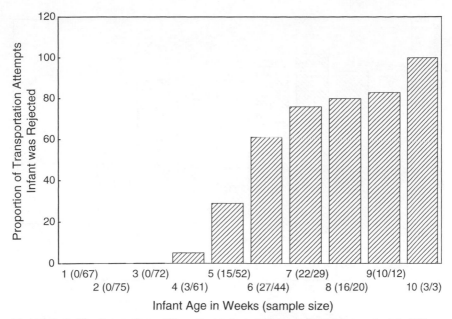

Figure 5–6 The Proportion of Time that Infants Wanted to be Transported, but Were Denied from 1 to 10 Weeks of Age*

* The number in parentheses represents the number of transportation attempts rejected over the total number of transportation attempts.

is an exception, though. Its exceptionally large size at birth and its unprecedented rate of postnatal growth may make the cost of transportation greater than the cost of lactation, despite the low conversion coefficient for lactation. On the other hand, studies have shown that milk quality in primates that park is much higher than in species that transport their infants (Haring & Wright 1989; Tilden 1993) because of their need for rapid postnatal growth.

INFANT PARKING

During the infants' first two months of life they were parked during 54.67% of all observations. Infant parking involved the mother transporting the infant in her mouth, placing it on a branch, and then departing. There were no statistically significant differences in the frequency that male and female offspring were parked overall (X^2=.2749, p=.6001, df=1). Figure 5–7 illustrates the changes in the amount of time infants were parked during weeks one through ten. There were several statistically significant changes in the amount of time that infants were parked when comparing between adjacent

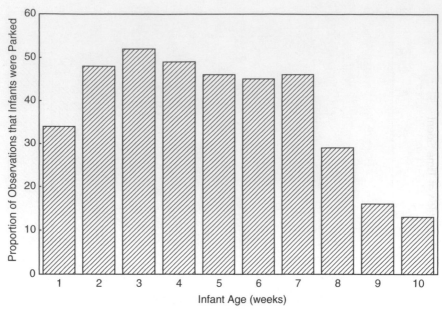

Figure 5–7 TThe Proportion of Time Infants Were Observed Parked Per Week of Infant Life

weeks. The first major change in infant parking occurred between weeks one and two. This was followed by a relatively constant period (nonsignificant changes) of time parked between weeks four and seven before a decline occurred between weeks seven and eight. Week six marks the time when the mother begins to solicit her infant to follow her and thus marks the beginning of the end of infant parking. Nonetheless, occasional occurrences of infant transport and infant parking continue to occur through ten weeks. Figure 5–8 illustrates the proportion of time that infants were parked, transported, and independent over the first ten weeks. Infants locomoted independently during their third week of life. The proportion of time that infants locomoted independently increased substantially between weeks three and ten.

No quantitative measures of the locations where infants were parked were taken besides height and substrate size. Qualitatively, I can say that the majority of the locations where the infants were parked were not well concealed. They did not offer much protection from the elements or predators. The tarsiers did not build any sort of nest in which to park their infants. Thus, unlike many other species (Emmons & Biun 1992), spectral tarsiers often leave their infants in open, unsheltered, and easy-to-reach locations. This suggests locations for parking are not chosen to minimize possible predation, but rather as a means of keeping the infant near the caretaker's foraging location.

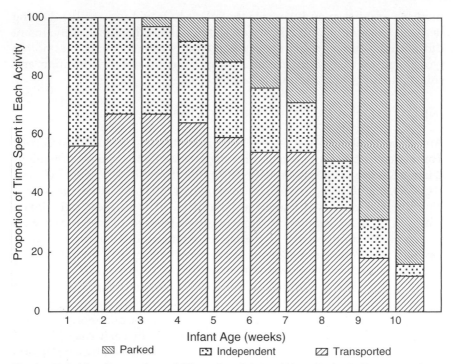

Figure 5–8 The Proportion of Time that Infants Were Parked, Transported, or Independent

Spectral tarsier mothers seemed to employ what I believe is best described as a "cache and carry" infant parking strategy. When the mother left her nest, she carried the infant in her mouth to her first foraging location. When the infant was very young, the infant was frequently parked within the same tree where the mother was observed foraging. This enabled the mother to remain relatively close to her infant. Each time the female decided to move on to a new foraging location, she picked up her infant and moved to a new location. At this new location she would then park her infant in the tree and then continue her nightly foraging nearby, but within the same tree. The number of locations where infants were parked initially increased slightly as the infants matured. As the infants attained independence, the mean number of minutes infants were parked increased, and the number of parked locations began to decrease.

As the infant matured, when the mother decided the foraging patch had been depleted, the mother did not always transport her infant to the new foraging location (e.g., two trees away), but began soliciting the infant to follow her with a series of vocalizations and movements. A typical solicitation sequence involved the mother vocalizing while traveling toward the infant, followed by the mother slowly retreating from the infant's parked location. After traveling a short distance away from the infant, the mother would stop and wait for the infant to travel toward her. During her wait she would emit a series of additional vocalizations. If the infant did not travel independently to the mother's new location, the mother would return to a short distance away from the infant's location and solicit it to follow with vocalizations and travel.

INFANT FALLING FROM PARKED LOCATIONS

Among spectral tarsiers at my study site, infant falling frequently occurred. This indicates it is not a behavioral pattern restricted to captive populations (Haring & Wright 1989; Roberts 1994). For the 18 infants who were followed regularly, infant falling was observed on a total of 111 occasions. No serious injury or mortality was known to have resulted from these falls. Infant falling in the wild population rarely occurred because of maternal neglect (i.e., mother's dropping babies during locomotion). In 48 of the 111 occurrences, a very young infant (less than one month of age) fell from its parked location. The fall resulted from the infant losing its grasp on the substrate where it was parked. The mother retrieved the fallen infant during 33 of the 48 falls, whereas another group member retrieved the infant during the remaining 15 falls. Thus, until the infant was at least one month old, the infant was always quickly retrieved after a fall. In each case of infant retrieval, the infant was transported orally. When retrieved by a nonmaternal individual, the infant was also transported orally and was brought back to a location near where it was originally parked.

After one month of age, infant falling continued to occur with surprising frequency. Sixty-three observations were made of a young infant falling as it began exploring its environment from its parked location. After one month of age, infant retrieval following a fall occurred only occasionally. In only 33 of the 63 falls was the infant retrieved. In 15 instances, retrieval was by the mother; in the other 18 instances, retrieval was by a subadult group member. In all instances of retrieval by the mother, the infant was transported in the mother's mouth to a new location. Seven times, when another group member retrieved an infant it was transported in the group member's mouth to a new location. In the other cases, the group member went down to the ground where the infant had fallen and solicited the infant to follow her or him to another location. Once the infant and the group member were up several meters in the canopy, the other group member then proceeded to groom the infant. In the additional thirty cases in which no group member retrieved the infant following a fall, the infant hopped on the ground toward the nearest tree and then climbed upward where it then rested and gathered its wits.

The mean height from which infants fell was 4.5 meters. The mean substrate size from which infants fell was 4.5 centimeter. Initially, I hypothesized that infants were more likely to fall when the diameter of the substrate size was too large for them to get their hands around. However, the substrate size that the infants held onto when they were parked was not an important variable affecting infant falling. As the infants aged and began exploring their environments, the cause of infant falling had more to do with the infant learning which substrates could hold their weight, and how far on a branch limb they could go before the limb gave way underneath them.

Infant falling has been described as a major sources of infant mortality in other parking species such as the ruffed lemur (Morland 1990). It has also been described in primates that transport their infants. For example, Wright (1985) observed a *Callicebus* infant to fall 30 meters. The father eventually went to the ground to check on the infant and the infant climbed back onto his back.

INFANT ALARM/DISTRESS CALLS

Infants gave alarm calls in several situations, including the first few times the infant came into visual contact with certain rats, snakes, and birds, as well as when the mother had not returned from foraging to nurse or be with the infant. Figure 5–9 illustrates the change in the mean frequency infants gave alarm/distress calls per hour of observation and infant age.

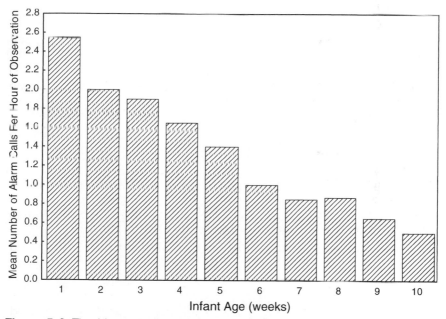

Figure 5–9 The Mean Number of Alarm Calls that Infants Emitted Per Hour of Observation, Per Week of Infant Life

In the first two weeks, numerous alarm-type calls were given. After this time, the frequency that alarm calls were given decreased with infant age.

INFANT ENVIRONMENTAL EXPLORATION AND DEVELOPMENTAL CHANGES

The first or neonatal stage of infant development is characterized by constant mother–infant contact. It is exceptionally short in the spectral tarsier relative to other primates. Figure 5–10 illustrates the frequency infants were observed in physical contact with their mothers per week of the infant's life. As expected, as the spectral tarsier infant became older, the amount of time spent in physical contact with the infant decreased. During the first two weeks, the mother spent nearly 60% of her time in physical contact with the infant and was always the group member nearest to the infant. Figure 5–11 also illustrates the mean distance (1 m, 3 m, 5 m, 10 m) between mother and infant. As the infant grows older, the mean distance between the mother–infant pair increases. Initially, the high amount of contact with the mother and the unusually low amount of contact between the infant and other group members stems from the fact that, shortly before giving birth, expectant mothers seem to move to a new sleeping location (tree) and sleep apart from the group. Although other group members occasionally

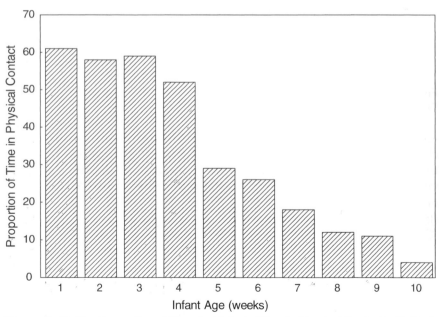

Figure 5–10 The Proportion of Time that Infants Were in Physical Contact with Their Mothers Between 1 and 10 Weeks of Age

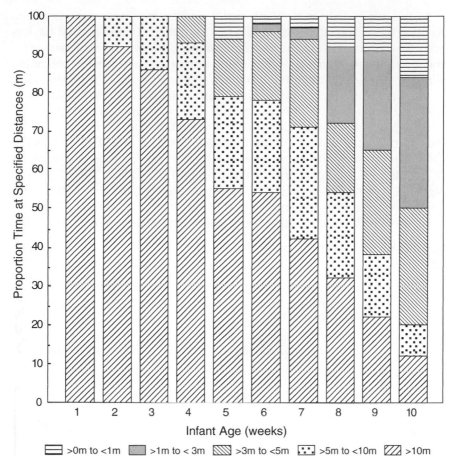

Figure 5–11 The Mean Proportion of Time the Mother and Infant Spent at Specified Distances from One Another During the Infant's First 10 Weeks of Life

identified where the female was sleeping and tried to join her, she actively chased them away. The mother's new sleeping location was kept secret for the first few days by not always joining the group during early morning vocal calls. This may be a strategy employed by mothers to minimize infanticidal attempts (van Schaik & Dunbar 1990) or to reduce predation risk (Janson 1992). This behavioral pattern has also been observed in galagos (Charles-Dominique 1977).

Environmental exploration and play are thought to be important behaviors that broaden the infant's experience and facilitate its behavioral development (Baldwin 1986) through the development of perceptual and motor skills, physical exercise, coordination, development of predator defense skills, and generally overcoming helplessness by developing competence in the environment.

In this study, I defined infant exploration as any movement from the location where the infant was parked by its mother. Infant spectral tarsiers were first observed to explore their environment, a developmental marker for the second phase of infant development, during the third week of infant life (Figure 5–12). In comparison, *L. catta* has also been observed exploring their environment between the second and third week (Gould 1990). There were no sex differences in the frequency that male and female infants explored their environment overall ($X^2=0.6787$, p=.4100 df=1). The mean substrate diameter utilized during environmental exploration was 1.73 centimeter. Note that this substrate size is substantially less than the substrate diameter of infants who had fallen down from their parked location. The mean substrate diameter utilized during environmental exploration was not significantly different than the mean substrate diameter utilized during other behaviors such as grooming (t=0.3347, p=.3972), nursing (t=0.5388, p=.3427), transport (t=0.3739, p=.3861) or parking (t=3.3600, p=.0921).

It was during the second phase of infant development that infants reached several important developmental markers including first attempts at independent locomotion, first successful leap, first attempt at capturing a prey, and first successful prey capture. As can be seen from Table 5–4, the infant's first successful leap was taken at a mean of 32 days. Similarly, their first swipe at prey was on 39 days and their first successful prey capture was taken on 47 days. In captive *Tarsius spp.* Wright noted that infants began

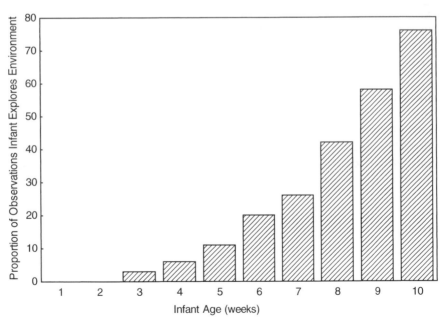

Figure 5–12 The Proportion of Time that Infants Explored Their Environment During the First 10 Weeks of the Infant's Life

Table 5–4 Developmental Markers for 18 Infant *T. Spectrum**

Infant ID	Age at First VCL	Age at First Attempted Forage	Age at First Successful Forage
C600-226	28	36	44
F600-046	39	43	58
F600-864	26	39	49
M600-571	37	44	48
M300-686	29	38	46
J750-110	34	37	54
I450-050	30	45	50
K50-231	30	42	47
G350-627	32	34	51
J700-914	35	29	34
E950-897	28	37	37
L200	33	40	51
S100	29	34	42
I50	32	37	49
I550	33	38	46
O300	29	36	53
A500	28	43	48
G200	37	41	41
Mean Age (in days)	31.6	38.5	47.1

* All data are plus or minus 4 days, the maximum amount of time that passed between consecutive focal follows for each study individual.

foraging independently by 40 days. Roberts (1994) reported the following developmental markers for captive *T. bancanus*: first leaps by 26 days, last age transported between 41 and 43 days, weaned between 68 and 82 days, first attempt at prey capture between 30 and 49 days, and first successful prey capture between 36 and 57 days. In young *T. spectrum*, as well as in *T. bancanus*, the infant's use of quadrupedal locomotion precedes bipedal leaps.

INFANT GROOMING

Infants were groomed on average during 8.5% of all observations. There were no statistically significant differences in the frequency that male and female infants were involved in bouts of grooming ($X^2=3.0461$; p=.0809; df=1). The lack of sex differences in grooming frequency remains when comparing the frequency of grooming in males and females between adjacent one-week age intervals. Figure 5–13 illustrates the decline in infant grooming

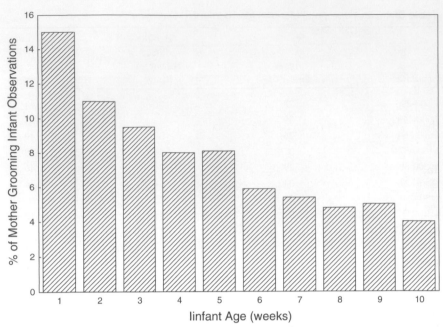

Figure 5–13 The Proportion of Time that Infants Were Groomed by the Mother During the First 10 Weeks of the Infant's Life

as a function of increasing infant age. Although the amount of time infants were groomed by the mother decreased with infant age, there was a corresponding increase in infant grooming by other group members (subadult and juveniles) as infants increased in age. This will be addressed in Chapter 6.

Bouts of grooming occurred throughout the night, but were most frequently observed between 2200 and 0200 hours, with another peak at the time of wake up, 1700 hours. When the mother grooms her infant, she uses her incisors in a comblike fashion while performing a slow biting movement. Her hands are not used in grooming as is observed in the simian primates. This is a very important observation because as cladists we use the lack of a toothcomb in the tarsiers to ally them with the monkeys and apes, as Haplorhines, despite the fact that the tarsiers still groom in the same way as other prosimians.

An individual may approach another and sit beside it to invite grooming or be groomed without apparent solicitation. The groomer usually starts on the head and neck picking through the fur, and occasionally using its mouth. Niemitz (1984) recorded fifty-three occurrences of allogrooming in the Bornean tarsier. The duration of the grooming bouts lasted seven minutes. His data show that the Bornean tarsiers seem to prefer to groom at heights greater than they seem to travel and forage. My data also indicate that grooming takes place at greater heights than many other behaviors.

INFANT MORTALITY

Infant mortality was average for a primate population (Cowlishaw & Dunbar 2000). In Table 5–5, I present the mortality schedule from birth to one year, recorded every two weeks, for the wild infant spectral tarsiers observed in this study. Infant mortality is restricted to the first two months of life, with most of the mortality concentrated shortly after birth and within the first month of life. After the first two months, the probability the infant

Table 5–5 The Mortality Schedule of Wild Spectral Tarsiers at 2–week Intervals from Birth Until One Year of Age (n=46)

Age Interval	n_x	d_x	q_x	l_x
0–2 weeks	46	10	0.217	1.000
3–4 weeks	36	4	0.111	0.783
5–6 weeks	32	2	0.063	0.672
7–8 weeks	30	1	0.033	0.639
9–10 weeks	29	2	0.069	0.570
11–12 weeks	27	0	0.000	0.570
13–14 weeks	27	1	0.037	0.533
15–16 weeks	26	0	0.000	0.533
17–18 weeks	26	1	0.038	0.495
19–20 weeks	25	0	0.000	0.495
21–22 weeks	25	0	0.000	0.495
23–24 weeks	25	1	0.040	0.455
25–26 weeks	24	0	0.000	0.455
27–28 weeks	24	1	0.042	0.413
29–30 weeks	23	0	0.000	0.413
31–32 weeks	23	0	0.000	0.413
33–34 weeks	23	0	0.000	0.413
35–36 weeks	23	0	0.000	0.413
37–38 weeks	23	0	0.000	0.413
39–40 weeks	23	0	0.000	0.413
41–42 weeks	23	0	0.000	0.413
43–44 weeks	23	0	0.000	0.413
45–46 weeks	23	0	0.000	0.413
47–48 weeks	23	0	0.000	0.413
49–50 weeks	23	0	0.000	0.413
51–52 weeks	23	0	0.000	0.413

* n_x represents the number of infants born into the population that were observed over a 52-week period; d_x represents the number of infants that died during any 2-week period; q_x represents the relative proportion of infants that died during any specific 2-week period; l_x represents the relative proportion of infants that survived from birth to a specified 2-week period.

will survive through each successive age interval remained constant until one year of age. Because males and females disperse from their parent's territory between one and two years, it is difficult to distinguish between mortality and successful dispersal. Therefore, mortality after one year of age is not reported here. Data on dispersal is presented in Chapter 7.

Table 5–6 presents the mortality schedule, from birth to one year, for the captive population of Bornean tarsiers at the National Zoological Park, as

Table 5–6 The Mortality Profile of Captive *T. Bancanus* Based on Literature Records (Roberts & Kohn 1993; Roberts 1994)

Age Interval	n_x	d_x	q_x	l_x
0–2 weeks	12	5	0.416	1.000
3–4 weeks	7	1	0.143	0.584
5–6 weeks	6	0	0.000	0.501
7–8 weeks	6	0	0.000	0.501
9–10 weeks	5	1	0.200	0.400
11–12 weeks	4	0	0.000	0.400
13–14 weeks	4	0	0.000	0.400
15–16 weeks	4	0	0.000	0.400
17–18 weeks	4	0	0.000	0.400
19–20 weeks	4	0	0.000	0.400
21–22 weeks	4	0	0.000	0.400
23–24 weeks	4	0	0.000	0.400
25–26 weeks	4	0	0.000	0.400
27–28 weeks	4	0	0.000	0.400
29–30 weeks	4	0	0.000	0.400
31–32 weeks	4	0	0.000	0.400
33–34 weeks	4	0	0.000	0.400
35–36 weeks	4	0	0.000	0.400
37–38 weeks	4	0	0.000	0.400
39–40 weeks	4	0	0.000	0.400
41–42 weeks	4	0	0.000	0.400
43–44 weeks	4	0	0.000	0.400
45–46 weeks	4	0	0.000	0.400
47–48 weeks	4	0	0.000	0.400
49–50 weeks	4	0	0.000	0.400
51–52 weeks	4	0	0.000	0.400

* An additional infant that was 3–4 weeks old was also observed.

** n_x represents the number of infants born into the population that were observed over a 52-week period; d_x represents the number of infants that died during any 2-week period; q_x represents the relative proportion of infants that died during any specific 2-week period; l_x represents the relative proportion of infants that survived from birth to a specified 2-week period.

extracted from published papers (Roberts & Kohn 1993; Roberts 1994). Once again, infant mortality seems to be restricted to the first two months of life, during which time mortality is extremely high. Most infant mortality in this captive population is centered around birth with three stillbirths, and three deaths within three weeks after birth. From the mortality schedule, once an infant survives the first three months of life, the probability the captive-born infant will survive through each successive age interval remains constant for several years of adulthood.

Figure 5–14 presents the survival function of the wild *T. spectrum* and the captive *T. bancanus*. The actual shape of the survival functions for the two populations are quite similar, with almost all mortality centered around the first two months of life.

Perhaps the most striking result of the mortality patterns is the similarity in the survival functions for the captive Bornean and the wild spectral

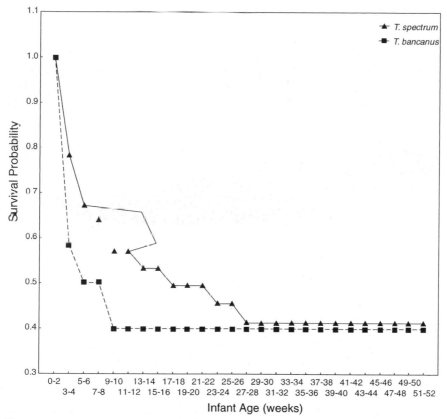

Figure 5–14 The Survival Probability Function for Wild Spectral Tarsiers and Captive Bornean Tarsiers from Birth to 1 Year of Age

tarsier populations. This is especially interesting given the vastly different environments and living conditions between captivity and natural habitat, as well as the noted behavioral differences between the two species (Niemitz 1984; Nietsch & Niemitz 1994; Gursky 1995). In both species, infant mortality is restricted to the first two to three months of life, and is concentrated in the first three weeks of life. In captivity, if an infant survived the first three months of life, then the probability of it surviving to adulthood is quite high. In the wild spectral tarsier population, if an infant survived the first two months, the probability it would survive until one year of age was also quite high. Yet, survival in those first few months, especially at birth and the first three weeks, seems exceptionally tenuous, both in captivity and in the wild. Wright (1995) argues that increasing investment (i.e., higher quality milk or increased length of lactation) will not necessarily decrease the infant's probability of mortality that results from either predation or infanticide. Consequently, "there may be increased selection pressure for mothers to keep some resources in reserve (bet hedging), so that a female will be in sufficiently good health to produce an infant at the next cycle, if she loses an offspring. Further, by keeping some resources in reserve, she probably can extend her total reproductive life span" (p. 850).

Despite the similarities, there is a significant difference in the level of infant mortality during the first two months: Although mortality seems to be restricted to this period, the relative number of infants that die is initially considerably higher in the captive Bornean tarsier population than in the wild spectral tarsier population. It is this exceptionally high infant mortality that has made captive tarsier breeding so difficult. It is unclear at this time whether the difference in infant mortality between the two populations is the result of species differences, or habitat differences (wild vs. captivity), or some combination of the two.

MOTHER–INFANT RELATIONSHIP IN GALAGOS AND LORISES

The mother–infant relationship observed in the spectral tarsier infants is quite similar to that reported for galago infants, but distinct from lorisid infants (Charles-Dominique 1977; Charles-Dominique et al., 1980; Nekaris 2003). In *T. spectrum* and *G. demidovii*, the female often—although not always (four out of six cases in the spectral tarsier)—isolates herself from the group before giving birth and rejoins the group one to two weeks later (Charles-Dominique 1977). The new location may have been as far away as 100 meters from the standard sleeping tree.

Initially there is intensive contact between the mother and her infant. This is also true of *G. demidovii* (Charles-Dominique 1977). Charles-Dominique reports that during the first week after birth, the mother carries her infant out of the nest at dusk and parks it in the vegetation where it remains immobile. This behavior has been observed with *G. alleni*, too. Charles-Dominique also reports that while the infant *G. demidovii* is parked the mother feeds in the nearby vicinity, often in the same tree. If the mother moves on to another feeding area, she comes to collect the infant and then redeposits it in the vegetation in the new area. At dawn, she carries the infant to the nest with her.

In contrast, Charles-Dominique (1977) reports that the mother–infant relationship in wild lorisids is quite distinct. Rasmussen (1986) made similar observations about captive lorisids. In lorisids, before the infant is one week old, the mother begins to park her baby at dusk and never returned before dawn. Nekaris (2003) found that slender loris females transported their infants for the first four weeks of life. After four weeks, mothers began parking their infants for the entire night. In contrast to galagos and the tarsiers, the lorisid mother does not exhibit a cache-and-carry strategy. She does not return to retrieve the infant until dawn approaches. In other words, the infant is basically left alone for the majority of the night. Charles-Dominique does not report whether there is any baby-sitting or infant guarding by other groups members. He only indicates that the mother does not return to the infant until morning. Nekaris (2003) does note that adult males visited and played with parked infants. This is very distinct from the type of infant parking exhibited by the spectral tarsier or the galagos, and is much more reminiscent of the form of infant parking exhibited by tree shrews.

MODELING MATERNAL TIME BUDGETS: WHY PARK?

The goal of this section is to address whether female spectral tarsiers have enough time in their night to obtain the additional energy necessary if they were to nurse and transport their infants. This will be achieved through a detailed analysis of their activity budget. By activity budget, I am referring to the amount of time the focal females spend in each of several predefined behaviors over the course of the study. In this section, I will first present the time budget of all females. The following subsection provides a detailed discussion of the model (Altmann 1980). Using the time budget model, I then present the calculations for the total time females need to forage, F_t, if they were providing all of the infant's nutritional needs through lactation. Then, following the methods of Dunbar (1988), I will incorporate the additional time a female would need to forage if she transported and nursed her infant. From this amended time budget, I then will determine if there is enough time in a night for spectral tarsier females to obtain the additional food necessary if she was to nurse and continually transport her infants.

To test the energetic hypothesis that female spectral tarsiers do not have enough time in their daily time budget to deal with the costs of continual infant transport, I modified Altmann's model of maternal time budgets (1980), a time allocation model. That is, it examines how animals expend their time (in terms of duration and scheduling) across a wide variety of behaviors. The aim of time allocation models is to determine whether the duration and scheduling of each behavior is predictable with respect to variables such as sex, age, weight, reproduction, and other aspects of the environment.

Time allocation models are founded on the basic economic assumption that time and resources are limited and have alternative uses. In order to survive and reproduce, an individual must find food, avoid predators, find a mate, and raise offspring. Each of these activities often prevents an individual from engaging in other activities at the same time. That is, time spent providing parental care is time lost to searching out food or other mating opportunities. In addition to opportunity costs, individuals can also incur resource costs (Hames 1992). A resource cost is measured as the amount of time or other resources (calories) that an individual expends while performing an activity. The goal of time allocation models is to assess the factors that determine the (opportunity and resource) costs and (fitness) benefits of these behavioral trade-offs (Hames 1992).

Models are often described as oversimplistic and somewhat unrealistic (Dupre 1987; Richardson & Boyd 1987). On the other hand, the simplifications found in mathematical models provide a modifiable framework such that the effects of modifying different variables can be explored in a quantifiable fashion. Models allow one to take apart complex systems and evaluate relationships between various components in the model. Given that the world is so complex, being able to make certain assumptions so that one can explore the relationship between variables is worthwhile. These simplifying assumptions not only permit testing predictions, but make modeling the ability of tarsiers to care for their offspring possible.

Following Altmann (1980), the model used in this chapter makes numerous simplifying assumptions. (For additional detail, see Altmann 1980). Altmann calculated the average time budget for female baboons, *Papio cynocephalus*. She then calculated the total time a female must forage, F_t to meet her own metabolic needs and the energetic cost of nursing. This was based on the formula:

$$F_t = A\,m^{.75} + \frac{A\,(i_o + \Delta_i)^{.75}}{E}$$

where A is a constant that converts energy requirement into time spent feeding, and can be calculated from $F_p/(m + i_o)^{.75}$, where F_p is the percentage of time spent feeding at parturition, m is the mother's body weight in kilograms, i_o is the infant's weight at birth in kilograms, and Δ_i is the increment in the infant's weight due to growth in kilograms per day, t is the infant's age in days, and E is the net efficiency of maternal lactation (Brody 1945; Blackburn & Calloway 1976; McClure 1987; Thompson 1992).

Using this formula, Altmann plotted the total time a female baboon needed to feed, F_t to maintain her own body and that of her infant from birth to eight months on the female's time budget. When the infant is eight months old, the model predicts that lactating females would need to spend between 60 and 65% of their time foraging compared to 43% in nonlactating and nonpregnant females. Altmann observed that lactating *Papio* must forage during time previously spent resting to meet her own nutritional needs as well as her infant's energetic needs. The conclusion Altmann reached is that even with conservative estimates of energetic demands, a mother could not provide all caloric requirements for herself and her infant beyond six to eight months without severe costs to herself. It is worthwhile to note that it is between six to eight months that baboon mothers wean their infants from the nipple. In the following sections of this chapter, I will apply this model to the female spectral tarsier and calculate the total amount of time she needs to forage to meet the energetic cost of nursing her infant.

TIME BUDGET OF ADULT FEMALE SPECTRAL TARSIERS

The data presented in this section are based on a subset of the total data collected throughout my research. The data is primarily based on eight females who were observed for varying lengths of time. As illustrated in Figure 5–15, females (all reproductive states pooled) spent approximately 53.38% of their time foraging, 25.69% traveling, 14.70% resting, and 6.23% socializing. Thus, for the calculation of F_t, " F_p " equals 53.38.

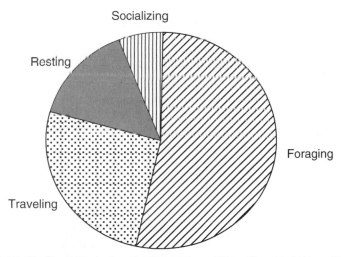

Figure 5–15 Pie Chart Illustrating the Proportion of Time Spent in Various Behavioral Categories for Female Spectral Tarsiers, Lumped for All Reproductive Conditions

In the actual collection of the data, numerous other behavioral states were recognized and recorded when conducting the scans. Thus, it was necessary to condense my data into the four categories utilized in this model. In this figure, foraging includes all searching behaviors as well as actual feeding events; resting includes not only resting behavior but also self-grooming; travel includes only traveling behavior; and social behavior includes nursing, scent-marking, vocalizations, allogrooming, and playing. The definitions of each of these behavioral states are given in Chapter 1. Using the original behavioral states recognized during data collection, nonreproductive adult female spectral tarsiers spent 6.23% of their time eating, 46.39% foraging, 25.69% traveling, 14.70% resting, 1.28% grooming, 0.64% playing, 1.93% scent-marking, and 2.38% vocalizing.

ADULT FEMALE BODY WEIGHT

The body weight of all the females captured in the mist nets was determined prior to the attachment of a radio collar. The body weight of the individual females are presented in Table 2–6. On average, adult female spectral tarsiers weighed 105.6 grams, but ranged from 86 to 121 grams (S. D. ± 6.10). It is noteworthy that the body weights presented in this book are significantly less than the adult weights reported in frequently cited papers such as Harvey et al. (200 g; 1987) and Fleagle (140g; 1988), and are much more similar to the body weights reported for the spectral tarsiers' sister species, *T. bancanus* and *T. syrichta* (Harvey et al., 1987; Fleagle 1988). The body weights obtained in this study are also comparable to those reported by Nietsch and Niemitz (1992). Thus, for the calculation of F_t, "m" equals 105.6 grams.

INFANT BIRTH WEIGHT AND INFANT GROWTH

Given the difficulty and risk involved in capturing newborn infants, no infant birth weights were obtained in this study. Captive data from infants in other tarsier species range from 23.0 to 27.3 grams (Haring & Wright 1989; Wright 1990; Roberts & Kohn 1993; Roberts 1994) (Table 5–7). From these data, a weighted mean (Sokal & Rohlf 1981) of 23.7 grams was derived and will be used as the infant birth weight. Based on infant weights obtained from wild spectral tarsiers measured at approximately one week of age, the mean weight derived from these other captive species is probably also fairly representative of infant weights in wild spectral tarsiers.

The infant growth rate for two spectral tarsiers was recorded at two-week intervals from one week to nine weeks of age. It was impossible to determine the sex of the infant prior to the first capture; by chance, only male infants were captured. Although the body sizes of males and females are sexually dimorphic, these initial growth rates may still be representative of both sexes as dimorphism in growth rates often, but not always, begins later in physical maturation than three months of age (Glassman et al., 1984).

Table 5–7 Birth Weights of Infant Tarsiers in Captivity

Mean Infant Birth Weight	Range	Sample Size	Tarsier Species	Reference
27.3	n/a	2	T. bancanus	Wright 1990
23.0	19.0–25.0	4	T. bancanus	Roberts 1994
T. bancanus Weighted Mean=24.43 g				
23.2	20.0–31.5	9	T. syrichta	Haring and Wright 1989
Total Weighted Mean = 23.69 g				

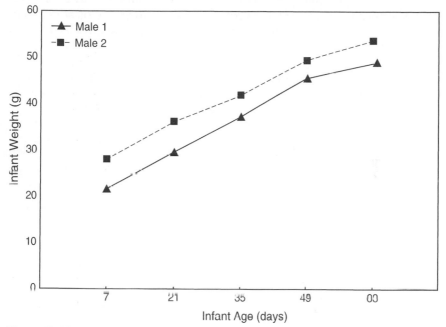

Figure 5–16 The Infant-growth Rates Obtained from Two Wild Male Infant Spectral Tarsiers

The growth rates of the two infant males from one to nine weeks, taken at two-week intervals, is presented in Figure 5–16.

Growth from birth to maturity in mammals generally is best represented by a complex curve (Zullinger et al., 1984; Kirkwood 1985). However, the portion of the curve under consideration here is essentially linear. The mean rate of infant growth for spectral tarsiers is approximately .3286 g/day from birth to 1 week, .4430 g/day from 1 to 3 weeks, .4660 g/day from 3 to 5 weeks, .4850 g/day from 5 to 7 weeks, and .4410 g/day from 7 to 9 weeks. After 9 weeks, because of the infant's drastically improved mobility, and the lack of time that infants were parked, capture became more difficult and weighing was discontinued. There is obviously some variation in the growth rates of the spectral tarsiers over the first 2 months of life. Glassman et al. (1984) found that body weight growth rates in baboons varied considerably over the course of an animal's life. For male baboons, growth rates averaged .01 kg/day during the first year and fell to .008 during the second and third year and then up to .017 during the fifth year during an adolescent growth spurt.

In comparison, Roberts (1994) reports data for the infant growth rates of several captive Bornean tarsiers, and Haring and Wright (1989) present growth data on a hand-raised Philippine tarsier (*Tarsius syrichta*; Mandarin). A comparison of the body weights of the three species, with data on body weight in *T. bancanus* and *T. syrichta* from Kappeler (1990) and data on *T. spectrum* from this study, indicates that there are no statistically significant differences between the species in terms of adult body size (Table 5–8); therefore, direct comparison of the actual growth curves is possible. Figures 5–17a and b illustrate the growth curves of the Bornean and Philippine tarsier species at approximately one to two week intervals. It is evident from this figure that, on first examination, the three sister species show growth curves that are close approximations of one another.

Table 5–8 ANOVA Results Comparing Mean Body Weight among Three Tarsier Species

Source	df	SS	MS	F-test
Between Groups	2	291.97	145.99	1.808
Within Groups	23	1857.14	80.75	p=.1865
Total	25	2149.12		

Comparison	F-value
T. bancanus & *T. syrichta*	0.0342
T. bancanus & *T. spectrum*	1.7095
T. syrichta & *T. spectrum*	1.2200

Species	Mean Body Weight (g)	Sample Size (n)	S.D.	Range	Source
T. spectrum	116.94	49	10.69	86–136	This study
T. bancanus	125.88	8	10.27	112–140	Crompton & Andau 1987; Izard et al., 1985
T. syrichta	124.33	3	4.04	120–128	Ulmer 1963

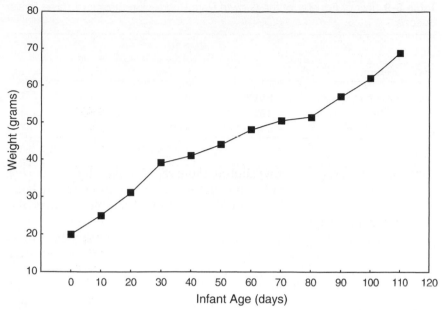

Figure 5–17a The Infant-growth Rate for a Single Hand-raised *Tarsius syrichta* Infant, Based on Data Taken from Haring & Wright (1989)

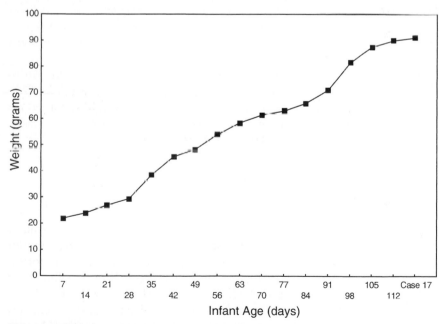

Figure 5–17b The Mean Infant-growth Rate for Mother-reared *Tarsius bancanus* Infants, Based on Data Taken in Captivity from Roberts (1994)

Table 5–9 Test of Equality of the Growth Rate Regression Slopes in Three Tarsier Species

Species Comparison	Fs	df First Species	df Second Species	$F_{.01}$
T. spectrum & T. bancanus	0.0126	46	6	7.72
T. spectrum & T. syrichta	4.6316	46	9	5.11
T. bancanus & T. syrichta	0.9086	9	6	7.98

T. bancanus does seem to grow slightly more rapidly than does *T. syrichta*. The most likely explanation for this discrepancy has to do with the latter being a hand-reared individual. Similarly, the small sample size may also be affecting the analysis.

To compare the rates of growth between species statistically, the growth curves for each species were further smoothed by least-squares regression (Sokal & Rohlf 1981). The regression lines for each of the spectral tarsier males was $Y=.4614x + 20.9000$, $r^2 = .9829$ and $Y=.4643x + 25.55$, $r^2 = .9946$. The regression lines for the captive hand-raised Philippine tarsier was $Y=.3853x + 20.3048$, $r^2 = .9790$. The regression lines for the captive hand-raised Bornean tarsiers was $Y=.6593x + 19.9608$, $r^2 = .9878$. The slope represents the growth velocity for each species. A test for equality of these three regression lines following the methods of Snedcor and Cochran (1989) yielded no significant difference (Table 5–9). At the .01 level of significance, the null hypothesis that there is no difference between the growth rates of the three tarsier species cannot be rejected.

Based on the mean tarsier infant birth weight reported in the literature (Haring & Wright 1989; Wright 1990; Roberts 1994), the model's "i_o", infant birth weight, will equal 23.7 grams. The mean weight obtained on the two infant spectral tarsier males in this study will be used to represent the increase in infant weight at new ages, represented as $_i$.

ESTIMATING THE ENERGETIC EFFICIENCY OF LACTATION (E)

One of the most important—but extremely costly—types of postnatal parental investment in primates and other mammals is lactation (Kleiman 1985). The energy requirements of lactating human females are reported to increase 20% to 50% (Portman 1970; Buss & Voss 1971; Coelho 1974; Nicholson 1987; Thompson 1992; Tilden 1993). Similarly, the basal metabolic rate of many lactating rodents and other mammals (Thompson 1992) have been shown to increase considerably during lactation. Madagascan primates, with their low basal metabolic rates and high prenatal maternal investment, are reported to raise their metabolic rates as much as

Table 5–10 The Calculation of the Parameters to Determine the Total Time, F_t, Females Need to Forage to Meet Their Own Needs and Those of Their Infant's Energetic Needs Through Lactation

Infant Age in Days (t)	A^*	$m\ (g)^*$	$i_o\ (g)^*$	$i\ (g)^*$	$F_p{}^*$	E^*	$F_t{}^*$
0	1.41	108.2	23.7	—	53.38	.60–.80	66.23–72.54
7	1.41	108.2	23.7	.3286	53.38	.60–.80	67.59–74.36
21	1.41	108.2	23.7	.4430	53.38	.60–.80	71.57–79.66
35	1.41	108.2	23.7	.4660	53.38	.60–.80	75.33–84.68
49	1.41	108.2	23.7	.4850	53.38	.60–.80	79.19–89.82
63	1.41	108.2	23.7	.4410	53.38	.60–.80	81.18–92.48

* A represents a constant that converts energy requirement into time spent feeding, and can be calculated from $F_p/(m + i_o)^{.75}$, where F_p is the percentage of time spent feeding at parturition (represented by nonreproductive females in this study), m is the mother's body weight, i_o is the infant's weight at birth. E represents the net efficiency of maternal lactation.

75% during reproduction (Young et al., 1990). The cost of lactation varies widely across species by raising the female's energetic requirements accordingly (Jenness 1974).

Compared to gestation, lactation is a relatively inefficient use of energy. Blackburn and Calloway (1976) estimate that in humans the conversion ratio for lactation (the efficiency with which energy ingested by the mother is converted into energy in milk) is only 80%. Brody (1945) gives a value for mammals of only 60%. This means that the mother has to consume 25% to 66% more energy than her infant actually needs to ensure that the infant obtains the energy that it requires. Some authors have found that the conversion efficiency of lactation is significantly less when corrections are made for fat deposition (Randolph et al., 1980; McClure 1987; Weiner 1987).

In this model, E represents the net efficiency of maternal lactation, the ratio of milk calories to lactational increment in maintenance calories and of assimilation by the infant. There have been no studies of the net efficiency of maternal lactation in tarsiers, so I use both estimates of E (Blackburn and Calloway 1976; Brody 1945) to bracket the model's predictions throughout this chapter (Table 5–10).

CALCULATING TIME SPENT FORAGING F_t FOR ADULT FEMALE SPECTRAL TARSIERS

Recall that the calculation of F_t (the total time that a female must forage to meet her own needs plus the energetic cost of nursing her infant) is based on the following formula:

$$F_t = Am^{.75} + \frac{A\ (i_o + t\Delta_i)^{.75}}{E}$$

Each parameter in this formula was calculated above, based on the data collected in this study, or based on data obtained from the literature. Using these estimates of the parameters in the formula provides estimates of F_t for a variety of spectral tarsier infant ages and weights. These are presented in Tables 5–11a and 5–11b.

The model predicts that when the infant is born the mother will have to increase the amount of time she forages for food by 10% to 17%, or will have to forage for 66% to 73% of her night just to meet her own energetic needs and those of her infant's (Figure 5–18). By one week of age, the new mother will have to increase the amount of time she forages for food by 12% to 18% or will have to forage for 68% to 74% of her night. This increases to 16% to 24% additional time, or 72% to 80% total time, when the infant is only three weeks of age. When the infant is five weeks old, the mother will have to forage an additional 19% to 29% for a total of more than 75% to 85% of her time. When the infant is seven weeks old, the mother will have to forage an additional 23% to 34% to meet her own and her infant's needs for a total of 79% to 90% of her time. By nine weeks of age, if the female was still nursing her infant, she would be required to forage for 81% to 92% of the night just to maintain

Table 5–11a   Daily Energy Expenditure for a Female Spectral Tarsier Weighing 108 g

Behavior	Estimated Energy	KJ/day Expenditure KJ/min.	Kcal/day
Sleep	.0396	28.54	119.51
Rest	.0544	6.53	27.34
Forage and Feed	.0931	37.52	157.12
Travel	.0102	6.12	25.63
Social	.0317	1.36	5.70

Table 5–11b   The Estimated Cost of Infant Transport for a Female Weighing 108 g

Infant Age	Estimated Energy Expenditure KJ/min.	KJ/day	Kcal/day
Birth	.0119	7.14	29.90
One Week	.0120	7.21	30.19
Three Weeks	.0125	7.50	31.41
Five Weeks	.0130	7.79	32.62
Seven Weeks	.0134	8.05	33.71
Nine Weeks	.0137	8.25	34.55

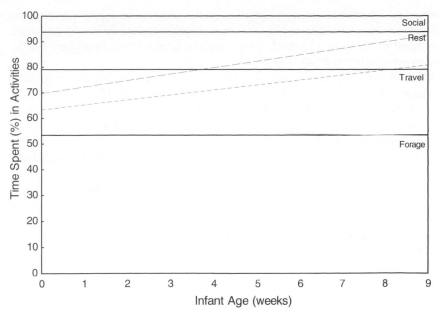

Figure 5–18 Maternal Time Budget for Spectral Tarsiers, *T. Spectrum*

* The average time budget is indicated by the horizontal lines. The predicted increase in
  the mother's feeding time due to the energetic cost of lactation using Brody (1945) and
  Blackburn & Calloway's estimates are indicated by long- and short-dashed lines, respectively.

her own body weight and provide adequate milk for her growing infant.
This leaves only 8% to 19% of the night to travel, socialize, and rest whereas
previously the female had more than 45% of her night for these other activities. In other words, the female must now spend an additional third of her
night foraging for food. These numbers suggest that the cost of lactation, in
terms of the additional time a female needs to forage, is quite high.

In comparison, Altmann's work on baboons shows that female baboons
normally forage for 43% of their day. This increases to 66% during the
infant's eighth month. This is a 23% increase in the time female baboons
need to forage to maintain their own bodies and provide adequate nutrition for their infants. The amount of time a female needs to forage by the
infant's ninth month may be even greater if the infant is growing faster
than .005 kg/day as has been observed in some captive populations
(Snow 1967; Buss & Reed 1970).

THE COST OF INFANT TRANSPORT

Robin Dunbar (1988) modified Altmann's model by incorporating the additional cost of infant transport, in terms of the additional time a mother
would need to forage if she was continually transporting her infant. Dunbar

tested whether or not female tamarins could, from an energetic perspective, transport their twin infants, lactate, and maintain their own energetic needs, without the help of a male. In other words, is male care necessary for the successful rearing of twin tamarin infants?

Following Altmann's model, Dunbar used Terborgh's average time budget for female saddle-back tamarins (Terborgh 1983). He then calculated the additional time needed to forage in order for the female to meet the nutritional needs of one and two infants, and then added this to the female's time budget.

The calculation of the cost of infant transport in terms of the additional time the transporter needs to forage is slightly complicated to compute. In 1980, Taylor demonstrated a proportionality between the energetic cost of carrying a load and the transporter's body mass. In other words, he observed a 10% increase in oxygen consumption when the load carried was equal to 10% of the transporter's body mass. It was based on this research that Dunbar reasoned that a newborn tamarin infant weighing 10% of adult weight would increase the transporter's energy requirements by 10%, thereby increasing the time the transporter would need to forage by 10%, Dunbar therefore added the additional time the transporter would need to forage, if the female was transporting one and two infants, onto the female tamarin's time budget. Dunbar concluded that while female tamarins do possess enough time in their daily time budget to transport and provide milk for a single infant, and meet their own nutritional needs, they do not have enough time in their daily time budget to provide the same maternal investment for two infants. Dunbar (1988) uses this model to explain the evolution of male care in tamarins, which makes an important difference: by increasing the reproductive success of both the male and female, it becomes possible for tamarins to produce two infants instead of one.

In this section, the additional cost of infant transport based on infant growth data, and the reasoning stated above, is added to the female's time budget. At birth, the infant spectral tarsier weighs (23.7 grams) almost 22% of adult female body weight (108.2 grams). By 1 week of age, the infant weighs approximately 24% of adult body weight. With each successive 2-week interval in infant age (3, 5, 7, and 9 weeks), the infant spectral tarsier weighs 30.5%, 37.0%, 43.9%, and 47.6% of adult body weight (Figure 5–19). This is an extraordinarily high infant weight ratio for birth and afterward.

Following Dunbar's reasoning (that a newborn infant weighing 10% of adult weight would increase the transporter's energy requirements by 10%, thereby increasing the time the transporter would need to forage by 10%), a newborn infant weighing 22% of adult female body weight would increases the time a female spectral tarsier would need to forage by an additional 22%. Given the calculation of F_t for the additional time a female needs to forage to meet her own needs as well to provide adequate milk

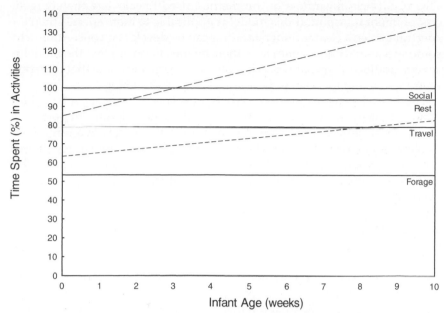

Figure 5–19 Predicted Amount of Time Female Spectral Tarsiers Need to Forage Given the Additional Energetic Costs from Lactation and Infant Transport*

* This figure is based on Altmann (1980) and Dunbar (1988) and data collected during this study. The short-dashed line represents the predicted increase in time needed to forage as a result of lactation, while the long-dashed lines represent the predicted increase in time needed to forage as a result of lactation and infant transport. This figure graphically illustrates the maximum predicted increase in time needed to forage. The bottom end of the predicted increase ranges from 88–129%.

for her newborn infant (66–73%), this brings the total amount of time a female would need to forage each night up to 88–95%. Although this is possible, and still leaves the female with approximately 5% to 12% of her time to travel, rest, and socialize, it makes it easier to understand why female spectral tarsiers do not continuously transport their young as do so many other primates, but prefer to utilize a cache-and-carry infant caretaking strategy. Mothers transport their infants (carry), deposit them on branches (cache), and forage in the nearby vicinity, returning at various intervals depending on the infant's age.

DISCUSSION AND CONCLUSIONS

Plotting the additional costs of lactation and transportation on the female's time budget demonstrates that, while a female spectral tarsier can comfortably feed her infant despite the heavy costs of lactation, she would be hardpressed if she had to bear the additional costs of transporting them as well.

This result held regardless of the method used to calculate the energetic cost of infant transport. If this model is applicable to more species than the spectral tarsier, a clearer understanding can be developed concerning why some species park and some carry their infants. I also applied the model to several additional primate species, some that park and some that transport their infants, and found that the result held (Gursky 1997).

These results raise a question: Why has the spectral tarsier evolved a life history strategy in which infants have already done a significant portion of their growth at birth and following birth continue to grow at a rapid rate? I believe that having large newborns may be an important strategy to get the offspring into the juvenile stage of development as quickly as possible and thereby minimize infant mortality. Recall from the section on infant mortality, in both wild spectral tarsiers and captive Bornean tarsiers, the highest probability of mortality occurred during the first two months of the infant's life. There is an obvious advantage to fast growth: If some target size defines the end of juvenility, then the faster an animal grows the less time it spends as a vulnerable juvenile. Clearly, the greater the growth constant, the smaller the time to maturity. Janson and van Schaik (1993) argue that an animal facing very high overall mortality must mature very fast to maximize the probability that it will survive to reproduce at all.

I want to point out that this life history strategy of spectral tarsiers contrasts sharply with that of most other primates. Janson and van Schaik (1993) note that primates have lower growth rates than other mammals if body size is taken into account. They argue that lower growth rates are expected when increased growth rates lead to rapid increases in mortality. Natural selection favors a maximal growth constant if mortality increases linearly or less than linearly with the growth constant. Thus, it is quite probable that the life history schedule of spectral tarsiers is dictated by the high risk of mortality.

6

The Cost of Nonmaternal Caretakers

Paternal and Subadult Infant Care

(Photo by the author)

In the previous chapter I showed that, although it is possible for adult females to both transport their young and also provide adequate nutrition for their infants through lactation, at least for the first three weeks, female spectral tarsiers would be extremely hard-pressed or energetically challenged to do so. Female primates seem to utilize two different strategies to minimize or eliminate the cost of infant transport. These are allotransport and infant parking. Thus, since I have shown how difficult it would be for spectral tarsier females to transport their infants given the already high energetic cost of lactation, the next logical question is whether other group members could provide the necessary infant transport. In other words, is infant parking the only available option left to the female spectral tarsier? In this chapter, I address whether adult males or subadult group members could provide the necessary transport for infants.

INTRODUCTION TO MALE CARE

Historically, all discussions of the roles of adult male mammals revolved around the topics of dominance and sexual behavior while discussions of the roles of adult females revolved around the topic of maternal care (DeVore 1965). Adult males were rarely perceived as infant caretakers. Yet, some adult male mammals are known to exhibit extensive male care of their infants. Kleiman and Malcolm (1981) estimate that 10% of all mammalian genera exhibit some form of direct male care of infants. They estimate that in the order Primates, nearly 40% of all genera exhibit some form of direct male interaction with infants.

Today, male care is recognized to be a common behavioral pattern found in numerous primate species (Taub 1984; Clutton-Brock 1992). Male primates often contribute to the costs of rearing their offspring in three general ways. First, males can provide direct assistance to the female by helping to transport, feed (through provisioning foods), and/or care for the infants (e.g., play, grooming) (Wright 1984; Tardif et al., 1993). Second, males can provide indirect help by actively providing the female and the offspring with protection against predators (vigilance and alarm calls) and conspecifics (territory defense against intruders) (van Schaik & van Noordwijk 1989; van Schaik & Dunbar 1990). Third, it has been suggested that males contribute to parental care by defending a territory that provides the female and her offspring exclusive access to essential resources (MacKinnon & MacKinnon 1980).

Three factors are frequently hypothesized to be associated with the evolution of male parental investment in primates: (1) female choice (Janson 1984; Smuts 1985), (2) paternity certainty (Daly & Wilson 1983; Wright 1990), and (3) a high infant–maternal weight ratio (Kleiman 1977; Wright 1990).

One primary factor that might predispose a primate species to male parental investment is female choice: Females may prefer to mate with males who invest in their offspring. For example, among capuchin monkeys, females often actively choose their mating partners (Janson 1984). Females in estrus solicit copulations from the males. During the first four days of estrus, the female follows the dominant male of the group. On the last two days of estrus, the female begins to solicit copulations from other males in the group. The dominant male then begins to aggressively prevent other males from approaching the female. Janson (1984) suggests that the

> . . . strong active solicitation by the female of the dominant male may be explained by direct benefits that she or her offspring might receive from him. Because the dominant male controls access to many food sources during periods when food is scarce, his tolerance of a particular female or her offspring could be an important component of fitness for them.

Paternity certainty is another factor that may predispose a species to exhibit paternal care. When the male is confident of his paternity, he may be more likely to provide care: by aiding his own offspring's survival, he increases his own reproductive success. Thus, a male provides care when its benefits—his long-term genetic representation—outweigh its costs (Hamilton 1964; Maynard Smith 1977). Monogamous social systems are often associated with exclusive territories and mate guarding, thereby improving paternal certainty (Wittenberger & Tilson 1980). Thus, in primates exhibiting a monogamous social structure paternal certainty is generally thought to be higher. However, it is important to state that paternity certainty alone is not enough for male care to evolve (Wright 1990)—it is only a prerequisite, it is not causal. Male care will only evolve when the benefit of male care, in terms of reproductive success and infant survival, outweighs the costs in terms of additional mating opportunities for the male (Maynard Smith 1977).

A third factor that is often hypothesized as necessary for the evolution of male care is the infant–adult weight ratio (Kleiman 1977; Vogt 1984; Wright 1990). That is, the ratio of the infant's weight divided by the adult weight is believed to determine whether male care is necessary. In most small monogamous primates, male care, specifically male transport of infants, is thought to play an integral role in infant development because of the unusually large size of infants at birth (Kleiman 1977; Leutenegger 1980; Wright 1985). In many of these species, the combined birth weight of the twin infants can amount to as much as 20% of adult weight (Goldizen 1987). Having large newborns may be an important strategy to get the offspring into the juvenile stage of development as quickly as possible and to minimize infant mortality.

At a proximate level, male care has a hormonal basis. Elevated levels of the hormone prolactin, usually associated with lactation, has been implicated in predisposing individuals to providing nonmaternal care (Ma et al.,

2005; Reburn & Wynne-Edwards 1999; Sussman in press). Prolactin levels fluctuate based on the quality of the males relationship with his mate.

Saguinus, Cebuella, and *Callithrix* all exhibit infant carrying by fathers as early as the first day after birth (Epple 1975; Ingram 1977; Cleveland & Snowdon 1984; Tardif et al., 1993). In *Callicebus moloch* (Wright 1984), the father is the primary transporter of the infant. By the end of the third week, fathers transported the infant 92% of the time. At twelve weeks of age the infant weighed as much as 40% of adult weight, yet was still transported by the father 38% of the time. A similar pattern was observed in *Aotus trivirgatus.* In captive *Saguinus oedipus,* fathers transport infants over 30% of the time (Tardif et al., 1993). Similarly, in *Saguinus mystax,* Garber et al. (1984) observed a statistically significant relationship between the number of adult males in a group to help transport and provide food for the offspring, and the number of surviving infants.

FORM AND QUANTITY OF PATERNAL CARE

Male care in spectral tarsiers is very limited. Males were only occasionally observed cuddling with the infant in the sleeping nest. On no occasion was the male observed to carry the infant or to passively or actively share food with the infant. On the other hand, males were never aggressive toward young infants as has been observed among captive populations of Bornean tarsiers (Haring & Wright 1989; Wright 1990; Roberts 1994), whose bouts of aggression resulted in the death of the infant. Male aggression was reserved for other males and subadult sons.

Males occasionally were observed grooming and playing with the infant, although much less frequently than the females, or other group members. These data are comparable to observations on the frequency that males groomed and played with infants in *C. moloch* (Wright 1984). Figure 6–1 illustrates the mean percentage of time that males were observed grooming the infants at several age intervals. When analyzing the data using a Kolmogorov-Smirnov test (Sokal & Rohlf 1981), the amount of time that adult males spent grooming the infant was significantly not uniformly distributed across the weeks of infant age ($N_1N_2D=$ 4.992; $D_{.01}=1.1022$). There were no statistically significant differences in the mean percentage of time that males groomed male and female infants overall ($X^2=0.8543$; $p=.3553$; $df=1$).

Figure 6–2 illustrates the mean percentage of time that males were observed playing with the infants at specified age intervals. When analyzing the data using a Kolmogorov-Smirnov test (Sokal & Rohlf 1981), the amount of time that adult males spent playing with the infant was significantly not uniformly distributed across the weeks of infant age ($N_1N_2D=$ 3.000; $D_{.01}=1.1889$). That is, males maintained a low level of direct care of the infants from birth through week ten. They did not significantly increase the amount of time they groomed or played with the infant to aid

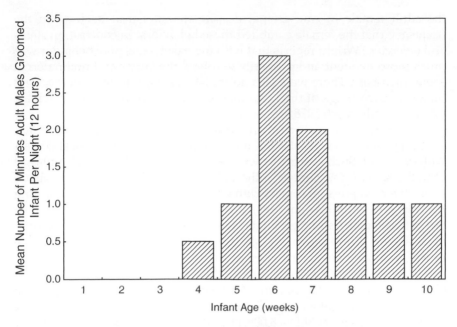

Figure 6–1 The Mean Number of Minutes (Per Night) that Adult Males Were Observed Grooming Infants from Ages 1 to 10 weeks

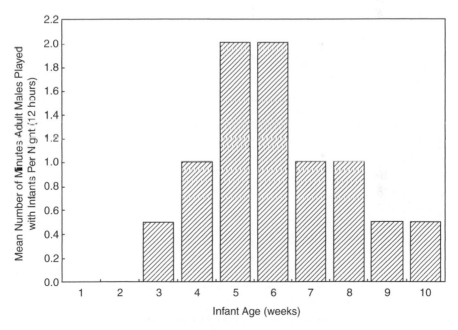

Figure 6–2 The Mean Number of Minutes (Per Night) that Adult Males Were Engaged in Play with Infants over the First 10 Weeks of the Infant's Life

the adult female in care giving, despite the statistical declines in the frequency that the female exhibited these behaviors. In contrast, in *Aotus* and *Callicebus*, Wright reports that with increasing age, play behavior was much more frequent and primarily involved the father and nonmaternal group members. There were also no statistically significant differences in the mean percentage of time that males played with male versus female infants overall ($X^2 = 0.5278$; $p = .4675$; $df = 1$).

Males were rarely in physical contact with the infant. Figure 6–3 illustrates the proportion of time that adult males were observed in physical contact with the infant. Such low frequency of male contact with infants is unheard of in the small monogamous anthropoid primates. For example, in *Aotus*, infants were in physical contact with the male over 51% of the time during the first week of life (Wright 1984). Exceptionally high rates of physical contact between males and their infants has also been observed in the majority of small New World primates (*Callicebus, Saguinus, Callithrix*; Rylands 1993) as well as in a monogamous primate, *Eulemur rubriventer* (Overdorff 1992), and in *Hapalemur griseus* (Wright 1990). Using the Kolmogorov-Smirnov test (Sokal & Rohlf 1981), the amount of time that adult males spent in physical contact with the infant was significantly not uniformly distributed across the weeks of infant age ($N_1N_2D = 8.008$; $D_{.01} = 0.7316$).

Males were infrequently the nearest neighbor of the infant. Figure 6–4 illustrates the percentage of time that males were the infant's nearest

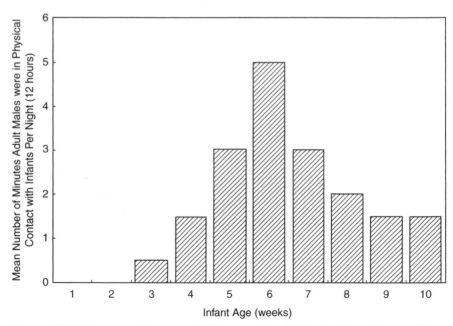

Figure 6–3 The Mean Number of Minutes (Per Night) that Adult Males Were Observed in Physical Contact with Infants over the First 10 Weeks of the Infant's Life

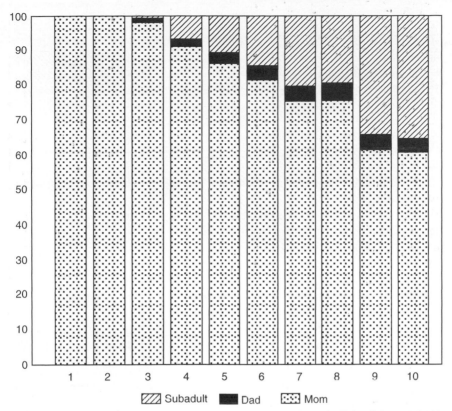

Legend: ▨ Subadult ■ Dad ⦂⦂⦂ Mom

Figure 6–4 The Mean Percentage of Time that the Adult Male, Subadult, and Adult Female Were Each the Infant's Nearest Neighbor over the First 10 Weeks of the Infant's Life

neighbor at specified age intervals. When analyzing the data using a Kolmogorov-Smirnov test (Sokal & Rohlf 1981), the amount of time that adult males were the infant's nearest neighbor was significantly not uniformly distributed across the weeks of infant age ($N_1 N_a D = 11.000$; $D_{.01} = 0.7113$). There were also no statistical differences in the frequency that males were the nearest neighbors of male and female infants ($X^2 = 0.7857$; $p = .3754$; $df = 1$). The fact that males were so rarely the infant's nearest neighbor is somewhat surprising as males frequently traveled with an adult female and her infant. This was discussed more fully in Chapter 4 in the section on gregariousness.

Another important aspect of male care involves scanning for predators and giving alarm calls. Males are known to give predator alarm calls to warn other group members. Figure 6–5 illustrates the mean number of alarm calls males gave each night when there was an infant in their group and when there was no infant. Notice that males gave significantly more alarm calls each night when there was an infant in their group compared to the mean number of alarm calls given when no infant was present ($X^2 = 8.3925$; $p = .0038$; $df = 1$).

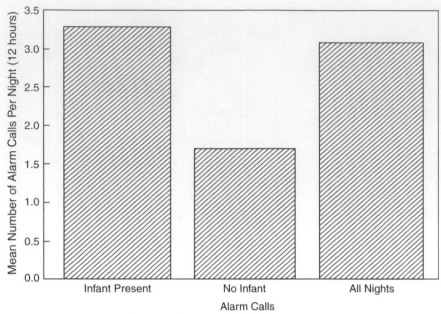

Figure 6–5 The Mean Number of Alarm Calls Given (Per Night) by Males on Nights When There Was an Infant in Their Group Compared with Nights When There Was No Infant in their Group

Vigilance behavior in the form of giving alarm calls also seems to be an important component of spectral tarsier male care. The spectral tarsiers in Tangkoko Nature Reserve are primarily threatened by four main types of predators: birds of prey, civets, monitor lizards, and snakes. Researchers studying hunting behavior have suggested that a predator's chances of successfully capturing prey are low if the prey detects the predator before the predator is close enough for attack (Caro 1986; Alvard 1993). Detecting predators before they are close enough to attack requires constant vigilance. It is this behavior that the adult male spectral tarsiers seem to increase when there is an infant in their group, suggesting that males are providing an important form of paternal care.

It is interesting to note that van Schaik and van Noordwijk (1989) found that, in *Macaca fasicularis*, vigilance behavior was incompatible with feeding and foraging. This may also be true in the spectral tarsier. Thus, the observation that adult males spend increasing amounts of time giving alarm calls when an infant is part of the group suggests that they are experiencing either an increased cost by not feeding and foraging, and/or they are increasing their own risk of predation by calling attention to their own location (Sherman 1977).

Figure 6–6 illustrates the mean number of loud calls males gave when there was and was not an infant in their group. These results were not

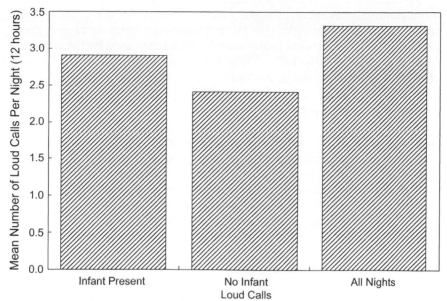

Figure 6–6 The Mean Number of Loud Calls Given (Per Night) by Males on Nights When There Was an Infant in Their Group Compared with Nights When There Was No Infant in Their Group

statistically significant (X^2=0.4337; p=.5102; df=1). That is, males did not significantly increase or decrease the number of loud calls they gave each night according to the presence or absence of an infant. This probably reflects the fact that loud calls are thought to be territorial in nature (MacKinnon & MacKinnon 1980). These results suggest that while adult males spend increasingly more time watching for predators when they have an infant nearby, they do not increase the number of loud calls they emit. This may be because loud calls are not utilized as contact calls between adult males and infants.

From the above discussion on the form and quantity of male spectral tarsiers' interactions with their infants, it seems clear that male care of infants is restricted to less than 5% of the observations. It is far from intensive male care (infant transport and/or food sharing) that would be predicted in a small-bodied monogamous primate species that gives birth to exceptionally large infants and has costly caretaking patterns. Such low frequency of male contact with infants is unheard of in the small monogamous anthropoid primates. For example, in *Aotus*, infants were in physical contact (in terms of being transported) with the male over 51% of the time during the first week of life. Exceptionally high rates of physical contact between males and their infants is observed in the majority of the small New World primates (*Callicebus, Saguinus, Callithrix*) as well as in a monogamous prosimian primate, *Eulemur rubriventer* (Overdorff 1992), and in *Hapalemur griseus* (Wright 1990). This is even more surprising given that, in contrast to females, males are not already stressed by the energetic costs of lactation (Daly 1979). Thus, the question remains: Why is male care in the spectral tarsier so limited?

ENERGETICS OF MALE CARE

To follow up the question of why male care in spectral tarsiers is so limited, I hypothesize that males do not have enough time in their night to obtain the additional food needed to meet their own maintenance costs as well as the additional energetic costs of infant transport, despite the fact that they are not burdened by the costs of lactation. To test this hypothesis, I use a modified time budget model (Altmann 1980; Hames 1992). First, I present data on the activity time budgets of males. Following Taylor (1970, 1980) and Dunbar (1988), to estimate the additional amount of time adult males will need to forage to meet the energetic costs of infant transport, I present the weight of adult males and the weight of infants, as well as the weight ratio of infants at specified ages to adult males. Using these figures, I estimated the predicted amount of time that adult males would need to forage given the estimated energetic cost of transporting an infant of a specified weight from birth through nine weeks.

MALE ACTIVITY BUDGETS AND DIFFERENCES
WITH FEMALES

Adult males spent approximately 53.47% of their night foraging, 30.30% traveling, 11.34% resting, and 4.89% socializing. The activity budgets of males differed significantly from that of females (forage $X^2=3.6342$, $p=.0566$, df=1; rest: $X^2=3.6692$, $p=.0571$, df=1; travel $X^2=6.7540$, $p=.0118$, df=1; social $X^2=4.2503$, $p=.0436$, df=1;). Males spent slightly less time foraging and resting than did females, although these results were not statistically significant. In contrast, males spent significantly more time traveling and socializing than did females. Additional information on the social interactions, traveling, and foraging behavior are presented in Chapters 3 and 4.

Using this activity budget and Dunbar's reasoning to determine the energetic cost of infant transport, the male would need to increase the time he spends foraging by the additional proportion of weight he is now transporting. In other words, the male would need to increase the time he spends foraging based on the male–infant weight ratio. Table 2–6 illustrates the range in adult male body weights. The mean body weight is 125.9 grams with a S. D. of 5.05. Given an infant birth weight of 23.7 grams, the male–infant weight ratio ranges from approximately 19% to 37% in only nine weeks. Thus, if males transported their infants at birth they would need to increase the time they spend foraging by almost 19%. Therefore, following the infant's birth males would need to spend more than 72% of their night foraging. This leaves 28% of their night for travel, rest, other social behaviors, territory defense, and mating opportunities. By the time the infant is only nine weeks of age, the time a male needs to forage to ensure adequate energy to transport his offspring increases to 89% of the night (Figure 6–7). In other words, by nine weeks, males would have only 11% of their night to devote to nonforaging activities. Thus, the energetic hypothesis suggests that although males potentially could transport their infants, especially following birth, they would be extremely stressed to do so, having only one-quarter of their night to spend resting, traveling, and socializing. In short, the costs may be too high. For example, males might lose mating opportunities, especially following birth, given the postpartum estrus shown by many primates, including the tarsier (Wright et al., 1986). Similarly, adequate time required to patrol the group's territory boundaries may be another factor preventing spectral tarsier males from investing in their young by providing infant transport.

The observation that males may be capable of providing some paternal care to the infant, at least initially, raises the question concerning what other forces play a role in decreasing the male's incentive to do so. As already noted, the cost to the male in terms of lost mating opportunities, the need

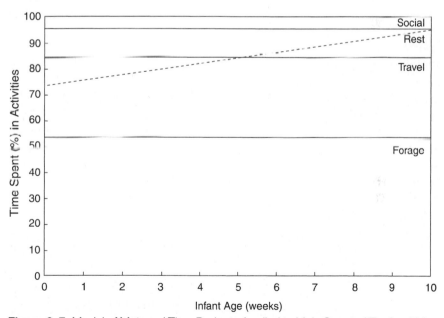

Figure 6–7 Model of Maternal Time Budgets Applied to Male Spectral Tarsiers Using Dunbar's (1988) Methods to Estimate the Cost of Infant Transport

for time to patrol the group's territory boundaries, and the additional mobility and foraging costs may prevent the male from providing this energetically expensive care. My observations on group size and composition suggest that reduced paternity certainty may account, in part, for the limited paternal investment provided by spectral tarsier males. This was discussed more fully in Chapter 4.

One option that has not yet been addressed concerns sharing the burden of infant care. Obviously, adult females cannot share the burden of lactation with their partner (Daly 1979). However, they could share infant transport (Clutton-Brock 1992), a behavioral strategy employed to some extent by tamarins (Rylands 1993; Sussman 2000). As will be seen throughout this chapter, spectral tarsiers (adults, not subadults) do not share the cost of infant transport.

There are several possible explanations for the lack of cost sharing by spectral tarsiers. First, there is no permanent association between adult males. This contrasts sharply with that of tamarins (Goldizen 1987), which often are characterized by permanent association between two adult males. The permanent association between, and sometimes even a genetic link to, adult males means that there are additional future opportunities for them to share both the costs and benefits. The lack of permanent association in spectral tarsiers hinders any known future interactions. Another possibility is that the cost of parking the tarsier infant may not be as high as I perceive it to be. That is, the cost of infant falling, predation, and/or infanticide is not as high as the cost of continual infant transport. The extraordinarily high cost of continual infant transport may result from the spectral tarsier's foraging style. Transporting an infant while foraging for mobile insects is a lot different than transporting an infant while searching for a stationary fruiting tree. It has been noted in night monkeys that the cost of infant transport toward foraging efficiency of insects is drastically reduced (Wright 1985). Since spectral tarsiers only consume insect prey, it may not make a difference who carries the infant—the cost in foraging efficiency might be too high.

MALE CARE: DISCUSSION AND CONCLUSIONS

The results of this section indicate that male care in the spectral tarsiers is very limited. Males were neither observed transporting infants nor food sharing with their infants. Other social behaviors such as grooming, playing, and physical contact occur infrequently. Males were also infrequently the nearest neighbor of the infant. Male care seems to be restricted to defending the territorial boundaries, scanning for predators, and giving alarm calls.

I hypothesized that males are energetically unable to transport their infants. Note that this hypothesis only accounts for the lack of male transport. It does not account for why the males were not the nearest neighbors or otherwise involved in infant care. Data on time budgets, weight, and infant growth rates were presented to test this hypothesis. The results indicate that although males possibly could provide this costly form of infant care, they would be hard-pressed to do so.

SUBADULT SPECTRAL TARSIERS

In the previous section I have shown that although it is possible, albeit difficult, for adult male spectral tarsiers to provide care for their young, were rarely observed engaging in this behavior. Since adult males do not provide substantial amounts of paternal care to their infants, perhaps the task of infant care falls to other group members such as subadults. In this section, I address whether subadult spectral tarsiers could provide the necessary care for infants, and well as provide data to demonstrate whether subadults do in fact exhibit this behavior.

ALLOMATERNAL CARE IN PRIMATES: HYPOTHESES

Compared to other mammals, primate infants are born in a relatively altricial state (Eisenberg 1981), one consequence of which is the need for large amounts of care. Although in the majority of primate species infant care is given solely by the mother, a number of species exhibit considerable allomaternal care, or care given to infants by individuals other than the mother (Poirier 1972; Hrdy 1977, 1979; McKenna 1979, 1981; Altmann 1980; Terborgh & Goldizen 1985; Goldizen 1987; Nicholson 1987; Periera et al., 1987; O' Brien & Robinson 1991; Gould 1992; Watt 1994; Nash pers. comm.). Allocare is given in the form of transport, food sharing, guarding or baby-sitting, play, allonursing, and grooming.

Allomaternal behavior entails costs to the alloparent. An altruistic behavior (sensu Trivers 1971) is not expected to evolve unless the benefits outweigh the costs. If individuals are selected to act in their own self-interest, then the presence of allocaretaking behavior necessitates asking why these individuals provide care for offspring that are not their own. At present, there have been four general mechanisms proposed to explain the evolution of alloparental care: (1) mutualism (Lancaster 1971), (2) reciprocity (Axelrod & Hamilton 1981), (3) kin selection (Hamilton 1964); and (4) benefits of philopatry (Stacey & Ligon 1990).

Mutualism

Mutualism is one of the primary hypotheses proposed to explain the evolution of a seemingly altruistic behavior such as alloparental care (e.g., Lancaster 1971). One form of mutualism posits that benefits to the allocaretaker may be realized if, by gaining experience (learning to mother), an allocaretaker can increase its reproductive success when it reproduces on its own (Lancaster 1971). In this case, benefits most likely will be realized for young nulliparous females. The learning-to-mother hypothesis does not explain the development of allocaretaking behavior in multiparous females, or in any males, but only in nulliparous females (Hrdy 1977; Morland 1990; Gould 1992). The behavior is of course also beneficial to the infant, the recipient of the care.

For example, Kurland (1977) noted that in Japanese macaques alloparenting is primarily by nulliparous females. In 122 of 140 instances, the behavior was directed at *unrelated* individuals. Kurland therefore suggested that alloparenting in Japanese macaques is a selfish act that helps to prepare young females to be better mothers when their chance comes.

Similarly, it has been shown that in vervet monkeys, young females practice their play-mothering skills on young infants (Lancaster 1971). Of 347 allomaternal contacts, 295 were initiated by young nulliparous females between one and three years of age. Lancaster argues, ". . . that although maternal care may possess innate basic components, it is a sufficiently difficult and complex activity to require practice. Play-mothering is one of the final episodes of the socialization process that provides the necessary practice for young nulliparous females."

Direct support for the learning-to-mother hypothesis also comes from the recent observation that young female vervet monkeys who have had the opportunity to act as allocaretakers have higher survivorship of their own young than females who have not previously acted as allocaretakers (Fairbanks 1993). Similarly, in captive adult callitrichids, individuals do not care properly for young if they have not had the opportunity to gain experience at infant care by helping to raise their siblings (Epple 1975; Hoage 1978). Fairbanks also observed that nulliparous females preferentially provided allocare to very young infants (under three months), as these infants required the most care and experience handling. Similarly, nulliparous females also showed greater interest in providing care to the infants than did the juvenile males. All of these examples provide support for the learning-to-mother hypothesis (Fairbanks 1993).

The relationship between female primates and newborn infants varies widely within the primate order. Hrdy (1976) refers to the spectrum of mother–infant relations as the "nurture–abuse continuum." Some authors have observed that excessive or incompetent allomothering, particularly by immature females, is detrimental to the survival of an infant and therefore may be costly to the mother's reproductive success. Hrdy (1976) hypothesized that allomothering is a selfish act that prepares a young female to be a better mother, but is costly to the infant and its mother. The eagerness of pregnant and nulliparous females in some species to take infants, and the reluctance of the mother to surrender her infant to allomothers is often cited as evidence of the selfish play-mothering benefits to young females.

Reciprocity

Reciprocity has also been proposed as a primary mechanism for the evolution of alloparental care (Axelrod & Hamilton 1981). Reciprocity can be in the form of tit for tat in which the benefits of the same fitness units are exchanged or in which benefits of different types are exchanged. There are several ways in which an allocaretaker may gain direct fitness benefits from its behavior. For instance, the helper may increase its chance of surviving by remaining in its natal territory where he or she knows the terrain and food supply (Woolfenden & Fitzpatrick 1984).

Alternatively, benefits to the allocaretaker may be realized by increasing chances to breed in the future. Adult male baboons often form special relationships with certain infants within their troop. Smuts (1985) found that after forming a relationship with the infants, adult males had higher than expected mating success with the infant's mothers. Thus, this alloparental behavior is a form of mating effort. Males trade infant care in the present for sex in the future with the infant's mothers. The males' behavior functions for the mother and infant as allocare, but because the benefits are delayed in time, the relationship is based on reciprocity (Wasser 1982).

In reciprocal allocare, the allocare may be either costly to the allomother or produce delayed benefits, but will always be beneficial to the infant. In such systems, relatedness between the allocaretaker and the recipient is unimportant.

Kin Selection

A third mechanism that has been proposed to explain the evolution of an altruistic behavior such as alloparental care is kin selection (Hamilton 1964). The basis of this theory is that selection favors the differential representation of an individual's genes in subsequent generations and that those genes can occur in nondescendent, as well as descendent, kin. Hamilton's quantitative model states that altruistic behavior should evolve when $B/C > 1/r$ where r represents the degree of relatedness between the donor and recipient of the altruistic behavior. In simple terms, the benefits to the recipient divided by the cost to the donor of an act should be greater than one divided by the degree of relatedness between the donor and recipient. It predicts that relatives should preferentially receive aid and that closer relatives should receive more aid.

Studies of the white-fronted bee eater (Emlen and Wrege 1989) have demonstrated that the primary benefit to allocaretakers is the increased probability of survival to the related but nondescendent offspring. This benefit (increased survival) has also been proposed for tamarins (Goldizen 1987). Goldizen suggests that as long as their help does not decrease their own chances of future reproduction, helpers increase their younger siblings' probability of survival, and therefore of future reproduction.

Gould (1992) also suggests that allocaretaking is preferentially given to related infants in *Lemur catta*. Possibly as a result of the high degree of terrestriality (approximately 30%) exhibited by this species, infants often jumped on the backs of nearby individuals in the presence of aerial predators.

O'Brien and Robinson (1991) found similar results in *Cebus olivaceus* in Venezuela. They observed that relatedness between the allocaretaker and the infant was the most important determinant of the presence of allocare. Sibling females were four times more likely to participate in allocare than other nonsibling females. They were especially active in carrying and associating with the infant. Although they found that young juveniles and nulliparous adults interacted more with infants than parous adults, the effect of age was relatively unimportant. These results provide additional support for the kin selection hypothesis and not the learning-to-mother hypothesis.

Benefits of Philopatry

A fourth mechanism that has been proposed to explain the evolution of alloparental care is the benefit of philopatry. Stacey and Ligon (1990) suggest that variation in territory quality is the primary factor affecting infant-caretaking patterns in acorn woodpeckers. In acorn woodpeckers, the number of storage holes in the trees within a territory determines the amount of food a group can store over the winter season. Since the number of storage holes is positively correlated with survivorship, Stacey and Ligon (1990) refer to territories with large numbers of storage holes as high-quality, and those with few storage holes as low-quality territories. The probability that offspring remained in their natal territory and acted as helpers to future siblings is dependent on the quality of the territory. Offspring are philopatric in high-quality territories, but generally disperse at reproductive maturity in low-quality territories. This is because the probability of mating, reproducing, and surviving is low when an offspring disperses to a lower quality territory than the natal territory. Thus, it benefits offspring to remain in their natal territory to help care for their siblings, and gain some inclusive fitness, than to disperse to a territory where the probability of survivorship is low. This is an offshoot of the kin selection or the reciprocity hypotheses.

ALLOMATERNAL CARE IN THE PROSIMIAN PRIMATES

The next logical question is, do the prosimian primates exhibit allomaternal care and, if so, are these hypotheses also applicable to the form of allo-care observed in prosimians? Although not all prosimians exhibit infant parking behavior, researchers have assumed that this strategy precludes allocaretaking behavior (Charles-Dominique 1977; Vogt 1984). That is, historically it was thought that parked infants were left completely alone and were given little or no care (Martin 1990). Recent research on prosimian primate behavior has illustrated that several prosimian species that park their infants do in fact exhibit allomaternal care in the form of play, grooming, and maintaining spatial proximity to the parked infant as well as food sharing and infant transport (Charles-Dominique 1977; Clark 1985; Periera et al., 1987; Morland 1990; Wright 1990; Nash 1991; Gould 1992; Gursky 1994).

Allocaretaking involving infant guarding or vigilance is recognized in two prosimian species: *V. variegata* and *O. crassicaudatus*. Morland observed that young infants were very clumsy, and were occasionally observed falling. Morland (1990) suggested that watchfulness over infants by adult males and other group members may simultaneously improve the mother's foraging efficiency and increase the likelihood of survival for cached infants. These results support the hypothesis advanced by Jones (1980) and Vogel (1985) that the advantage of allomothering is that, by allowing a mother to feed and travel unencumbered by her infant, she can enhance her nutritional status during early lactation. Thus, the adaptive significance of allomothering in at least some nonhuman primates may be a reciprocal altruistic relationship between the adult females of a group. Such intragroup cooperative behavior would be an additional benefit of female–female bonding that is already seen as an important element in some primate species' social systems.

This hypothesis is further supported by observations in other studies. Specifically, Whitten (1982) found that in vervet monkeys (*Cercopithecus aethiops*), mothers obtained more food, measured in mouthfuls, when unencumbered by infants than they did while carrying an infant. Similarly, Wright (1984) reports that *Callicebus* males transporting infants captured significantly fewer insects compared to times when they were not transporting infants. This reduced foraging success also occurred when the infant was in close proximity to their fathers (Wright 1984). Stanford (1992) reported similar results for capped langurs (*Presbytis pileata*).

Allocaretaking behavior also has been observed in *Otolemur crassicaudatus*. Clark (1985) noted that adult females, and juveniles of both sexes, maintained frequent proximity to cached infants while the mother foraged. The infant caretaking strategy of *T. spectrum* may be characterized by a similar form of allocaretaking, involving infant guarding by older siblings (juveniles).

The results of a recent preliminary study of the parenting behavior in spectral tarsiers (Gursky 1994) suggest that this species exhibits allocaretaking behavior. When infants were in spatial proximity to a group member, juveniles were more often in proximity to the infant than other group members, including the mother. This relationship holds true even when the mother was absent. This suggests that juveniles may be baby-sitting or guarding infants when the parents are out foraging. Similarly, MacKinnon and MacKinnon (1980) qualitatively noted that "infants were visited and played with at intervals throughout the night, not only by the mother between hunting trips, but also by other family members of both sexes. In particular, one infant was visited and played with by four different group members in a two hour period."

Gould (1992) also observed allocaretaking behavior in *Lemur catta* at Berenty, Madagascar. Allocaretaking seems to be a major component of the infant caretaking systems in this species. According to Gould (1992), group members of all age and sex classes were found to participate to varying degrees in alloparental care to infants. The rank and/or sex of the infant did not affect the amount of alloparental care it received. Specifically, Gould found that alloparental behaviors were performed most often by nulliparous adult females and by other mothers, supporting the learning-to-mother hypothesis. Unrelated adult females with offspring were found to provide allomaternal care much more frequently than expected, and more frequently than other age–sex classes.

Allocaretaking behavior is also a major component of the infant caretaking system in the red-bellied lemur, *Lemur rubriventer* (Overdorff 1992). Overdorff (1992) found that fathers and subadults transported twin infants for a significant portion of the day as well as tolerated "theft" of food by the infants.

Another prosimian that exhibits substantial amounts of allomaternal care is *Hapalemur griseus*. This is a very intriguing species, in part because males are often observed transporting their infants (Wright 1990). In addition, males and female *Hapalemur* have also been observed parking their infants.

From these examples, it is evident that allocare is found in prosimians that park their infants and in those that continually transport them. The type of allomaternal care, and the frequency that it is exhibited, differs between prosimians that park and those that transport their young. In parkers, infant care seems to be restricted to baby-sitting and guarding, playing and grooming. Very little infant transport and food sharing have been observed in prosimians that park their young. In contrast, in prosimians such as the red-bellied and ring-tailed lemurs that transport their young, infant transport and active food sharing are the primary forms of allomaternal care. Unfortunately, too few studies on the form of allocare have been conducted to try and determine whether different mechanisms can explain the development of allocare in parkers and transporters.

Gittleman and Oftedal (1987) observed that the amount of allocare provided in carnivore species is related to their rate of postnatal growth. Ross and MacLarnon (1995) observed a similar relationship in Haplorrhine primates and suggest that it reflects the fact that females assisted with the burden of infant transport are able to provide nutritional resources to the infant faster than females who care for infants without any allocaretakers. This result is interesting in light of the results found by Tilden (1993), who observed that, within Strepsirhine primates, more-rapidly growing species did not have higher milk protein or calcium levels than more-slowly growing species. In contrast, Tilden found that the best predictor of milk energy content was the infant rearing strategy (park or carry). Species that parked their infants had significantly higher milk energy concentration than did species that transported their young. This is because parked infants may nurse at less frequent intervals than transported infants, which may nurse continuously. This implies that the rearing strategy of prosimians (parking or transporting) is not necessarily related to the infant's growth rate.

ALLOMATERNAL CARE BY SUBADULT FEMALE SPECTRAL TARSIERS

Infant Transport

I observed infant transport by subadult individuals on only thirty-three occasions. During thirty-two of these occasions, a young infant (less than two months old) had fallen from its parked location. The subadult nearest the infant responded by transporting the infant to a new location, near where the infant was originally parked. In each observation, the subadult transported the infant orally. Clearly, infant transport by subadults is minimal and is not a major infant care strategy and is primarily limited to infant falling. On one occasion, I observed a young infant and subadult playing in a tree when the subadult observed a snake nearby. The subadult proceeded to transport the infant (less than one month old) away from the snake, alarm called, and then began mobbing the snake.

There may be sex differences in whether male or female subadults transport the infant. During my observations, only female subadults were observed to retrieve infants following a fall. On the other hand, on no occasion when the subadult males were the nearest neighbor did the infant fall from its parked location. Thus, these observations may not necessarily indicate a sex bias in infant care, but rather may represent the fact that the males may not have had the opportunity to provide this form of infant care.

Food Sharing

In the previous chapter I stated that the life history schedule of spectral tarsiers may be dictated by this species' high risk of mortality. One strategy that adult primates use to reduce the vulnerability of their offspring is to subsidize their food intake by sharing. However, food sharing, passive or active, was never observed between mother and infant, or father and infant. It might be expected that mothers would share food with infants during weaning from breast milk, but this was never observed. I suspect that female spectral tarsiers time their reproduction (reproduce seasonally) so that weaning occurs when weaning foods are most available for their juvenile offspring (Janson & van Schaik 1993; Goldizen et al., 1988). Similarly, it might be expected that fathers might share food with infants as a way of sharing the burden of infant care with adult females, but this too was never observed. However, I did observe eleven instances of passive food sharing between an infant and a subadult group member. These observations occurred four times during an infant's fifth week, five times during its sixth week, and twice during the infant's seventh week of life. During each observation, the subadult caught a relatively large insect (greater than 3 cm) and the infant grabbed a small piece of the insect. There was no vocal reprimand by the subadult following this activity, nor did the subadult move to a new perch to prevent the infant from consuming a portion of the prey. In contrast, on obtaining the insect, the subadult moved to the branch where the infant was parked. Thus, the subadult may have expected the infant to try and eat a piece of the insect. However, the subadult was never observed emitting a food call to encourage the infant to come and eat the insect.

Food sharing, passive as well as active, by subadult group members with infants was also observed in many of the small New World monkeys such as *Aotus, Saguinus,* and *Callithrix* (Wright 1984; Tardif et al., 1993). In *C. jacchus, S. oedipus,* and *S. fuscicollis,* siblings are reported to provide more food to infants than do mothers or fathers (Cebul & Epple 1984; Wright 1984; Simek 1988). In *Aotus,* juveniles shared food with infants as much as the mother, but significantly less than the father (Wright 1984).

Passive food sharing has also been observed between mothers and their infants in *G. demidovii* (Charles-Dominique 1977) and between infants and juveniles and their siblings and mothers in *G. s. braccatus* (Nash 1991). Charles-Dominique (1977) and Nash (1991) both argue that food sharing functions to allow younger individuals to learn appropriate foods. Charles-Dominique (1977) referred to this behavior as dietary conditioning. These observations of food sharing in other primate species differs substantially from that observed in spectral tarsiers in that I never observed any food sharing between infants and adults of either sex.

Food sharing by older subadults, or older siblings, is a very costly behavior. Food that could be consumed by the subadult is eaten by the infant. Similarly, time spent foraging for food that is given or shared with the infant is time that could be spent searching for a mate. Nonetheless, spectral tarsier subadults occasionally chose to share food with infants that are their siblings. If paternity certainty is not 100%, then the probability that the adult male is the father of both the infant and the subadult is even lower. One implication of this is that the cost of providing allocare in the form of food sharing, infant transport, and a variety of other methods, is much higher to the subadult provider than if the infant and subadult had been full siblings and not, potentially, half-siblings.

There may also be sex differences in whether male or female subadults share food with the infant. Once again, infants were only observed taking food from the mouths of female subadults. On no occasion did a subadult male return to the perch of a parked infant after capturing a large insect. Nonetheless, the sample size (n=11) is too small to draw any more conclusions or conduct any statistical analyses. It is interesting to note that food sharing by subadult *Callicebus* and *Aotus* is primarily by males and not by females.

Play

Poirier (1972) and Baldwin (1986) emphasize the importance of play behavior in the social development of primates. Poirier suggests that play helps the infant to adjust to the groups social milieu. Baldwin notes that social skills that develop from play include social bonding, cooperative relations, social perception, sex roles, and parental and communication skills. In other words, infant play is an opportunity for young animals to acquire, practice, and perfect skills that will be useful in adulthood in social and other activities, according to this definition, play is considered a form of allocare.

I frequently observed play behavior between infants and subadult individuals. Figure 6–8 illustrates the mean percentage of time that subadults were observed playing with the infant every two weeks of the infant's life, relative to all observations. Using a Kolmogorov-Smirnov test (Sokal & Rohlf 1981), the amount of time that subadults spent playing with infants was significantly not uniformly distributed across the weeks of infant age ($N_1N_2D=10.9560$; $D_{.01}=0.6795$). The major changes in the mean percentage of time that the subadults played with the infant occurred between the second and third weeks, and fourth and fifth weeks of the infant's life.

Grooming

Infant grooming by older siblings was frequently observed. Figure 6–9 illustrates the mean percentage of time that subadults were observed to groom the infant every week of the infant's life, relative to all observations. Using a Kolmogorov-Smirnov test (Sokal & Rohlf 1981), the amount of time that subadults spent grooming infants was significantly not uniformly distributed across the weeks of infant age ($N_1N_2D=6.006$; $D_{.01}=0.9057$).

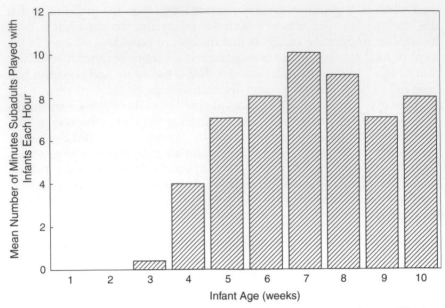

Figure 6–8 The Mean Number of Minutes (Per Hour) that Subadult Spectral Tarsiers Engaged in Play Behavior with the Infant over the First 10 Weeks of the Infant's Life

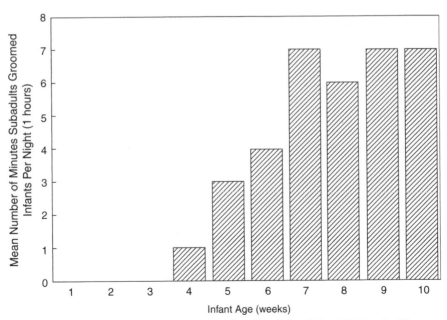

Figure 6–9 The Mean Number of Minutes (Per Hour) that Subadult Spectral Tarsiers Groomed the Infant over the First 10 Weeks of the Infant's Life

In particular, there was a substantial increase in grooming between the third and fourth week of the infant's life. It is interesting to note that while Niemitz (1984) recorded fifty-three occurrences of allogrooming between adult individuals in the Bornean tarsier, he did not observe allogrooming of infants by other group members. All occurrences of allogrooming involved the mother grooming the infant, or grooming during copulation and during fights.

Allogrooming behavior by subadults has also been observed in several other prosimian species including the ruffed lemur (*Varecia variegata*) and the ring-tailed lemur (*Lemur catta*) (Gould 1990; Morland 1990). In *Lemur rubriventer*, the red-bellied lemur, grooming of infants by subadults has also been observed (Overdorff 1992).

Distance

Figure 6–10 illustrates the mean percentage of time subadults were in physical contact with the infant as a function of infant age. Using a Kolmogorov-Smirnov test (Sokal and Rohlf 1981), the amount of time that subadults were in physical contact with infants was significantly not uniformly distributed across the weeks of infant age ($N_1 N_2 D = 17.051$; $D_{.01} = 0.5584$). The major increases in the mean percentage occurred between the infant's second and

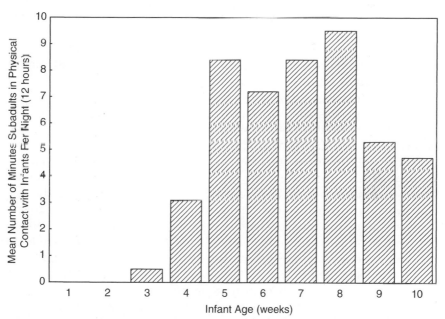

Figure 6–10 The Mean Number of Minutes (Per Hour) that Subadults Were in Physical Contact with the Infant over the First 10 Weeks of the Infant's Life

fifth weeks. It was not until the third week that subadults were observed in physical contact with the infant. At this time, other nonmaternal group members also started being the nearest neighbor to the infant. The unusually low amount of contact between the infant and other group members stems from the fact that, slightly before birth, fourteen females separated themselves from the group and moved to another sleeping location prior to parturition. The new location may have been as far away as 100 meters from the standard sleeping tree. The female used this location consistently until approximately one week following birth. After this time, the female alternated her days irregularly between the group's main sleeping tree and the new sleeping site. MacKinnon and MacKinnon (1980) do not report any observations of the mother changing the sleeping site prior to or after birth. Females isolating themselves prior to the birth of their infants have also been reported in *G. demidovii* (Charles-Dominique 1977) and *O. crassicaudatus* (Clark 1985).

Although other group members occasionally located the female's sleeping site and tried to join her, she actively chased them away. The mother's new sleeping location was kept secret for the first few days by her not always joining the group during early morning vocal calls. During these first few days, the mother frequently gave alarm calls at the slightest approach of any individual tarsier or other animal. After one week, the frequency she gave alarm calls decreased and she slowly permitted other group members into the tree. MacKinnon and MacKinnon (1980) also report that the mother had trouble protecting the baby from overly inquisitive members of the family that repeatedly tried to lick and mark the baby. The mother avoided other members of the family by taking the baby in her mouth and jumping to a new resting perch. As the infant matured, the mother was more willing to let other group members near and interact with the infant.

After the first two weeks of infant life, the mean percentage of time subadults were the infant's nearest neighbor increased, as Figure 6–11 illustrates for specified age classes; a noticeable increase in frequency occurred between the infant's fourth and fifth week.

O'Brien and Robinson (1991) found that allocare in capuchins accounts for a large portion of infant care and results in the maintenance of high levels of infant care even as maternal care declines. Mothers are the sole caregivers during the first three months; from four to six months, allocare becomes more pronounced and is especially important as the infant capuchin becomes independent, a finding also observed in this study. In the first three weeks, interactions between the infant tarsier and other group members are limited. As the infant matures, its interactions with nonmaternal group members increase in frequency, especially after five weeks. The frequency that nonmaternal group members interact with the infant increases through ten weeks of age, at which time this study ended.

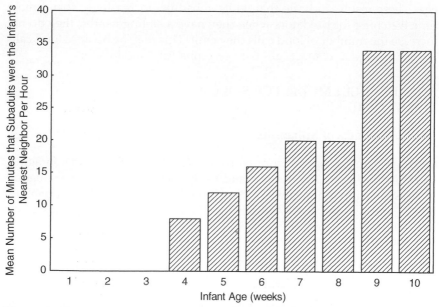

Figure 6–11 The Mean Number of Minutes (Per Night) that Subadults (vs. Parents) Were the Infant's Nearest Neighbor, over the First 10 Weeks of the Infant's Life

Alarm Calls

Another potentially important aspect of subadult allocare involves scanning for predators and giving alarm calls. There were no statistical differences in the frequency that subadult allocaretakers gave alarm calls and the sex of the infant in the group (X^2=0.0017; p=.9670; df=1). The most important result is that the frequency that subadults gave alarm calls when an infant was in the group was significantly greater than during nights when there was no infant present (X^2=6.6901; p=.0097; df=1). This result suggests that subadults may spend more time scanning for potential predators when there are infants compared to times when there are none, and are actively providing allocare.

There were also no statistical differences in the frequency that subadult allocaretakers gave loud calls, which are thought to be territorial in nature (MacKinnon & MacKinnon 1980), versus the sex of the infant in the group (X^2=0.0322; p=.8576; df=1). In contrast to the alarm calls, however, there was also no statistical increase in the frequency that subadults gave loud calls during nights when an infant was in the group and nights when no infant was in the group (X^2=2.4634; p=.1165; df=1). That is, subadults did not increase or decrease the frequency that they gave loud calls depending on the presence/absence of an infant in the group nor based on the infant's age. These results indicate that while subadults increasingly spend more time watching for predators when they have a sibling nearby, they do not increase the number of loud calls they emit. This may be because loud calls are not utilized as contact calls between subadults and infants.

A TIME BUDGET MODEL FOR SUBADULT INFANT CARE

Activity Budgets of Subadults

Subadult females spend approximately 55.19% of their time foraging, 16.22% traveling, 13.83% resting, and 14.76% socializing, whereas subadult males spend approximately 52.16% of their time foraging, 24.49% traveling, 15.72% resting, and 7.63% socializing (Figure 6–12). Although these sex

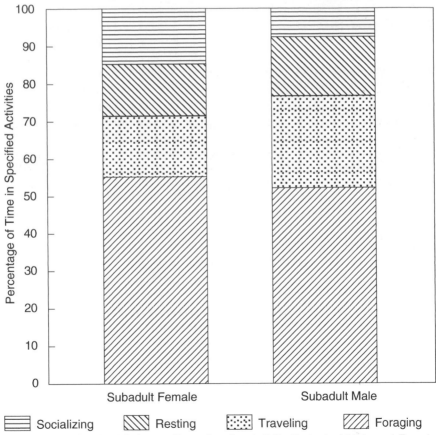

Figure 6–12 Stacked Columns Illustrating the Activity Budget of Male and Female Subadult Spectral Tarsiers

differences in the activity budgets of subadults are intriguing, the sample size is too small to explore whether these findings represent real differences.

Subadult Body Weight

The body weight of all subadults individuals captured in the mist nets was determined prior to giving them a radio collar (see Table 6–1). On average, the subadult males weighed 91 grams, whereas the subadult female weighed 86 grams. The observation that adult males and adult females exhibit sexual size dimorphism suggests that the size differences observed here will also be maintained with larger sample sizes. Thus, for the calculation of F_t, m equals 86 grams for the subadult female and 91 grams for the subadult males.

Time Allocation Model

Although subadults cannot provide allocare in the form of lactation to the infants, theoretically, they are physically capable of providing infant transport. In this section, the additional cost of infant transport based on infant growth data, presented in previous chapters, will be added to the subadult's time budget. At birth, the infant spectral tarsier weighs (23.7 grams) 28% of subadult female body weight (86 grams) and 26% of subadult male body weight. By 1 week of age, the infant weighs approximately 30% and 29% of subadult male and female body weight. With each successive 2-week interval in infant age, (3, 5, 7, and 9 weeks), the infant spectral tarsier weighs 38.4%, 46.5%, 55.2%, and 59.8% of subadult female body weight, and 36.3%, 43.9%, 52.2%, and 56.6% of subadult male body weight.

Table 6–1 The Body Weight (g) of Subadult Spectral Tarsiers

ID	Sex	Body Weight (g)
Blue/Black	F	85
Red/Red	F	88
Yellow/Red	F	89
Red/Black	F	87
Green/Blue	F	83
Red/Orange	F	84
Green/Yellow	M	94
Blue/Orange	M	93
White/Black	M	87
Black/Yellow	M	90
Blue/White	M	91

Following Dunbar's reasoning that a newborn infant weighing 10% of adult weight would increase the transporter's energy requirements—and therefore the time it would need to forage—by 10%, then when the infant is one week old and weighs 28% of the subadult female's and 26% of the subadult male's body weight, the time that subadults would need to forage increases by 28% and 26%, respectively. Given the average amount of time that subadults need to forage to meet their own needs (52%–55%), this increases the time allocated to foraging each night by up to 83%–78% for females and males, respectively. This still leaves the subadults, at the infant's birth, with 17% to 22% of their time to travel, rest, and socialize. Figures 6–13 and 6–14 illustrate the time a subadult female and subadult male would need to forage if they transported an infant from birth to nine weeks of age. It is not until the infant is approximately seven weeks of age that the amount of time a subadult would need to forage is longer than the number of hours in the night, assuming they can forego all travel, resting, and socializing behavior. Nonetheless, the fact that at the infant's birth, between 17% and 22% of the subadult's time could be allocated to travel, rest, and socializing illustrates how difficult it would be for a subadult to transport an infant. This type of analysis makes it easier to understand

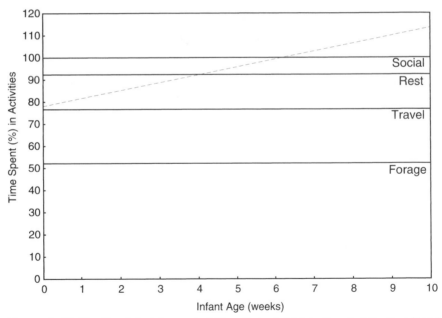

Figure 6–13 The Predicted Amount of Time Subadult Male Spectral Tarsiers Need to Forage Given the Additional Cost of Infant Transport*

* This figure is based on data collected during this study and a modified version of Altmann's time budget model (1980). The energetic cost of transport was calculated following Dunbar (1988).

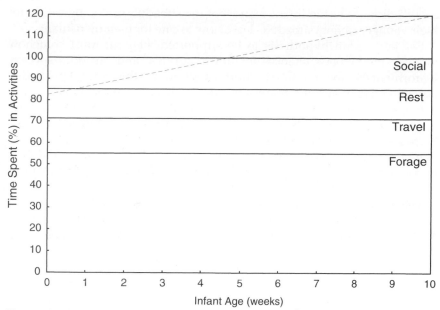

Figure 6–14 The Predicted Amount of Time Subadult Female Spectral Tarsiers Need to Forage Given the Additional Cost of Infant Transport*

* This figure is based on data collected during this study and a modified version of Altmann's time budget model (1980). The energetic cost of transport was calculated following Dunbar (1988).

why subadult spectral tarsiers do not transport infants and why spectral tarsiers prefer a cache-and-carry strategy.

SUBADULT ALLOCARE: DISCUSSION AND CONCLUSIONS

Why Do Spectral Tarsiers Provide Allocare?

As stated earlier, there are four general hypotheses that have been proposed to explain the evolution of alloparental care: (1) learning-to-mother, one form of mutualism (Lancaster 1971); (2) reciprocity (Axelrod & Hamilton 1981); (3) kin selection (Hamilton 1964); and (4) benefits of philopatry (Stacey & Ligon 1990). Which hypothesis best explains the presence of allomaternal care in the spectral tarsiers?

The first hypothesis is supported by the observation that subadult female spectral tarsiers provide more care than do subadult males. No food sharing by a subadult male was observed. Female subadults were also observed to retrieve fallen infants and transport them orally to a new location. Similarly, subadult females were more likely to play with, groom, or be located within a close distance to the infant than were the subadult males. By caring for their younger sibling, subadults learn how to care for their own infant.

For the second hypothesis to be supported, helping must somehow increase the helper's chances for future survival and breeding success. Unfortunately, the relatively short duration of this study precluded obtaining data that could discern this delayed benefit to the helper.

For the kin selection hypothesis (number three) to be supported, helping must increase the offspring's chances of survival, without affecting the helper's own chances for future reproduction one-half as much. Unfortunately, the small sample sizes as well as the relatively short duration of this study prevented determining whether helping does in fact increase the offspring's chances for survival.

The fourth hypothesis, the benefit of philopatry hypothesis, may also be correct. Subadults may provide care to infants as payment to their parents for permitting them to remain in their natal territory. Although one group did have a subadult male, he dispersed shortly after the study began and formed his own group. Consequently, because of the early age at which males disperse (one year) and the fact that females delay dispersal until about two years (MacKinnon & MacKinnon 1980; pers. obser.), subadult males were rarely available to provide care to the infants.

At a proximate level, elevated levels of the hormone prolactin, usually associated with lactation, has been implicated in predisposing individuals to providing nonmaternal care (Snowdon 2004). In particular, Sussman (in press) argues that if cooperation is rewarding, such that physiological and neurological feedback systems reinforce social tolerance and cooperative behavior, then social group-living can persist in the absence of any conscious recognition that material gains might also flow from mutual cooperation.

Could Subadults Continually Transport the Infants?

Using the time budget model discussed earlier, and Dunbar's calculations for the energetic cost of infant transport, the additional amount of time subadults would need to forage if they transported the infant from birth through nine weeks would be 26%–60%. Following the infant's birth, subadults would have to spend 78%–83% of their time foraging just to meet their own maintenance needs and the additional energetic costs of infant transport. Although it can be argued that this still leaves the subadult with 17% to 22% of their night to travel, rest, and socialize, these numbers make it much easier to understand why so little infant care in the form of transport is provided.

I want to point out that this model assumes that the subadults are responsible for the totality of infant carrying. Callitrichids are known to share responsibility for infant transport among several group members

(Goldizen 1987; Rylands 1993). When there are two adult males in a group, both males are responsible for infant transport. Similarly, when there is one adult male and a subadult, they share responsibility for infant transport. A future permutation of this model might evaluate how group members could potentially share the costs of infant transport.

CHAPTER SUMMARY

This chapter was broken down into four main parts. Part one reviewed the theoretical basis of male care, followed by a detailed description of male care in spectral tarsiers. The data basically demonstrate that adult males provide little, if any, care to infants. Next, I used a modified version of Altmann's time budget model to evaluate whether adult males could in fact provide care to an infant. The model suggests that although males could provide paternal care, they would be energetically challenged if they did. I suggest that the primary reason adult males do not provide paternal care stems from their lack of paternity certainty. I then reviewed the theoretical basis for allocare by subadults, followed by a detailed description of subadult allocare in spectral tarsiers. The data basically demonstrate that spectral tarsier subadults provide little, if any, care to infants. Finally, I used a modified version of Altmann's time budget model to evaluate whether subadults could in fact provide care to an infant. The model suggests that although subadults could provide allocare, they would be energetically challenged if they did.

7

Conservation Status of Spectral Tarsiers

In today's world, it is impossible to study primate behavioral ecology without being concerned about a species' conservation status. Thus, in this chapter I present data on the spectral tarsier's population density and captive conservation. I evaluate how this species' population density and habitat have fared over the last decade. In addition, I provide several suggestions for improving the spectral tarsier's survival probability.

INTRODUCTION

Studies of the population density of tarsiers as well as their distribution are critical if we are to develop any conservation schemes for the tarsiers The conservation status of the five accepted tarsier species are presently categorized as either Low Risk (least concern), Low Risk (conservation dependent), or Data Deficient. Following a workshop organized by Myron Shekelle and the Pusat Primata Schmutzer in Jakarta, Shekelle, Gursky, and Nietsch (nd) compiled and reanalyzed data on each species' distribution, abundance, and conservation status. Using IUCN criteria for calculating conservation status (estimates of the amount of land within each species' distribution), we determined that *T. bancanus* should be listed as low risk, conservation dependent (LR cd); *T. syrichta T. spectrum,* and *T. dianae* as vulnerable (VU); and *T. pumilus* as data deficient (DD). We recognize that using the criteria of the "amount of land available within each species' distribution" is problematic for several reasons. First, not all land is appropriate for the tarsiers. Second, because we did not have satellite images, we could not distinguish between low and high altitude, nor were we able to determine the amount of land that has already been converted from forested area to developed area. Thus, our estimates of "available land" were clearly overestimates, making the resulting conservation status extremely conservative.

POPULATION DENSITY

In 1994, I found that the spectral tarsiers within Tangkoko Dua Saudara Nature Reserve were relatively abundant (Table 7–1). I located 14 groups in the 25 one-hectare plots surveyed. I observed a total of 39 individuals within these 14 groups. The mean number of groups per sampled home range (ha) was .56. The mean number of individuals per sample hectare is 1.56. The number of groups estimated in the entire study area (100 hectare) is 56. I estimated that the population density within the study area was 156 tarsiers per square kilometer.

It should be noted that the estimate of population density that I obtained in 1994, 156 individuals per square kilometer, was one-half of the lowest estimate calculated by Bearder (1987) (300–1,000 individuals per square kilometer, per 100 hectare) based on density estimates determined by MacKinnon and MacKinnon (1980) of 3 to 10 individuals per hectare in north Sulawesi. There are three possible explanations for the discrepancy in the density estimates recorded by Bearder (1987) and those I calculated in 1994. First and foremost, different methods were used. MacKinnon and MacKinnon's work was not based on systematic surveying of a predefined area, it was based on observations in numerous habitat types throughout the northern arm of Sulawesi, as well as at different altitudes.

Second, MacKinnon and MacKinnon's population density estimate was based on home range estimates that were considerably smaller than those observed during my research. Niemitz (1984) computed (using a published figure by MacKinnon and MacKinnon) that the spectral tarsier's home range was slightly greater than one hectare. Similarly, MacKinnon and MacKinnon's determination of this species' home range size was based on spot observations of individuals and not on systematic observations of ranging behavior. The third possibility for the discrepancy in our estimates is that there has been an actual decrease in population density. Unfortunately, it is not possible to actually determine which of these factors is the primary explanation.

The possibility that the population has declined significantly because of habitat destruction is quite disturbing. Thus, I decided to estimate population density for the reserve, within the same study area, in 1999 and again in 2003–2004. In 1999 I found that population density had decreased

Table 7–1 Results of the 1994 Population Census for the Spectral
Tarsier in Tangkoko Dua Saudara Nature Reserve

Quadrat #	Group Observed in Quadrat
1	Present
2	Absent
3	Present
4	Present
5	Present
6	Present
7	Absent
8	Absent
9	Present
10	Absent
11	Present
12	Present
13	Absent
14	Absent
15	Present
16	Present
17	Absent
18	Present
19	Present
20	Absent
21	Absent
22	Absent
23	Present
24	Absent
25	Present
Total Number of Groups Observed	14
Total Number of Animals Observed	39
Mean Number of Individuals Per Sample Quadrat	1.56
Mean Number of Groups Per Sample Quadrat	.56
Estimated Number of Groups in 100 Quadrats	56
Estimated Population in Sampled Area (1 km^2)	156

to 87 individuals per square kilometer and 83 individuals per square
kilometer in 2003–2004. This is substantially lower than any previous estimate of the population density of this species (MacKinnon & MacKinnon
1980; Bearder 1987; Gursky 1998b).

In comparison, studies of *T. bancanus* have also yielded varying estimates of population density. Crompton and Andau (1987) determined

that there are between 14 and 20 individual tarsiers per square kilometer. On the other hand, Niemitz (1979, 1984) reports an estimate of 80 individual tarsiers per square kilometer. Given the significantly larger home range of individuals observed by Crompton and Andau in their study, the reduced number of individuals estimated to be present in a given area can be better understood.

Population surveys of the Philippine tarsier have also been quite variable. Neri-Arboleda (2001) estimated the density of the Bohol Philippine tarsier as approximately 57 individuals per square kilometer. Lagapa (1993) used a line transect method to estimate the population density of tarsiers in Bohol to be 1 to 3 individuals per hectare, or 100 to 300 individuals per square kilometer. Dagosto and Gebo (1998) calculated a similar estimate of 0.5 to 2 individuals per hectare based on the home ranges of 4 radio-tracked animals in Leyte. Rickart et al. (1991) argue that tarsiers are common in the Philippines. However, it would be erroneous for the densities to be extrapolated to determine the total population of tarsiers over the whole of the respective islands, because the projection would be based on the assumption that all forests are suitable habitat for the tarsiers.

In a study of the population density of *T. dianae*, I estimated the population density at Kamarora as 129 individuals per square kilometer. Stefen Merker's long-term study of Dian's tarsier produced population density estimates of approximately 136 groups per square kilometers. At present there has been no population density survey of the Sulawesian pygmy tarsier.

These values are somewhat deceptive because tarsier population density is known to change substantially with both altitude and habitat type. For example, the population density of Dian's tarsier was significantly lower at higher altitudes than lower altitudes (Gursky 1998b). The population density of Dian's tarsier was estimated to be 180 individuals per square kilometer between an altitude of 500–1000 meter, and 57 individuals per square kilometer between an altitude of 1000–1500 meter. Altitude did not significantly affect the population density of spectral tarsiers, but this could reflect the fact that no spectral tarsier populations were censused that resided over 1000 meter.

For both species, I found that population densities were higher in the secondary forest than in the primary forest. The population density of Dian's tarsier in the secondary disturbed forest was approximately 250 individuals per square kilometer, but only 22 individuals per square kilometer in the primary forest. The population density of spectral tarsiers in the secondary forest was also estimated to be about 208 individuals per square kilometer, but was only 100 individuals per square kilometer in the primary forest. Similar results were observed by Stefen Merker, who found that the density of Dian's tarsiers was greatest in habitat he characterized as "small plantations." However, areas that were logged, even selectively, had densities one-third to one-half that of nonlogged forest habitats.

At first glance, the population density estimate calculated in this book suggests that the spectral tarsier is not in imminent danger of extinction. Nonetheless, several additional factors must be considered when discussing the conservation status of this species. This includes: (1) the species distribution, (2) the size of area that is protected where this species occurs, and (3) the degree to which the "protected areas" are in fact protected.

The spectral tarsier, as discussed previously in Chapter 1, has a very limited distribution that is becoming even more limited as new Sulawesian tarsier species are identified. With each new species that is identified, the range of the spectral tarsiers decreases.

In addition, although several reasonably large protected areas have been set up within the spectral tarsier's range in Sulawesi, these protected areas are still undergoing serious deforestation. For example, when Tangkoko Nature Reserve was initially set up in 1980, it comprised almost 9,000 hectare and was surrounded by a similar amount of forest in the form of a buffer zone (MacKinnon & MacKinnon 1980). By 1990, the buffer zone was completely destroyed, and the amount of forest in the reserve was recognized to be down to 7,800 hectare because of encroaching coconut plantations of the villages that surround the reserve. More recently (1995), an additional 1,300 hectare was downgraded from nature reserve to recreation forest, thereby removing protection from an additional segment of forest. Consequently, I believe that, although the spectral tarsier is presently found in relatively large numbers within protected areas in Sulawesi, habitat destruction is a significant threat. As a result, I believe that the conservation status of the spectral tarsier should be changed from indeterminate and insufficiently known (Wolfheim 1986; IUCN 1994) to vulnerable. Dian's tarsier, the lowland Sulawesian tarsier species in central Sulawesi, occurs in two large protected areas in central Sulawesi: Lore Lindu National Park and Morowali Nature Reserve. Although the animals are in protected areas, the tarsiers are opportunistically hunted and the forest is still undergoing major deforestation and destruction (pers. obser.; Merker et al., 2004). For example, Lore Lindu National Park is surrounded by agrarian communities that still hunt within the park's boundaries, obtain most of their income from both the timber and rattan industry, and also burn the forest to convert it to cocoa and coffee plantations. Similarly, a group of traditional slash-and-burn horticulturalists reside within Morowali Nature Reserve. Not only do the Wana opportunistically hunt the tarsiers with dogs and blowguns, but they burn large tracts of land for dry rice agriculture. Thus, although Dian's tarsier is presently found in relatively large numbers within protected areas in Sulawesi, habitat destruction and hunting are significant threats. Similarly, although Dian's tarsier is found at high densities at the lower altitudes, it occurs at noticeably lower densities at higher altitudes. This discrepancy needs to be considered in any determination of the species' conservation status because approximately 70% of the protected areas in which Dian's tarsier occurs are located between 1,000 and 1,500 meter (Nature Conservancy 1994). As a result, I believe that the conservation status of *T. dianae* should be changed from data deficient to lower risk: conservation dependent. Its classification within the low-risk category should be conservation dependent given the hunting pressure, intensive habitat destruction within the protected areas, and the substantially lower densities of this species at higher altitudes (most of its range).

POPULATION VIABILITY ANALYSIS

At present, there have been no population viability analyses (PVA) of spectral tarsiers. However, Neri-Arboleda conducted a PVA of *T. syrichta* using the metapopulation model Analysis of the Likelihood of Extinction (ALEX). Given the values of the life history and environmental parameters used for the analysis (Neri-Arboleda 2001), and in the absence of environmental catastrophe, the minimum habitat area that could attain a less than 5% probability of extinction within hundred years is 60 hectare. Therefore, 60 hectare can be considered the minimum viable habitat area for the Philippine tarsier. Each tarsier has a home range of approximately 2.5 hectare with little overlap; thus, the minimum viable habitat area of 60 hectare contains twenty-four female individuals. Neri-Arboleda noted that the model's output was very sensitive to changes in adult mortality. Slight increases in adult mortality made the population very unstable and caused substantial increases in the probability of extinction.

This estimate of 60 hectare assumes that the whole forested area is fully occupied, which in the wild is most often not the case. This estimate is also based on life history parameters derived from one 8-month study in Bohol. Long-term fieldwork is clearly warranted to distinguish variation in the parameters used.

CAPTIVE CONSERVATION

As a result of their uncertain conservation status, numerous attempts have been made to maintain both the Bornean and the Philippine tarsier species in captivity (Ulmer 1963; Wright et al., 1986, 1988; Roberts & Kohn 1993; Roberts 1994). Although many copulations and conceptions have occurred, infant survivorship has been quite poor. At present, only eight captive-born infants are reported to have been reared to weaning: one *T. syrichta* at the Frankfurt Zoo; two *T. syrichta* at the Cincinnati Zoo; one *T. syrichta* that was hand-reared at the Duke University Primate Center (Haring & Wright 1989); and four *T. bancanus* infants born at the National Zoological Park (Roberts 1994). No spectral tarsier, nor any other Sulawesian tarsier, has ever been maintained in captivity.

HABITAT DESTRUCTION

In addition to exploring how the population density of the spectral tarsiers has changed over the last decade, I also quantified the changes in the habitat within a 4-hectare study area. In 1994, within the 4-hectare vegetation plot (within the arca used by some of the spectral tarsiers), I calculated that there were a total of 33,898 trees. This value only included trees that were greater than 1 meter in height and 1 centimeter in diameter. Of the nearly 34,000 trees, I observed a total of 127 species. I plotted a species area curve to ascertain if a large-enough area had been sampled such that the number of species had already reached an asymptote (Figure 7–1). There were 10,084, 7,559, 8,394, and 7,861 trees, and a total number of 106, 115, 122, and 89 species, in each of the 4 hectares, respectively. In each hectare, the total number of trees with a dbh greater than or equal to 5 centimeter was 919, 752, 770, and 723 trees, respectively. The total number of trees within each hectare with a dbh greater than or equal to 10 centimeter was 481, 439, 425, and 382, respectively.

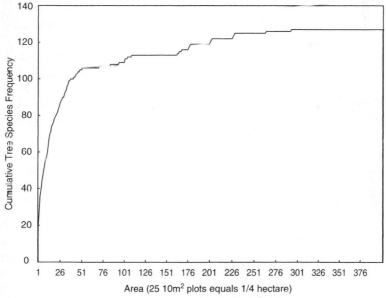

Figure 7–1 Species Area Curve for the Trees Sampled in Four 1-hectare Plots

Comparing this field site with data from other field studies in Sulawesi, Indonesia, and Malaysia where information on forest structure was also recorded may provide additional insight into the type of habitat the tarsiers in this field study were using. At Toraut in Dumoga Bone National Park in northern Sulawesi, there are approximately 408 trees per hectare with a dbh greater than or equal to 10 centimeter (Whitten et al., 1987). At Ketambe, Sumatra, the number of trees per hectare with at least a 10-centimeter dbh was only 287 (Whitten et al., 1987). At Kuala Lompat in Malaysia, there are approximately 307 trees per hectare with a dbh greater than 10 centimeter (Raemakers 1980). Thus, initially, the number of large trees in Tangkoko seems to be equivalent or slightly higher than the number of large trees found in other forest throughout Sulawesi, Indonesia, and Malaysia.

The importance value index (IVI) (Brower et al., 1990) for each of the tree species in the hectare plots within the study area in Tangkoko Nature Reserve was calculated. The analysis was only performed for trees greater than 10-centimeter dbh to permit easy comparison of the habitat with other field sites. The six most important species were *Leea indica*, *Morinda citrifolia*, *Piper aduncum*, *Palaquium obvatum*, *Barringtonia acutangula*, and *Vitex quinata*. Table 7–2 lists each tree species in terms of their relative density, relative frequency, relative coverage, and the importance value index using trees greater with a dbh greater than or equal to 10 centimeter.

In 1999, I redid the vegetation plot (Table 7–3). I found that the number of trees had significantly decreased (Friedman ANOVA: X^2=8.000; p=.0183; df=2). In addition, I found that the number of smaller-diameter trees had increased (Friedman ANOVA: X^2=8.000; p=.0183; df=2) and the number of large-diameter trees within this area had decreased (Friedman ANOVA: X^2=8.000; p=.0183; df=2). This pattern continued in the vegetation plot survey in 2003–2004. The number of trees decreased (Friedman ANOVA: X^2=8.000; p=.0183; df=2), the number of large-diameter trees decreased (Friedman ANOVA: X^2=8.000; p=.0183; df=2), and the number of small-diameter trees increased (Friedman ANOVA: X^2=8.000; p=.0183; df=2).

The data I have presented on population density and habitat destruction certainly suggest that the spectral tarsier population at Tangkoko is on the road to extinction. It is my opinion that the best way to reduce habitat destruction and prevent any additional declines in population density is to *enforce* the local rules concerning habitat usage. At present, the Indonesian government has very detailed rules concerning what forest can be used by local people and what forest cannot. However, these rules are not instituted by the local forestry officials. The local forestry officials are paid to protect the forest and thus they need to be held accountable for annual destruction to the local rain forest. Fining the local officials by regularly docking their pay, for small as well as large infractions, would be a sure way to prevent local officials from looking the other way—even if distant family members were involved.

Table 7–2 The Relative Density, Frequency, Coverage, and Importance Value Index (Brower et al., 1990) for All the Trees Within the Four-hectare Vegetation Plot at Tangkoko Nature Reserve Between 1994–1995

Tree Species	Relative Species Density	Relative Frequency	Relative Coverage	Importance Value (IV)
Acalypha caturus	.00090	.00375	.00036	.00501
Aglaia odoratissima	.00004	.00083	.00000	.00087
Aglaia sp.	.00020	.00125	.00000	.00145
Aglaia dookoo	.00553	.01541	.00028	.02122
Albizia saponaria	.00636	.00958	.00188	.01782
Alectryon sp.	.00204	.01000	.00009	.01213
Alstonia ranvolfia	.01503	.00167	.01053	.02723
Alstonia sumatrana	.01271	.01541	.00754	.03566
Anthrocephalus macrophyllus	.00067	.00583	.00754	.01404
Ardisia sp.	.00722	.01374	.00030	.02126
Ardisia rumphii	.02590	.01666	.00754	.05010
Areca vestiaria	.00020	.00083	.00000	.00103
Arenga pinnata	.00008	.00083	.00000	.00091
Artocarpus dadah	.00793	.01624	.00144	.02561
Averrhoa bilimbi	.00059	.00250	.00002	.00842
Barringtonia acutangula	.05036	.01666	.02491	.11754
Bombax valetonii	.00118	.00750	.00005	.00873
Breynia cernua	.00078	.00583	.00001	.00662
Bridellia minutiflora	.00809	.01541	.00175	.02525
Buchanania urborescens	.00008	.00125	.00000	.00133
Calophyllum soulattri	.00004	.00042	.00000	.00046
Cananga odorate	.00805	.01541	.03015	.05451
Canarium asperum.	.00075	.00541	.00000	.00616
Canarium hirsutum	.00424	.01499	.00110	.02033
Canarium vriesanum	.00106	.00375	.00001	.00482
Caryota mitis	.00522	.01541	.00305	.02368
Chisocheton kingu	.00102	.00708	.00005	.00815
Clausens excavata	.00259	.01041	.00003	.01303
Cordia mysea	.00004	.00042	.00000	.00046
Crateva nurlava	.00122	.00458	.00009	.00589
Cryptocarya celebica	.00479	.01249	.00033	.01761
Cryptocarya bicolor	.00259	.00916	.00009	.01184
Dendrocnide microstigma	.00396	.01458	.00305	.02159
Dillenia ochreata	.00043	.00292	.00004	.00339
Diospyros korthalsiana	.02426	.01666	.00429	.04521

(*Continued*)

Table 7–2 Continued

Tree Species	Relative Species Density	Relative Frequency	Relative Coverage	Importance Value (IV)
Diospyros rumphii	.00440	.01041	.00132	.01613
Dracontomelum dao	.00832	.01624	.02491	.04947
Dracontomelum mangiferum	.00173	.01000	.00025	.01198
Drypetes minutiflora	.00122	.00625	.00001	.00748
Drypetes longifolia	.00059	.00333	.00011	.00403
Erythrina sp.	.00004	.00042	.00000	.00046
Eugenia accuminatissima	.01307	.01374	.00150	.02831
Eugenia sp.	.04396	.01666	.03015	.09077
Eugenia sp.	.00012	.00042	.00000	.00054
Euodia minahassae	.00565	.01374	.00030	.01969
Ficus ampelas	.00012	.00083	.00000	.00095
Ficus annulata	.00004	.00042	.00016	.00062
Ficus benjamina	.00004	.00083	.00016	.00103
Ficus bracheata	.00004	.00042	.00000	.00096
Ficus calulocarpa	.00004	.00042	.00042	.00466
Ficus chrysolepsis	.00031	.01666	.00004	.01701
Ficus cordulata	.00004	.00042	.00001	.00047
Ficus drupacea	.00004	.00042	.00000	.00046
Ficus pubinervis	.00035	.00250	.00001	.00286
Ficus septica	.00059	.00458	.00002	.00519
Ficus tinctoria	.00098	.00500	.00011	.00609
Ficus variegata	.01295	.01583	.02491	.05369
Ficus virens	.00012	.00083	.00020	.00115
Ficus spp.	.00098	.00416	.00138	.00236
Garcinia tetrandra	.01723	.01583	.00195	.03501
Garcinia daedalanthera	.01860	.01249	.00182	.03291
Garcinia parvifolia	.00318	.01000	.00008	.01326
Garuga floribunda	.00973	.00042	.01221	.02236
Gastonia papuana	.00035	.01417	.00002	.01454
Glochidion philippicum	.00966	.00292	.00623	.01881
Gnetum gnemenoides	.00114	.01541	.00002	.01657
Gnetum sp.	.00008	.00042	.00000	.00050
Grewia koordersiana	.00451	.01333	.00033	.01817
Gymnocranthera forbesii	.00004	.00042	.00000	.00046
Harpullia cupaniodes	.00349	.01374	.00064	.01787
Harpullia arborea	.00157	.00667	.00014	.00838
Homalium celebicum	.00212	.00667	.00005	.00884

Table 7–2 Continued

Tree Species	Relative Species Density	Relative Frequency	Relative Coverage	Importance Value (IV)
Kjellbergiodendron celebicum	.00039	.00208	.00004	.00251
Kleinhovia hospita	.01613	.01374	.03893	.06880
Koodersiodendron pinnatum	.01609	.01583	.01800	.04992
Lagerstroemia ovalifolia	.00024	.00167	.00001	.00192
Leea aculeata	.00008	.00042	.00000	.00050
Leea indica	.10503	.01624	.26314	.38441
Leea rubra	.00895	.01374	.00305	.02574
Livistona rotundifolia	.01028	.01458	.00202	.02688
Macaranga philippicum	.03199	.01583	.01401	.06183
Macaranga mappa	.00216	.00875	.00008	.01099
Maesa perlaurius	.00706	.01124	.00009	.01839
Mallotus tanarius	.00157	.00584	.00012	.00753
Mangifera indica	.00016	.00125	.00000	.00141
Melanolepis ricinoides	.01036	.01500	.00100	.02636
Melia azedarach	.00636	.01333	.00527	.02496
Melochia ambellata	.00004	.00042	.00000	.00046
Memecylon sp.	.00020	.00208	.00000	.00228
Morinda citrifolia	.08191	.01624	.08994	.18809
Morinda bracteata	.00671	.01000	.00754	.02425
Palaquium obvatum	.04545	.01624	.10987	.17156
Pandanus sp.	.00035	.00125	.00000	.00160
Piper aduncum	.14031	.01624	.14954	.17857
Pipturus argentus	.00094	.00458	.00006	.00558
Pisonia umbellifera	.00082	.00250	.00012	.00156
Planconella oxyedra	.00059	.00416	.00001	.00476
Polyalthia rumphi	.00184	.00416	.00002	.00602
Polyalthia glauca	.01036	.01499	.00162	.02697
Polyalthia lateriflora	.00078	.00042	.00000	.00120
Pterocarpus indicus	.00039	.00125	.00000	.00164
Pterocymbium javanicum	.00102	.00583	.00020	.00705
Pterocymbium diversifolium	.00718	.01083	.00271	.02072
Pterocymbium javanicum	.00863	.01333	.03893	.06089
Rapanea sp.	.00126	.00708	.00001	.00835
Saccopetalum horsfieldii	.00400	.01166	.00018	.01584
Spathodea campanulata	.00255	.00583	.00003	.00841
Spondia sp.	.00004	.00042	.00001	.00047
Sterculia insularis	.00349	.01166	.00144	.01659
Sterculia comosa	.00075	.00541	.00004	.00620

(Continued)

Table 7–2 continued

Tree Species	Relative Species Density	Relative Frequency	Relative Coverage	Importance Value (IV)
Syzygium #1	.00506	.01333	.00202	.02041
Syzygium litorale	.00381	.01291	.00009	.01681
Syzygium polyanthra	.00479	.01166	.00028	.01673
Terminalia catappa	.00004	.00042	.00000	.00046
Terminalia celebica	.00149	.00666	.00023	.00838
Tetrameles nudifloria	.00243	.00416	.00012	.00671
Vitex quinata	.04545	.01583	.03893	.10021
Vitex cofassus	.00310	.00750	.00028	.01088
Zanthoxylum sp.	.00055	.00292	.00002	.00347
Zizyphus angustifolia	.00024	.00292	.00000	.00316
Unknown species 1	.00730	.01208	.00052	.01990
Unknown species 2	.00071	.00916	.00000	.00987
Unknown species 3	.00181	.01041	.00003	.01225
Unknown species 4	.00008	.00500	.00000	.00508
Unknown species 5	.00314	.01166	.00011	.01491
Unknown species 6	.00887	.00627	.00090	.01604
Unknown species 7	.00102	.00416	.00001	.00519

Table 7-3 Change in the Number of Trees, Number of Species, and dbh Frequency, in the Four-hectare Plots in Tangkoko Nature Reserve from 1994 to 2003

	# Trees	# Species	dbh <5 cm	dbh <10 cm	# Trees	# Species	dbh <5cm	dbh <10 cm	# Trees	# Species	dbh <5 cm	dbh <10 cm
Plot 1	10084	105	919	481	9462	101	944	451	8976	99	953	435
Plot 2	7559	115	752	439	6186	99	777	359	6041	96	784	321
Plot 3	8394	122	770	425	7824	112	796	396	7533	108	787	366
Plot 4	7861	89	723	382	7263	84	749	353	7129	82	752	317
Total:	33898	127	3164	1727	30735	121	3266	1559	29679	117	3276	1439

8

Summary and Conclusions

My goal in this volume was to explore the behavior and conservation status of the spectral tarsier, *Tarsius spectrum*. I observed the behavior of this enigmatic primate at Tangkoko Nature Reserve in north Sulawesi for more than a decade.

In Chapter 1, I began by introducing the taxonomic history of the tarsiers. Over the last few centuries, there has been quite an upheaval in tarsier taxonomy. Questions concerning whether tarsiers are prosimian primates or whether they should be placed in the Haplorrhini with the monkeys and apes have not yet been resolved. New questions concerning whether the Sulawesian tarsiers should be in the same genus as the Philippine and Bornean tarsiers have been raised, as well as whether *spectrum* should be the species name for the northeastern-most Sulawesian tarsier population or whether *tarsier* has priority as the species name.

In Chapter 2 I introduced the field site where I conducted my behavioral observations and presented details about the forest where I worked. In addition, I also described in detail the methods that I used to observe the tarsiers, three of which distinguish my research. First, I regularly used radio tracking. This enabled me to locate my focal animals in the forest whenever and wherever they were located. Second, I observed my animals' behavior using simultaneous focal follows whereby all adult group members were observed simultaneously. Finally, I conducted numerous predator experiments and recorded the focal animal's response to the presence of different types of predators.

Chapter 3 presented information on the size of tarsier groups as well as their composition. I found that the majority of groups contained an adult male–female pair, but approximately 15% of the groups contained two adult females. I argue that the social system of spectral tarsiers is best represented as facultative monogamy, as some groups are in fact polygynous. This conclusion is supported by the morphometric data on sexual size dimorphism present in this population.

Spectral tarsiers do not exhibit a monogamous breeding system, but rather one with greater male–male competition for access to females (as the presence of dimorphism suggests), as discussed in Chapter 3. The lack of a strictly monogamous breeding system may explain, at least in part, the limited nature of male care in this species. Specifically, it may be too risky for a male *T. spectrum* to provide energetically expensive paternal care to an offspring that is less likely to carry his genes.

The second part of Chapter 3 explored questions regarding gregariousness and group cohesion. To test whether nocturnal encounters between spectral tarsier group members, outside of the sleeping tree, are due to gregarious behavior or whether they are the result of chance, I utilized Waser's Random Gas Model. According to Waser's model, if group members' movements are random and independent (i.e., solitary foraging), then their territory can be considered a two-dimensional gas of tarsier individuals. I found that at all distance classes less than 50 meters, the tarsiers encountered one another more frequently than expected by chance alone. The increase in encounter frequency is true especially at the closer distance classes. According to Waser's Random Gas Model, the spectral tarsiers spent more scans in proximity to other group members than predicted by chance, given the size of their home range, their nightly travel speed, and their nightly path length.

Additional observations have shown that the tarsiers are gregarious foragers, that is, they were more likely to forage when near another group member than when alone. However, I found that the insect capture rate was substantially less for gregarious foragers than solitary foragers. This result naturally begs the question, if the tarsiers are experiencing substantial intragroup competition over food resources when foraging in close proximity to another adult, then why do they continue to forage in proximity? Group living is predicted to occur only when the benefits of living in a group outweigh the costs incurred (Krebs & Davies 1984; Dunbar 1988; Kappeler and Ganzhorn 1993). So, if living in a group is costly to tarsiers, then why don't they actively avoid one another while traveling throughout their territory? One possibility is that they forage in proximity only when this behavior's benefits outweigh the costs of intraspecific food competition (in the form of lower insect capture rates).

One situation in which it benefits the spectral tarsiers to be gregarious is when they are exposed to predators. Throughout my research, I have found that spectral tarsiers mob their predators as a group.

In the third part of Chapter 3, I explored how infant spectral tarsiers behave in the presence of potential predators. In addition to moving away from their parked location on encountering a predator, spectral tarsier infants also repeatedly gave a series of alarm calls in response to the predator models. Infants emitted an alarm call in response to all presentations of the model predators, regardless of their age. However, the type of alarm call they emitted varied depending on the type of potential predator. The infants consistently emitted a twittering alarm call in response to the bird-of-prey models and birds-of-prey vocalizations whereas they emitted a harsh loud call three times in rapid succession in response to the model snakes. Given that such young infants were capable of making the distinction between a snake and a bird of prey may suggest that the alarm calls are not predator-specific. Instead, following Hauser (1993), it is possible that these acoustic differences represent the infant's assessment of individual risk from a particular predator's attack. Twittering may be given in response to low-risk predator events whereas harsh loud calls are given to high-risk predator attempts. This behavioral pattern has been noted in ground squirrels (Owings and Hennessy 1984) and also suggested for vervet monkeys by Hauser (1993).

In the last section of Chapter 3, I evaluated how moonlight may affect a species' predation risk. Whereas most nocturnal mammals are lunar phobic, the majority of studies on the behavior of nocturnal primates have shown that nocturnal primates are lunar philic. Throughout my field work I have observed the spectral tarsier to be lunar philic. This behavioral response is intriguing because lunar phobia is generally believed to be a form of predator avoidance (Lockard & Ownings 1974; Fenton et al., 1977; Morrison 1978; Watanuki 1986; Nelson 1989; Bowers 1990; Daly et al., 1992; Kotler et al., 1993; Kramer & Birney 2001). Specifically, it has been argued that during full moons nocturnal animals are more easily seen and preyed on by nocturnal and diurnal predators, thereby increasing the risk of predation. If this hypothesis is accurate (nocturnal mammals are lunar phobic because of increased predation risk during full moons), and numerous studies suggest that it is, then by extension it implies that tarsiers and other nocturnal primates are increasing their exposure to predators when they increase their activity during full moons.

One possible explanation for the lack of lunar phobia exhibited by the spectral tarsiers is that full moons do not increase predation pressure for nocturnal primates. Nash (1986) has suggested that the nocturnal primates are actually safer from predators during full moons than they are during new moons. Although the tarsiers (and other nocturnal primates) would be more easily seen during a full moon, they would also be more likely to see their predators before the attack. It is well known that the probability of a successful hunt is tremendously decreased if the prey becomes aware of the predator prior to the attack. A major distinction between primates and other mammals is their highly developed visual system (Martin 1990; Fleagle 1999). This emphasis on visual systems, even in primates that still rely on olfaction, makes increased moonlight attractive.

The first section of Chapter 4 focused on the function of territoriality in spectral tarsiers. I found mixed support for both the mate defense and resource defense hypotheses, but slightly more support for the mate defense function. Supporting the mate defense hypothesis, there was an increase in the number of territorial encounters, as well as intragroup encounters, during the mating season compared to the nonmating season. Providing minor support for resource defense hypothesis, there was an increase in the number of intergroup encounters (territorial disputes) during the dry season.

In the second section of Chapter 4, I explore how spectral tarsiers modify their diet in response to seasonality. During the wet season, when resource abundance was higher, tarsiers ate Orthopterans and Lepidopterans with greater frequency and Coleoptera, Isoptera, and Hymenoptera with reduced frequency.

In this chapter, I also demonstrate that the majority of sleeping trees utilized by spectral tarsiers were *Ficus sp.*, with *Ficus caulocarpa* being used much more frequently than all other species. Spectral tarsiers primarily utilized one major sleeping site, although most groups had one alternate sleeping site as well. They also regularly slept in family groups in contrast to the other tarsier species. There was a lot of site fidelity between years. Based on data from bird-banding, I found that male–female dispersal distances were significantly different, with males dispersing much farther than females.

Chapter 5 describes infant development and maternal care during the first ten weeks of the infant's life. I found that wild spectral tarsiers have a mean gestation length of approximately 190 days, a mean weaning age of 78 days, and reproduce seasonally. Infants were almost always transported orally and were parked repeatedly throughout the night. I described the infant transport and parking behavior as a cache-and-carry strategy. There was noticeable conflict between the mother and infant concerning the cessation of transport, but less conflict surrounding the cessation of nursing. The mortality rate of wild spectral tarsiers was initially high during the first two months of life and then rapidly decreased. Captive Bornean tarsiers follow the same mortality schedule, but have a higher rate of mortality during the first two months.

The second half of Chapter 5 tested the hypothesis that spectral tarsiers park their infants because they do not possess sufficient time in their nightly activity period to meet the additional energetic costs of continual infant transport. I argued that infant parking behavior in the prosimian primates is an adaptive behavioral strategy designed to reduce the cost of continual infant transport. The null hypothesis was that spectral tarsiers exhibit infant parking behavior because it is an ancestral behavior pattern (Martin 1968; Eisenberg 1981; van Schaik & Kappeler 1994). To test the hypothesis, I used a modified version of Altmann's model of maternal time budgets (1980). Altmann's model is a simple time allocation model that predicts the total amount of time that a female would need to forage if she met all of her own maintenance needs and those of her infant's nutritional needs through lactation. The modified time budget model incorporates the additional time that the female would need to forage if she continually transported her infant. Using Dunbar's (1988) method for estimating the energetic cost of infant transport I found that female spectral tarsiers do not have sufficient time to forage to meet the energetic costs of continual infant transport.

In the first half of Chapter 6, I reviewed the observation that many small primates also exhibit paternal transport of infants when the cost of infant transport and lactation together become prohibitive for the female to handle alone. I presented data illustrating the amount of paternal care provided and showed that spectral tarsier males were never observed transporting their infants. I then incorporated all the parameters for males into the modified time budget model to ascertain whether they possess enough time in the night to forage to meet their own foraging needs as well as the energetic cost of transporting their infant. The data showed that males should be able to continually transport their young. Thus, the hypothesis that adult males could not provide paternal transport of infants because of energy and time limitations is rejected.

In the second part of Chapter 6, I reviewed allocare, another strategy that small primates employ when the energetic cost of infant transport becomes prohibitive. I presented data on the form and frequency of allocare in the spectral tarsiers to illustrate how limited allotransport is in this species. I then incorporated all the parameters for subadults into the modified time budget model to ascertain whether subadults possess enough time in the night to meet their own foraging needs as well as the energetic cost of transporting the infant. Using Dunbar's (1988) method for calculating the energetic cost of infant transport, the model predicted that subadults do not have sufficient time to forage to meet the energy costs of continual infant transport.

In Chapter 7, I present the population density of the spectral tarsier over a ten-year period. I found that the density had significantly decreased over time from 156 to as low as 83 individuals per square kilometer. In the nineteenth century, Alfred Russell Wallace (1869) recognized the threat of humans to these wonderful creatures: "[S]hould civilized man ever reach these distant islands . . . we may be sure that he will so disturb the nicely-balanced relations of . . . nature as to cause the disappearance, and finally the extinction, of these very beings whose wonderful structure and beauty he alone is fitted to appreciate and enjoy." The data I have presented on population density and habitat destruction certainly suggest that the spectral tarsier population at Tangkoko is on the road to extinction. That is, if population density continues to decline and habitat destruction continues at its present rate, then it is doubtful that the tarsiers at Tangkoko will be around in the twenty-second century.

It will be a shame if spectral tarsiers go extinct just as scientists and laymen alike are finding out how wonderful they truly are. With each research project that I have undertaken, several additional questions about spectral tarsiers have begun to plague my brain. There is the question of the phylogenetic relationship of tarsiers to other primates, both living and fossil (Beard 1998, 2004; Ross 1994; Beard & Wang 1990; Ginsburg & Mein 1986; Simons & Bown 1985). When I first began studying tarsiers I was convinced that they were more closely related to anthropoids. However, after observing their behavior I became convinced that they were more closely related to prosimians.

Another question that requires future attention is why *T. spectrum* are so much more social than the other tarsier species. Is it a reflection of their different habitat? *T. bancanus* and *T. syrichta* live in dipterocarp forests that fruit on seven-year cycles whereas the Sulawesian tarsiers live in forests with very few dipterocarps, and higher proportions of figs that fruit year-round. As the tarsiers consume insects that are attracted to the fruit of these trees, this may account for some of the differences. Note that the Sulawesian tarsiers are east of Wallace's line whereas the other tarsier species are west of Wallace's line. Crompton (1989) believes it may have to do with the different types of insects that each species consumes; *T. bancanus* eats large ground-dwelling insects whereas *T. spectrum* consumes more flying and colonial insects. Research is needed to determine which, if any, of these explanations can account for the different social systems in these sister species. It is my hope that this monograph will inspire a new generation of students to study one of the most enigmatic of all primates, the spectral tarsier.

References Cited

Aiello, L. 1986. The Relationship of the Tarsiiformes: A Review of the Case for the Haplorhini. In ed. B. A. Wood, L. B. Martin, and P. J. Andrews. *Major Topics in Primate and Human Evolution,* Cambridge: Cambridge University Press.

Altmann, J. 1974. Observational Study of Behavior: Sampling Methods. *Behaviour* 49: 227–267.

Altmann, J. 1980. *Baboon Mothers and Infants.* Cambridge: Cambridge University Press.

Altmann, J., and A. Samuels. 1992. Costs of Maternal Care: Infant Carrying in Baboons. *Behavioral Ecology and Sociobiology* 29: 391–398.

Alvard, M. 1993. *Testing the Ecologically Noble Savage Hypothesis: Conservation and Subsistence Hunting in Amazonia Peru.* Ph.D. dissertation, University of New Mexico, Albuquerque.

Amlaner, C. Jr., R. Sibley, and R. McCleery. 1979. Effects of Telemetry Weight on Breeding Success in Herring Gulls. In *Proceedings 2nd International Conference on Wildlife Biotelemetry,* ed. F. Long, 254–259. University of Wyoming.

Anderson, C. 1981. Subtrooping in a Chacma Baboon (*Papio ursinus*) Population. *Primates* 23. 445–458.

Audley-Charles, M. 1981. Geological History of the Region of Wallace's Line. In *Wallace's Line and Plate Tectonics,* ed. T. C. Whitmore. Oxford: Clarendon Press.

Axelrod, R., and W. Hamilton. 1981. The Evolution of Cooperation. *Science* 211: 1390–1396.

Baldwin, J. 1986. Behavior in Infancy: Exploration and Play. In *Comparative Primate Biology, Vol. 2, Part A: Behavior, Conservation and Ecology.* ed. G. Mitchell and J. Erwin, 295–326. New York: Alan R. Liss.

Barlow, G. W. 1988. Monogamy in Relation to Resources. In *The Ecology of Social Behavior,* ed. C. N. Slobodshikoff, 55–79. New York: Academic Press.

205

Bartecki, U., and E. Heymann. 1987. Field Observations of Snake Mobbing in a Group of Saddleback Tamarins, *Saguinus fuscicollis nigrifrons. Folia Primatologica* 48: 199–202.

Bateman, A. 1948. Intra-sexual Selection in *Drosophila. Heredity* 2: 349–368.

Bearder, S. 1987. Lorises, Bush Babies, and Tarsiers: Diverse Societies in Solitary Foragers. In *Primate Societies*, ed. B. Smuts, D. Cheney, R. Seyfarth, R. Wrangham, and T. Struhsaker. Chicago: University of Chicago Press.

Bearder, S. 1999. Physical and Social Diversity among Nocturnal Primates: A New View based on Long-term Research. *Primates* 40(1): 267–282.

Bearder, S., Nekaris, K. A. I., and C. Buzzell. 2002. Dangers in the Night: Are Some Nocturnal Primates Afraid of the Dark? In *Eat or Be Eaten: Predator Sensitive Foraging Among Primates*, ed., L. Miller, 21–40. Cambridge: Cambridge University Press.

Bearder, S., and R. D. Martin. 1979. The Social Organization of a Nocturnal Primate Revealed by Radio-tracking. In *A Handbook on Biotelemetry and Radiotracking*, ed. D. W. Donald and C. J. Amlaner. Oxford: Pergamon Press.

Berman, C. 1980. Mother–Infant Relationships among Free-ranging Rhesus Monkeys on Cayo Santiago: With a Comparison among Captive Pairs. *Animal Behaviour* 28: 860–873.

Bibby, R., T. Southwood, and P. Cairns. 1992. *Techniques for Estimating Population Density in Birds*. New York: Academic Press.

Blackburn, M., and D. Calloway. 1976. Basal Metabolic Rate and Work Energy Expenditure of Mature Pregnant Women. *J Am Diet Assoc* 69: 29–37.

Boesch, C., and H. Boesch-Achermann. 2000. *The Chimpanzees of the Tai Forest*. Oxford: Oxford University Press.

Boinski, S. 1987. Habitat Use by Squirrel Monkeys (*Saimiri oerstedi*) in Costa Rica. *Folia Primatologica* 49: 151–167.

Bowers, M. 1988. Seed Removal Experiments on Desert Rodents: The Microhabitat by Moonlight Effect. *Journal of Mammalogy* 69: 201–204.

Bowers, M. 1990. Exploitation of Seed Aggregates by Merriam's Kangaroo Rats: Harvesting Rates and Predatory Risk. *Ecology* 71: 2334–2344.

Brander, R., and W. Cochran. 1971. Radio Location Telemetry. In *Wildlife Management Techniques*, ed. R. H. Giles. Washington, DC: Wildlife Society.

Brigham, M., and R. Barclay. 1992. Lunar Influence on Foraging and Nesting Activity of Common Poorwills. *Auk* 109: 315–320.

Brody, S. 1945. *Bioenergetics and Growth*. New York: Rheinhold.

Brooks, R. 1985. *Nocturnal Mammals: Techniques for Study*. School of Forest Resources, Research Paper #48. University Park: Pennsylvania State University Press.

Brower, J., J. Zar, and C. von Ende. 1990. *Field and Laboratory Methods for General Ecology*. Iowa: Wm. C. Brown.

Brown, J. 1964. The Evolution of Diversity in Avian Territorial Systems. *Wilson Bulletin* 76: 160–169.

Buffon, G. 1765. *Histoire naturelle, generale et particuliere. L'imprimeerie du Roi* 13: 87–91.

Burmeister, H. 1846. *Beitrage zur Kentniss der Gattung Tarsius.* Berlin: G. Reimer.

Buss, D. H., and O. M. Reed. 1970. Lactation of Baboons Fed a Low Protein Maintenance Diet. *Lab Anim Care* 26: 709–712.

Buss, D. H., and W. R. Voss. 1971. Evaluation of Four Methods for Estimating the Milk Yield of Baboons. *J Nutrition* 101: 901–910.

Butynski, T. 1984. Vertebrate Predation by Primates: A Review of Hunting Patterns and Prey. *Journal of Human Evolution* 11: 421–430.

Caldecott, J. 1986. Mating Patterns, Societies and the Ecogeography of Macaques. *Animal Behavior* 34: 208–220.

Caro, T. 1986. The Functions of Stotting in Thomson's Gazelles: Some Tests of the Hypotheses. *Animal Behavior* 34: 663–684.

Carter, S., and B. S. Cushing. 2004. Proximate Mechanisms Regulating Sociality and Social Monogamy, in the Context of Evolution. In *Origins and Nature of Sociality*, ed. R. W. Sussman, and A. R. Chapman, 99–121. New York: Aldine De Gruyter.

Cartmill, M., and R. Kay. 1978. Cranio-dental Morphology, Tarsier Affinities, and Primate Suborders. In *Recent Advances in Primatology, Vol. 3: Evolution*, ed. D. Chivers and K. Joysey, 205–214. London: Academic Press.

Castenholz, A. 1984. The Eye of *Tarsius.* In *Biology of Tarsiers*, ed., C. Niemitz, 303–318. Stuttgart: Gustav Fischer.

Catchpole, H., and J. Fulton. 1943. The Oestrus Cycle in *Tarsius. Journal of Mammalogy* 24: 90–93.

Cave, A. J. 1973. The Primate Nasal Fossa. *Biological Journal of the Linnean Society* 5: 377–387.

Cebul, M., and G. Epple. 1984. Father–Offspring Relationships in Laboratory Families of Saddle-back Tamarins (*Saguinus fuscicollis*). In *Primate Paternalism*, ed. Taub D. M. 1–19. New York: Van Nostrand Reinhold.

Chapman, C. 1986. Boa Constrictor Predation and Group Response in White-faced *Cebus* Monkeys. *Biotropica* 18: 171–172.

Charles-Dominique, P. 1977. *Ecology and Behavior of Nocturnal Primates.* New York: Columbia University Press.

Charles-Dominique, P., H. Cooper, A. Hladik, C. Hladik, E. Pages, G. A. Pariente, A. Petter-Rousseaux, and A. Schilling. 1977. *Nocturnal Malagasy Primates.* New York: Academic Press.

Charnov, E. 1976. Optimal Foraging: The Marginal Value Theorum. *Theor Popul Biol* 9: 129–136.

Cheney, D., and R. Wrangham. 1987. Predation. In *Primate Societies*, ed. B. Smuts, D. Cheney, R. Seyfarth, R. Wrangham, and T. Struhsaker. Chicago: Chicago University Press.

Clark, A. 1985. Sociality in a Nocturnal "Solitary" Prosimian: *Galago crassicaudatus.* *International Journal of Primatology* 6: 581–600.

Cleveland, J., and C. Snowdon. 1984. Social Development during the First Twenty Weeks in the Cotton-top Tamarin (*Saguinus oedipus*). *Animal Behavior* 32: 432–444.

Clutton-Brock, T. 1975. Ranging Behavior of Red Colobus (*Colobus badius tephrosceles*) in the Gombe National Park. *Folia Primatologica* 19: 368–379.

Clutton-Brock, T. H. 1992. *The Evolution of Parental Care*. Princeton: Princeton University Press.

Clutton-Brock, T. H., and P. Harvey. 1977. Primate Ecology and Social Organization. *Journal of Zoology* 183: 1–39.

Coehlo, A. 1974. Sociobioenergetics and Sexual Dimorphism in Primates. *Primates* 15: 263–269.

Colquhoun, I. 1998. Cathemeral Behavior of *Eulemur macaco macaco* at Ambato Massif, Madagascar. *Folia Primatologica* 69: 191–203.

Corbin, G., and J. Schmidt. 1995. Insect Secretions Determine Habitat Use Patterns by a Female Lesser Mouse Lemur. *American Journal of Primatology* 37: 317–324.

Cresswell, W., and S. Harris. 1988. The Effects of Weather Conditions on the Movement and Activity of Badgers (*Meles meles*) in a Suburban Environment. *Journal of Zoology* 216: 187–194.

Crompton, R. 1984. Foraging, Habitat Structure and Locomotion in Two Species of *Galago*. In *Adaptations for Foraging in Nonhuman Primates*, ed. P. Rodman and J. Cant. New York: Columbia University Press.

Crompton, R., and P. Andau. 1986. Locomotion and Habitat Utilization in Free-ranging *Tarsius bancanus*: A Preliminary Report. *Primates* 27: 337–355.

Crompton, R., and P. Andau. 1987. Ranging, Activity Rhythms, and Sociality in Free-ranging *Tarsius bancanus*: A Preliminary Report. *International Journal of Primatology* 8: 43–71.

Crompton, R., W. Sellers, and M. Gunther. 1993. Energetic Efficiency and Ecology as Selective Factors in the Salutatory Adaptation of Prosimian Primates. *Proc R Soc London B* 254: 41–45.

Curio, E. 1978. The Adaptive Significance of Avian Mobbing: Teleonomic Hypotheses and Predictions. *Z Tierpsychol* 48: 175–183.

Dagosto, M., D. Gebo, and C. Dolino. 2001. Positional Behavior and Social Organization of the Philippine Tarsier (*Tarsius syrichta*). *Primates* 42(3): 233–243.

Dagosto, M., and D. Gebo. 1998. A Preliminary Study of the Philippine Tarsier (*Tarsius syrichta*) in Leyte. *Am J Phys Anthrop Supplement* 26: 73.

Daly, M. 1979. Why Don't Male Mammals Lactate? *Journal of Theoretical Biology* 78: 325–345.

Daly, M., P. Behrends, M. Wilson, and L. Jacobs. 1992. Behavioral Modulation of Predation Risk: Moonlight Avoidance and Crepuscular Compensation in a Nocturnal Desert Rodent, *Dipodomys merriami*. *Animal Behavior* 44: 1–9.

Daly, M., and M. Wilson. 1983. *Sex, Evolution and Behavior*. Boston: Willard Grant Press.

Darwin, C. 1871. *The Descent of Man and Selection in Relation to Sex*. London: Murray.

Dettling, A., J. Feldon, and C. Pryce. 2002. Early Deprivation and Behavioral and Physiological Responses to Social Separation/Novelty in the Marmoset. *Pharmacology Biochemistry and Behavior* 73(1): 259–269.

DeVore, I. 1965. *Primate Behavior: Field Studies of Monkeys and Apes*. New York: Holt, Rinehart and Winston.

Doran, D. 1997. Influence of Seasonality on Activity Patterns, Feeding Behavior, Ranging and Grouping Patterns in Tai Chimpanzees. *International Journal of Primatology* 18(2): 183–207.

Doyle, G. 1979. Development of Behavior in Prosimians with Special Reference to the Lesser Bushbaby. In *The Study of Prosimian Behavior*, ed. G. Doyle and R. D. Martin. New York: Academic Press.

Dunbar, R. 1988. *Primate Social Systems*. Ithaca, NY: Cornell University Press.

Dupre, J. 1987. *The Latest on the Best: Essays on Evolution and Optimality*. Cambridge, MA: MIT Press.

Dutrillaux, B., and Y. Rumpler. 1988. Absence of Chromosomal Similarities between Tarsiers (*Tarsius syrichta*) and Other Primates. *Folia Primatologica* 50: 130–133.

Ebensperger, L. 1998. Strategies and Counterstrategies to Infanticide in Mammals. *Biol Rev* 73: 321–346.

Eisenberg, J. 1981. *The Mammalian Radiations*. Chicago: Chicago University Press.

Eisenberg, J., and T. Struhsaker. 1981. Census Methods for Estimating Densities. *Techniques for the Study of Primate Population Ecology*. Washington, DC: National Academy of Science Press.

Emlen, S., and L. Orings. 1977. Ecology, Sexual Selection and the Evolution of Mating Systems. *Science* 197: 215–223.

Emlen, S., and P. Wrege. 1986. Forced Copulation and Intraspecific Parasitism: Two Costs of Social Living in the White-fronted Bee Eater. *Z. Tierpsychol* 71: 2–29.

Emmons, L., and E. Biun. 1992. Maternal Behavior in Tree Shrews. *Research and Exploration* 1991: 60–81.

Engqvist, A., and A. Richard. 1991. Diet as a Possible Determinant of Cathemeral Activity Patterns in Primates. *Folia Primatologica* 57: 169–172.

Epple, G. 1975. Parental Behavior in *Saguinus fuscicollis*. *Folia Primatologica* 24: 221–228.

Erkert, H. 1974. Der Einfluss des Mondlichtes auf die Aktiviatsperiodik machtaktiver Säugetiere. *Oecologia* 14: 269–287.

Erkert, H. 1976. Beleuchtungsabhangiges Aktiviatsperiodik bei Nachtaffen (*Aotus trivirgatus*). *Folia Primatologica* 25: 186–192.

Erkert, H. 1989. Lighting Requirements of Nocturnal Primates in Captivity: A Chronobiological Approach. *Zoo Biology* 8: 179–191.

Erkert, H., and J. Grober. 1986. Direct Modulation of Activity and Body Temperature of Owl Monkeys (*Aotus lemurinus griseimenbra*) by Low Light Intensities. *Folia Primatologica* 47: 171–188.

Erxleben, J. 1777. *Systema regni animalis*, 1–636. Liepzig: Impensis Weygandianis.

Fairbanks, L. 1993. Vervet Monkey Grandmothers: Effects on Mother–Infant Relationships. *International Journal of Primatology* 9: 425–441.

Falk, D. 2000. *Primate Diversity*. New York: W. W. Norton.

Fenton, M., N. Boyle, T. Harrison, and D. Oxley. 1977. Activity Patterns, Habitat Use and Prey Selection by Some African Insectivorous Bats. *Biotropica* 9: 73–85.

Fischer, G. 1804. *Anatomie der Maki, und der ihnem verwandten Thiere*. Frankfurt: Andreaische Buchhd.

Fleagle, J. 1988. *Primate Adaptation and Evolution*. New York: Academic Press.

Fleagle, J. 1999. *Primate Adaptation and Evolution*. New York: Academic Press.

Fogden, M. L. 1974. A Preliminary Field Study of the Western Tarsier, *Tarsius bancanus* Horsfield. In *Prosimian Biology*, ed. R. D. Martin, G. A. Doyle, and A. C. Walker. London: Duckworth.

Ford, N. 1983. Variation in Mate Fidelity in Monogamous Birds. *Current Ornithology* 1: 329–356.

Garber, P. 1991. Seasonal Variation in Diet and Ranging Patterns in Two Species of Tamarin Monkeys. *Am J Phys Anthropol Suppl*. 12: 75.

Garber, P., L. Moya, and C. Malaga. 1984. A Preliminary Field Study of the Mustached Tamarin Monkey (*Saguinus mystax*) in Northeastern Peru: Questions Concerned with the Evolution of a Communal Breeding System. *Folia Primatologica* 42: 17–32.

Garrott, R., R. Bartmann, and G. White. 1985. Comparison of Radio Transmitter Packages Relative to Deer Fawn Mortality. *Journal of Wildlife Management* 49: 758–759.

Geoffrey, S. H. 1812. *Suite au tableau des quadrumanes*. *An Mus Hist Nat Paris* 19: 156–170.

Gilbert, B., and S. Boutin. 1991. Effect of Moonlight on Winter Activity of Snowshoe Hares. *Arctic and Alpine Research* 23: 61–65.

Gittleman, J., and O. Oftedal. 1987. Comparative Growth and Lactational Energetics in Carnivores. In *Reproductive Energetics in Mammals*, ed. A. Loudon and P. Racey, 41–77. Oxford: Oxford University Press.

Gladstone, D. 1979. Promiscuity in Monogamous Colonial Birds. *American Naturalist* 114: 545–557.

Glander, K., P. Wright, P. Daniels, and A. Merenlender. 1992. Morphometrics and Testicle Size of Rain Forest Lemur Species from Southeastern Madagascar. *Journal of Human Evolution* 22: 1–17.

Glassman, D., A. Coehlo, K. Carey, and C. Bramblett. 1984. Weight Growth in Savannah Baboons: A Longitudinal Study from Birth to Adulthood. *Growth* 48: 425–433.

Goldizen, A. W. 1987. Tamarins and Marmosets: Communal Care of Offspring. In *Primate Societies*, ed. D. Cheney, B. Smuts, R. Seyfarth, R. Wrangham, and T. Struhsaker. Chicago: University of Chicago Press.

Goldizen, A., J. Terborgh, F. Cornejo, D. Porras, and R. Evans. 1988. Seasonal Food Shortage, Weight Loss and the Timing of Births in Saddleback Tamarins. *J. Anim. Ecol*. 57: 893–901.

Goodall, J. 1986. *The Chimpanzees of Gombe*. Cambridge, MA: Harvard University Press.

Gould, L. 1990. The Social Development of Free-ranging Infant *Lemur catta* at Berenty Reserve, Madagascar. *International Journal of Primatology* 11: 297–318.

Gould, L. 1992. Allo-parental Care in Free-ranging *Lemur catta* at Berenty Reserve, Madagascar. *Folia Primatologica* 58: 72–83.

Greenwood, R., and A. Sargeant. 1973. Influence of Radio Packs on Captive Mallards and Blue-Winged Teal. *Journal of Wildlife Management* 37: 3–9.

Groves, C. 1998. Systematics of Tarsiers and Lorises. *Primates* 39: 13–27.

Groves, C. 2001a. *Primate Taxonomy.* Washington, DC: Smithsonian Institution Press.

Groves, C. 2001b. Getting to Know the Tarsiers: Yesterday, Today, and Tomorrow. Paper presented at the *International Society of Primatologists*, 14th Congress, Adelaide, Australia. January 7–12, 2001.

Gursky, S. L. 1994. Infant Care in the Spectral Tarsier, *Tarsius spectrum*: A Preliminary Analysis. *International Journal of Primatology* 15(6): 843–853.

Gursky, S. L. 1995. Group Size and Composition in the Spectral Tarsier, *Tarsius spectrum*: Implications for Social Organization. *Tropical Biodiversity* 3(1): 57–62.

Gursky, S. L. 1997. *Modeling Maternal Time Budgets: The Impact of Lactation and Gestation on the Behavior of the Spectral Tarsier, Tarsius spectrum.* Ph.D. dissertation, SUNY—Stony Brook.

Gursky, S. L. 1998a. The Effect of Radio Transmitter Weight on a Small Nocturnal Primate: Data on Activity Time Budgets, Prey Capture Rates, Mobility Patterns and Weight Loss. *American Journal of Primatology* 46: 145–155.

Gursky, S. L. 1998b. The Conservation Status of the Spectral Tarsier, *Tarsius spectrum*, in Sulawesi Indonesia. *Folia Primatologica* 69: 191–203.

Gursky, S. L. 2000a. Sociality in the Spectral Tarsier. *American Journal of Primatology* 51: 89–101.

Gursky, S. L. 2000b. Allo-care in a Nocturnal Primate: Data on the Spectral Tarsier. *Folia Primatologica* 71: 39–54.

Gursky, S. L. 2000c. Effects of Seasonality on the Behavior of an Insectivorous Primate. *International Journal of Primatology* 21: 477–495.

Gursky, S. L. 2002a. The Behavioral Ecology of the Spectral Tarsier. *Evolutionary Anthropology* 11: 226–234.

Gursky, S. L. 2002b. Predation on a Wild Spectral Tarsier by a Snake. *Folia Primatologica* 73. 60–62.

Gursky, S. L. 2002c. Determinants of Gregariousness in the Spectral Tarsier. *Journal of Zoology* 256: 1–10.

Gursky, S. L. 2003a. Lunar Philia in a Nocturnal Prosimian Primate. *International Journal of Primatology* 24(2): 351–367.

Gursky, S. L. 2003b. Predation Experiments on Infant Spectral Tarsiers. *Folia Primatologica* 74: 272–284.

Gursky, S. L. 2003c. Territoriality in the Spectral Tarsier, *Tarsius spectrum*. In *The Tarsiers: Past, Present and Future*, ed. P. Wright, E. Simons, and S. Gursky, 221–236. NJ: Rutgers University Press.

Haile, N. S. 1978. Reconnaissance Paleomagnetic Results from Sulawesi, Indonesia Bearing on Paleogeographic Reconstructions. *Tectonophysics* 46: 743–771.

Hames, R. 1992. Time allocation. In *Evolutionary Ecology and Human Behavior*, ed. E. Alden Smith, and B. Winterhalder. New York: Aldine de Gruyter.

Hamilton, W. D. 1964. The Genetical Evolution of Social Behaviour. *Journal of Theoretical Biology* 7: 1–52.

Harcourt, A. H., P. H. Harvey, S. G. Larson, and R. V. Short. 1981. Testis Weight, Body Weight and Breeding Systems in Primates. *Nature* 29: 55–57.

Harcourt, C. 1980. *Behavioral Adaptations of South African Galago*. MSc thesis, University of Witwatersrand, Johannesburg.

Harcourt, C. 1986. Seasonal Variation in the Diet of South African Galagos. *International Journal of Primatology* 7: 491–506.

Harcourt, C., and L. Nash. 1986. Social Organization of Galagos in Kenyan Coastal Forests: *Galago zanzibaricus*. *American Journal of Primatology* 10: 339–355.

Haring, D., and P. Wright. 1989. Hand-raising a Philippine Tarsier, *Tarsius syrichta*. *Zoo Biology* 8: 265–274.

Harlow, H. 1958. The Nature of Love. *Am Psychol* 13: 673–685.

Harrington, J. 1978. Diurnal Behavior of *Lemur mongoz* at Ampijoroa, Madagascar. *Folia Primatologica* 29: 291–302.

Harvey, P., and A. Harcourt. 1984. Sperm Competition, Testes Size and Breeding Systems in Primates. In *Sperm Competition and the Evolution of Animals Mating Systems*, ed. R. L. Smith. New York: Academic Press.

Harvey, P., R. Martin, and T. Clutton-Brock. 1987. Life Histories of Primates. In *Primate Societies*, ed. B. Smuts, D. Cheney, R. Seyfarth, R. Wrangham, and T. Struhsaker, 330–342. Chicago: University of Chicago Press.

Hauser, M. 1993. Do Vervet Monkey Infants Cry Wolf? *Animal Behavior* 45: 1242–1244.

Heymann, E. 1990. Reactions of Wild Tamarins, *Saguinus mystax* and *Saguinus fuscicollis* to Avian Predators. *International Journal of Primatology* 11(4): 327–337.

Hill, W. C. 1955. *Primates. Haplorhini, Tarsoidea*. New York: Interscience.

Hinde, R. 1956. The biological significance of the territories of birds. *Ibis* 98: 340–369.

Hladik, C. 1977. A Comparative Study of the Feeding Strategies of Two Sympatric Species of Leaf Monkeys: *Presbytis senex* and *Presbytis entellus*. In *Primate Ecology*, ed. T. H. Clutton-Brock, 324–353. New York: Academic Press.

Hladik, C., and P. Charles-Dominique. 1976. The Behavior and Ecology of the Sportive Lemur in Relation to its Dietary Peculiarities. *Prosimian Behaviour*, ed. R. D. Martin, G. A. Doyle, and A. C. Walker, 23–38. London: Duckworth.

Hoage, R. 1978. Social and Physical Maturation in Captive Lion Tamarins. *Smithsonian Contrib. Zool.* 364: 1–56.

Holenweg, A., R. Noe, and M. Schabel. 1996. Waser's Gas Model Applied to Associations between Diana Monkeys and *Colobus* Monkeys in Tai National Park, Ivory Coast. *Folia Primatologica* 67: 125–136.

Horsfield, J. 1821. *Zoological Research in Java and in the neighboring islands*. London: Kingsbury, Parbury and Allen.

Hrdy, S. 1976. The Care and Exploitation of Nonhuman Primate Infants by Conspecifics other than their Mother. In *Advances in the Study of Behavior*, ed. J. Rosenblatt, R. Hinde, E. Shaw, and C. Beer, 101–158.

Hrdy, S. 1977. *The Langurs of Abu: Female and Male Strategies of Reproduction*. Cambridge, MA: Harvard University Press.

Hrdy, S. 1979. Infanticide among Mammals: A Review, Classification, and Examination of the Implications for the Reproductive Strategies of Females. *Ethology and Sociobiology* 1: 13–40.

Ingram, J. C. 1977. Parent–Infant Interactions in the Common Marmoset *Callithrix jacchus*. In *The Biology and Conservation of the Callithricidae*, ed. Kleiman, D., 221–291. Washington, DC: Smithsonian Press.

Isbell, L. 1994. Predation on Primates: Ecological Patterns and Evolutionary Consequences. *Evolutionary Anthropology* 61–71.

IUCN. 1994. *Red Data Book*. New York: IUCN Press.

Iwamoto, T., and R. Dunbar. 1983. Thermoregulation, Habitat Quality and Behavioral Ecology of Gelada Baboons. *J Anim Ecology* 52: 357–366.

Iwaniuk, A., S. Pellis, and I. Whishaw. 1999. The Relationship between Forelimb Morphology and Behavior in North American Carnivores. *Canadian J. Zool.* 77: 1064–1074.

Izard, M., P. Wright, and E. Simons. 1985. Gestation Length in *Tarsius bancanus*. *Am J Primatol* 9: 327–331.

Jahoda, J. 1973. The Effect of the Lunar Cycle on the Activity Pattern of *Onychomys leucogaster breviauritius*. *Journal of Mammalogy* 54: 544–549.

Janson, C. 1984. Female Choice and Mating System of the Brown Capuchin Monkey *Cebus apella*. *Z. Tierpsychol* 65: 177–187.

Janson, C. 1988. Intraspecific Food Competition and Primate Social Structure: A Synthesis. *Behaviour* 105: 1–17.

Janson, C. 1990. Social Correlates of Individual Spatial Choice in Foraging Groups of Brown Capuchin Monkeys, *Cebus apella*. *Animal Behavior* 40: 910–921.

Janson, C. 1992. Evolutionary Ecology of Primate Social Structure. In *Evolutionary Ecology and Human Behavior*, ed. E. Alden-Smith and B. Winterhalder, 95–130. New York: Aldine.

Janson, C., and C. van Schaik. 1993. Ecological Risk Aversion in Juvenile Primates: Slow and Steady Wins the Race. In *Juvenile Primates*, ed. M. Pereira and L. Fairbanks, 57–74. Oxford: Oxford University Press.

Janzen, D. 1973. Sweep Samples of Tropical Foliage Insects: Effects of Seasons, Vegetation Types, Elevation, Time of Day and Insularity. *Ecology* 54(3): 687–708.

Jenness, R. 1974. The Composition of Milk. In *Lactation: A Comprehensive Treatise*, ed. B. Larson and V. Smith, 3–107. New York: Academic Press.

Jolly, A., H. Rasamimanana, M. Kinnaird, T. O'Brien, H. Crowley, C. Harcourt, S. Gardner, and J. Davidson. 1993. Territoriality in *Lemur catta* groups during the Birth Season at Berenty, Madagascar. In *Lemur Social Systems and Their Ecological Basis*, ed. P. Kappeler and J. Ganzhorn. New York: Plenum Press.

Jones, C. 1980. The Functions of Status in the Mantled Howler Monkey, *Alouatta palliata* Gray: Intraspecific Competition for Group Membership in a Folivorous Neotropical Primate. *Primates* 21: 389–405.

Jungers, W. 1985. Body Size and Scaling of Limb Proportions in Primates. In *Size and Scaling in Primate Biology*, ed. W. Jungers. New York: Plenum Press.

Kappeler, P. 1989. Sexual Dimorphism in Body Size among Prosimian Primates. *American Journal of Primatology* 16: 151–179.

Kappeler, P. 1990. The Evolution of Sexual Size Dimorphism in Prosimian Primates. *American Journal of Primatology* 21: 201–214.

Kappeler, P. 1991. Patterns of Sexual Dimorphism in Body Weight among Prosimian Primates. *Folia Primatologica* 57: 132–143.

Kappeler, P. 1997. Determinants of Primate Social Organization: Comparative Evidence and New Insights from Malagasy *Lemurs. Biological Review* 72: 111–151.

Kappeler, P., and J. Ganzhorn. 1993. *Lemur Social Systems and their Ecological Basis.* New York: Plenum Press.

Kaufmann, J. 1983. On the Definitions and Functions of Dominance and Territoriality. *Biological Reviews of the Cambridge Philosophical Society* 58: 1–20.

Kavanagh, M. 1978. The Diet and Feeding Behavior of *Cercopithecus aethiops tantalus. Folia Primatologica* 30: 30–63.

Kenward, R. 1987. *Wildlife Radio Tagging.* New York: Academic Press.

Kie, J., J. Baldwin, and C. Evans. 1996. CALHOME: A Program for Estimating Animal Home Ranges. *Wildlife Society Bulletin* 24: 342–344.

Kinnaird, M. 1992. Variable Resource Defense by the Tana River Crested Mangabey. *Behavioral Ecology and Sociobiology* 31: 115–122.

Kinnaird, M., and T. O'Brien. 1993. Species List of Trees Found within Tangkoko Nature Reserve. *Unpublished manuscript.*

Kirkwood, J. 1985. Patterns of Growth in Primates. *J Zoology London* 205: 123–136.

Kleiman, D. G. 1977. Monogamy in Mammals. *Rev Biol* 52: 39–69.

Kleiman, D. 1985. Paternal Care in New World Monkeys. *American Zoologist* 25: 857–859.

Kleiman, D., and J. Malcolm. 1981. The Evolution of Male Parental Investment in Mammals. In *Parental Care in Mammals*, ed. D. Gubernick and P. Klopfer, 347–387. New York: Plenum Press.

Klinger, H. 1963. The Somatic Chromosomes of Some Primates: *Tupaia glis, Nycticebus coucang, Tarsius bancanus, Cercocebus aterrimus, Symphalangus syndactylus. Cytogenetics* 2: 140–151.

Klopfer, P., and K. Boskoff. 1979. Maternal Behavior in Prosimians. In *The Study of Prosimian Behavior*, ed. G. Doyle and R. Martin. New York: Academic Press.

Kobayashi, T. 1987. Does the Siberian Chipmunk Respond to the Snake by Identifying It? *Journal of Ethol* 5: 137–144.

Kobayashi, T. 1994. The Biological Function of Snake Mobbing by Siberian Chipmunks: I. Does it Function as a Signal to Other Conspecifics. *Journal of Ethol* 12: 89–95.

Kobayashi, T. 1996. The Biological Function of Snake Mobbing by Siberian Chipmunks: II. Functions Beneficial for the Mobbers Themselves. *Journal of Ethol* 14: 9–13.

Kodric-Brown, A., and J. Brown. 1978. Influence of Economics, Interspecific Competition and Sexual Dimorphism on Territoriality of Migrant Rufous Hummingbirds. *Ecology* 59: 285–296.

Kotler, B. 1984. Risk of Predation and the Structure of Desert Rodent Communities. *Ecology* 65: 689–701.

Kotler, B., J. Brown, and O. Hasson. 1993. Factors Affecting Gerbil Foraging, Behavior and Rates of Owl Predation. *Ecology* 72: 2249–2260.

Kramer, K., and E. Birney. 2001. Effect of Light Intensity on Activity Patterns of Patagonian Leaf-eared Mice, *Phylottis xanthopygus*. *J. Mammal.* 82: 535–544.

Krebs, J., and N. Davies. 1984. *Behavioural Ecology: An Evolutionary Approach*. Mass: Sinauer Assoc.

Kurland, J. A. 1977. Kin Selection in the Japanese Monkey. *Contributions to Primatology*, Volume 12. Basel: Karger.

Lagapa, P. 1993. *Population Estimates and Habitat Analysis of the Philippine Tarsier, Tarsius syrichta, in Bohol*. Bachelor's thesis. University of Philippines, Los Banos.

Lancaster, J. 1971. Play-mothering: The Relations between Juvenile Females and Young Infants among Free-ranging Vervets. *Folia Primatologica* 15: 161–182.

LeGros Clark, W. 1924. Notes on the Living Tarsier (*Tarsius spectrum*). *Proceedings of the Zoological Society of London* 14: 216–223.

Leutenegger, W. 1980. Monogamy in Callitrichids: A Consequence of Phyletic Dwarfism. *International Journal of Primatology* 1: 95–98.

Leutenegger, W., and J. Cheverud. 1982. Correlates of Sexual Dimorphism in Primates: Ecological and Size Variables. *International Journal of Primatology* 3: 387–402.

Linnaeus, C. 1758. *Systema naturae per regna tria naturae, secundum classes, ordines, genera, species, cum characteribus et differentiis*, 10th ed., 1–823. Holmiae: L. Salvii.

Lockard, R., and D. Ownings. 1974. Seasonal Variation in Moonlight Avoidance by Bannertail Kangaroo Rats. *Journal of Mammology* 55: 189–193.

Loughry, W. 1988. Population Differences in how Black-tailed Prairie Dogs Deal with Snakes. *Behav Ecol Sociobiol* 22. 61–67.

Luckett, W. 1976. Comparative Development and Evolution of the Placenta in Primates. *Contributions to Primatology* 3: 142–234.

Ma, E. J. Lau, D. R. Grattan, D. A. Lovejoy, and K. E. Wynne-Edwards. 2005. Male and Female Prolactin Receptor mRNA Expression in the Brain of a Biparental and a Uniparental Hamster, *Phodopus*, Before and After the Birth of a Litter. *Journal of Neuroendocrinology* 17(2): 81–90.

MacArthur, R., and E. Pianka. 1966. On Optimal Use of a Patchy Environment. *American Naturalist* 100: 603–609.

MacDonald, D. W., and C. J. Amlaner. 1980. *A Handbook on Biotelemetry and Radio Tracking*. Oxford: Pergamon Press.

MacKinnon, J., and K. MacKinnon. 1980. The Behavior of Wild Spectral Tarsiers. *International Journal of Primatology* 1: 361–379.

MacPhee, R., and M. Cartmill. 1986. Basicranial Structures and Primate Systematics. In *Comparative Primate Biology, Vol. 1: Systematics, Evolution and Anatomy*, ed. D. Swindler and J. Erwin, 219–275. New York: Alan R. Liss.

Maestripieri, D. 2001. Is There Mother–Infant Bonding in Primates? *Developmental Review* 21(1): 93–120.

Martin, R. D. 1968. Reproduction and Ontogeny in Tree Shrews (*Tupaia belangeri*) with Reference to Their General Behavior and Taxonomic Relationships. *Z. Tierpsycholo.* 25: 409–495.

Martin, R. D. 1972. A Preliminary Study of the Lesser Mouse Lemur (*Microcebus murinus*). *Advances in Ethology* 9: 43–89.

Martin, R. D. 1990. *Primate Origins and Evolution*. Princeton: Princeton University Press.

Maynard Smith, J. 1977. Parental Investment: A Prospective Analysis. *Animal Behavior* 25: 1–9.

McClure, P. A. 1987. The Energetics of Reproduction and Life Histories of Cricetine Rodents (*Neotoma floridana* and *Sigmodon hispidus*). *Symp Zool Soc London* 57: 241–258.

McKenna, J. J. 1979. The Evolution of Allomothering Behavior among Colobine Monkeys: Function and Opportunism in Evolution. *Am Anthropologist* 81: 818–840.

McKenna, J. J. 1981. Primate Care-giving Behavior: Origins, Consequences and Variability with Emphasis upon the Common Indian Langur. In *Parental Care in Mammals*, ed. D. Gubernick, and P. Klopfer, 389–416. New York: Plenum Press.

Merker, S., I. Yustian, and M. Muhlenberg. 2004. Losing Ground but Still Doing Well—*Tarsius dianae* in Human-Altered Rainforests of Central Sulawesi, Indonesia. *Folia Primatologica* 299–311.

Miller, G., and F. Hollister. 1921. A Review of *Tarsius spectrum* from Celebes. *Proceedings of the Biological Society of Washington* 34: 103–.

Mitani, J., and P. Rodman. 1979. Territoriality: The Relation of Ranging Pattern and Home Range Size to Defendability, with an Analysis of Territoriality among Primate Species. *Behavioral Ecology and Sociobiology* 5: 241–251.

Morland, H. S. 1990. Parental Behavior and Infant Development in Ruffed Lemurs (*Varecia variegata*) in a Northeast Madagascar Rain Forest. *American Journal of Primatology* 20: 253–265.

Morrison, D. 1978. Lunar Phobia in a Neotropical Fruit Bat, *Artibeus jamaicensis* (Chiroptera, Phyllostomidae). *Animal Behaviour* 26: 852–855.

Muirhead-Thomson, R. C. 1991. *Trap Responses of Flying Insects*. New York: Academic Press.

Musser, G. 1987. The Mammals of Sulawesi. In *Biogeographical Evolution of the Malay Archipelago*, ed. T. C. Whitmore. Oxford: Clarendon Press.

Musser, G., and M. Dagosto. 1987. The Identity of *Tarsius pumilus*, a Pygmy Species Endemic to Montane Mossy Forests of Central Sulawesi. *American Museum Novitiates* 2867: 1–53.

Napier, J. 1967. Vertical Clinging and Leaping—A Newly Recognized Category of Locomotor Behavior in Primates. *Folia Primatologica* 6: 204–219.

Nash, L. 1986. Influence of Moonlight Level on Traveling and Calling Patterns in Two Sympatric Species of Galago in Kenya. In *Current Perspectives in Primate Social Dynamics*, ed. D. Taub and F. King, 357–367. New York: Van Norstrand Reinhold.

Nash, L. 1991. Development of Food Sharing in Captive Infant *Galago senegalensis braccatus*. *Primatology Today* 1991: 181–182.

Nature Conservancy. 1994. *Lore Lindu National Park and Morowali Nature Reserve Management Plan*. The Nature Conservancy, Palu, Indonesia.

Negraeff, O. E., and R. M. Brigham. 1995. The Influence of Moonlight on the Activity of Little Brown Bats (*Myotis lucifugus*). *Zeitschrift fur Saugetierkunde* 60(6): 330–336.

Nekaris, K. A. I. 2003. Spacing System of the Mysore Slender Loris (*Loris lydekkerianus lydekkerianus*). *American Journal of Physical Anthropology* 121: 86–96.

Nekaris, K. A. I. 2003. Observations of Mating, Birthing and Parental Behaviour in Three Subspecies of Slender Loris (*Loris tardigradus* and *Loris lydekkerianus*) in India and Sri Lanka. *Folia Primatologica* 74: 312–336.

Nelson, D. 1989. Gull Predation on Cassin's Auklet Varies with the Lunar Cycle. *Auk* 106: 495–497.

Neri-Arboleda, I. 2001. *Ecology and Behavior of Tarsius syrichta in Bohol, Philippines: Implications for Conservation*. MSc thesis, Department of Applies and Molecular Ecology, University of Adelaide.

Nicholson, N. 1982. *Weaning and the Development of Independence in Olive Baboons*. Ph.D. dissertation, Harvard University.

Nicolson, N. 1987. Infants, Mothers and Other Females. In *Primate Societies*, ed. B. Smuts, D. Cheney, R. Seyfarth, R. Wrangham, and T. Struhsaker, 330–342. Chicago: University of Chicago Press.

Niemitz, C. 1984. *Biology of Tarsiers*. Stuttgart: Gustav Fischer.

Niemitz, C., A. Nietsch, S. Warter, and Y. Rumpler. 1991. *Tarsius dianae*: A New Primate Species from Central Sulawesi (Indonesia). *Folia Primatologica* 56: 105–116.

Nietsch, A., and M. Kopp. 1998. The Role of Vocalization in Species Differentiation of Sulawesi Tarsiers. *Folia Primatologica* 69: 371–378.

Nietsch, A. 1999. Duet Vocalizations among Different Populations of Sulawesi Tarsiers. *International Journal of Primatology* 20(4): 567–583.

Nietsch, A., and C. Niemitz. 1992. Indication for Facultative Polygamy in Free-ranging *Tarsius spectrum*, Supported by Morphometric Data. *International Primatological Society Abstracts*: 1992: 318.

Nietsch, A., and C. Niemitz. 1994. Diversitat der Sulawesi-Tarsier. 67. *Hauptversammlung der DGS*, Tubingen. 45–46.

Nievergelt, C., T. Mutschler, and A. Feistner. 1998. Group Encounters and Territoriality in Wild Alaotran Gentle Lemurs (*Hapalemur griseus alaotrensis*). *American Journal of Primatology* 46: 251–258.

O'Brien T. G., and J. G. Robinson. 1991. Allo-maternal Care by Female Wedge-capped Capuchin Monkeys: Effects of Age, Rank and Relatedness. *Behaviour* 119(2): 30–50.

Ostfeld, R. 1985. Limiting Resources and Territoriality in Microtine Rodents. *American Naturalist* 126: 1–15.

Overdorff, D. 1992. *Ecological Correlates to Social Structure in Two Prosimian Primates,* Eulemur fulvus *and* Eulemur rubriventer. Ph.D. dissertation, Duke University.

Owings, D., and R. Coss. 1977. Snake Mobbing by California Ground Squirrels: Adaptive Variation and Ontogeny. *Behaviour* 62: 50–69.

Owings, D., and D. Hennessey. 1984. The Importance of Variation in Sciurid Visual and Vocal Communication. In *The Biology of Ground Dwelling Squirrels,* ed. J. Murie and G. Michener, 167–200. Lincoln: University of Nebraska Press.

Pallas, P. S. 1778. *Novae species quad e glirium ordinae cum illustrationibus variis complurium ex hoc ordinae animalium.* Erlangen: W. Walther.

Palombit, R. 1993. Extra-pair Copulations in a Monogamous Ape. *Animal Behavior* 47: 721–723.

Passamani, M. 1995. Field Observations of a Group of Geoffroy's Marmosets Mobbing a Margay Cat. *Folia Primatologica* 64: 163–166.

Pavey, C., and A. Smith. 1998. Effects of Avian Mobbing on Roost Use and Diet of Powerful Owls, *Ninox strenua. Animal Behaviour* 55: 313–318.

Pereira, M. 1991. Asynchrony within Estrus Synchrony among Ring-tailed Lemurs. *Physiol Behavior* 49: 47–52.

Pereira, M., A. Klepper, and E. Simons. 1987. Tactics of Care for Young Infants by Forest-living Ruffed Lemurs (*Varecia variegata variegata*): Ground Nests, Parking and Biparental Guarding. *American Journal of Primatology* 13: 129–144.

Peres, C. 1989. Costs and Benefits of Territorial Defense in Wild Golden Lion Tamarins, *Leontopithecus rosalia. Behav Ecol Sociobiol* 25: 227–233.

Petiver, J. 1705. *Gazophylacii naturae et artis.* London.

Plavcan, M., R. Kay, W. Jungers, and C. van Schaik. 2002. *Reconstructing Behavior in the Primate Fossil Record.* New York: Kluwer.

Pocock, R. I. 1918. On the External Characteristics of the Lemurs and of *Tarsius. Proceedings of the Zoological Society of London* 1918: 19–53.

Poirier, F. 1972. Introduction. In *Primate Socialization,* ed. F. Poirier, 3–28. New York: Random House.

Poorman, P., M. Cartmill, and R. MacPhee. 1985. The G-banded Karotype of *Tarsius bancanus* and Its Implications for Primate Phylogeny. *American Journal of Physical Anthropology* 66: 215.

Portman, O. 1970. Nutritional Requirement of Nonhuman Primates. In *Feeding and Nutrition of Nonhuman Primates,* ed. R. Harris, 87–115. New York: Academic Press.

Post, D. 1981. Activity Patterns of Yellow Baboons (*Papio cynocephalus*) in the Amboseli National Park, Kenya. *Animal Behavior* 29: 357–374.

Price, M., N. Waser, and T. Bass. 1984. Effects of Moonlight on Microhabitat Use by Desert Rodents. *Journal of Mammalogy* 65: 211–219.

Raemakers, J. 1980. Ecology of Sympatric Gibbons. *Folia Primatologica* 31: 227–245.

Ralls, K. 1977. Mammals in which Females Are Larger Than Males. *Quarterly Review of Biology* 51: 245–276.

Randolph, P., J. Randolph, K. Mattingly, and M. Foster. 1980. Energy Costs of Reproduction in the Cotton Rat, *Sigmodon hispidus*. *Ecology* 58: 31–45.

Rasmussen, D. T. 1986. *Life History and Behavior of Slow Lorises and Slender Lorises*. Ph.D. thesis, Duke University.

Reburn, C. J., and K. E. Wynne-Edwards, (1999). Hormonal Changes in Males of a Naturally Biparental and a Uniparental Mammal. *Hormones and Behavior* 35(2): 163–176.

Regelmann, K., and E. Curio. 1986. Why Do Great Tit (*Parus major*) Males Defend their Brood more Than Females Do? *Animal Behavior* 34: 1206–1214.

Reichard, U. 1995. Extra-pair Copulations in a Monogamous Gibbon (*Hylobates lar*). *Ethology* 100: 99–112.

Reichard, U., and V. Sommer. 1997. Group Encounters in Wild Gibbons (*Hylobates lar*): Agonism, Affiliation and the Concept of Infanticide. *Behaviour* 134: 1135–1174.

Remis, M. 1997. Western Lowland Gorillas (*Gorilla gorilla gorilla*) as Seasonal Frugivores: Use of Variable Resources. *Am J Primatol* 43: 87–109.

Richard, A. 1978. *Behavioral Variation: A Case Study of a Malagasy Lemur*. Lewisburg, PA: Bucknell University Press.

Richard, A. 1985. *Primates in Nature*. New York: Freeman.

Richardson, P., and R. Boyd. 1987. Simple Models of Complex Phenomena: The Case of Cultural Evolution. In *The Latest on the Best: Essays on Evolution and Optimality*, ed. J. Dupre. Massachusetts: MIT Press.

Rickart, E., L. Heaney, and R. Utzurrum. 1991. Distribution and Ecology of Small Mammals along an Elevational Transect in Southeastern Luzon, Philippines. *Journal of Mammalogy* 72: 458–469.

Roberts, M. 1994. Growth, Development, and Parental Care Patterns in the Western Tarsiers, *Tarsius bancanus*, in Captivity: Evidence for a Slow Life History and Nonmonogamous Mating System. *International Journal of Primatology* 15(1): 1–28.

Roberts, M., and F. Kohn. 1993. Habitat Use, Foraging Behavior and Activity Patterns in Reproducing Western Tarsiers, *Tarsius bancanus*, in Captivity: A Management Synthesis. *Zoo Biology* 12: 217–232.

Robinson, J. 1986. Seasonal Variation in the Use of Time and Space by the Wedge-capped Capuchin Monkey, *Cebus olivaceus*: Implications for a Foraging Theory. *Smithson Contrib Zool* 431: 1–60.

Rosenberger, A., and F. Szalay. 1980. On the Tarsiiform Origins of the Anthropoidea. In *Evolutionary Biology of the New World Monkeys and Continental Drift*, ed. R. Ciochon and A. Chiarelli, 139–157. New York: Plenum Press.

Ross, C. 1993. Predator Mobbing by an All-male Band of Hanuman Langurs (*Presbytis entellus*). *Primates* 34: 105–107.

Ross, C., and A. MacLarnon. 1995. Ecological and Social Correlates of Maternal Expenditure on Infant Growth in Haplorrhine Primates. In *Motherhood in Human and Nonhuman Primates*, ed. C. Pryce, R. Martin, and D. Skuse, 37–46. New York: Plenum Press.

Rowe, N. 1996. *A Pictorial Guide to the Living Primates*. New York: Pogonias Press.

Russell, L. 1977. *Behavior, Ecology and Environmental Physiology of a Nocturnal Primate, Lepilemur mustelinus.* Ph.D. dissertation, Duke University.

Rylands, A. 1993. *Tamarins and Marmosets.* Oxford: Oxford University Press.

Schultz, A. 1948. The Number of Young at a Birth and the Number of Nipples in Primates. *American Journal of Physical Anthropology* 6: 1–23.

Seyfarth, R., and D. Cheney. 1990. The Assessment by Vervet Monkeys of Their Own and Another Species' Alarm Calls. *Animal Behaviour* 40: 754–764.

Shekelle, M. 2003. *Taxonomy and Biogeography of Eastern Tarsiers.* Ph.D. thesis. Washington University.

Shekelle, M., S. Leksono, L. Ischwan, and Y. Masala. 1997. The Natural History of the Tarsiers of North and Central Sulawesi. *Sulawesi Primate Newsletter* 4(2): 4–11.

Sherman, P. 1977. Nepotism and the Evolution of Alarm Calls. *Science* 197: 1246–1253.

Shields, W. 1984. Barn Swallow Mobbing: Self-defense, Collateral Kin Defense, Group Defense or Parental Care? *Animal Behavior* 32: 132–148.

Simek, M. 1988. *Food Provisioning of Infants in Captive Social Groups of Common Marmosets (Callithrix jacchus) and Cotton-top Tamarins (Saguinus oedipus).* Unpublished Master's thesis, University of Tennessee, Knoxville.

Simpson, G. G. 1945. The Principles of Classification and a Classification of Mammals. *Bulletin American Museum Natural History* 85: 1–350.

Slagsvold, T., S. Dale, and G. Saetree, 1994. Dawn Singing in the Great Tit (*Parus major*): Mate Attraction, Mate Guarding or Territorial Defense? *Behaviour* 131: 11–138.

Smuts, B. 1985. *Sex and Friendship in Baboons.* New York: Aldine.

Snedcor, G., and W. Cochran. 1989. *Statistical Methods.* Iowa State University Press.

Snow, C. C. 1967. *The Physical Growth and Development of the Open-land Baboon, Papio doguera.* Ph.D. thesis, University of Arizona.

Snowdon, C. (2004). Affiliative Processes and Male Primate Social Behavior. *Paper presented at Annual Meetings of American Association for the Advancement of Science,* Seattle, February, 2004.

Sokal, R., and J. Rohlf. 1981. *Biometry.* New York: Freeman and Co.

Southwood, T. R. E. 1992. *Ecological Methods with Particular Reference to the Study of Insect Populations.* New York: Chapman and Hall.

Srivastava, A. 1991. Cultural Transmission of Snake Mobbing in Free-ranging Hanuman Langurs. *Folia Primatologica* 56: 117–120.

Stacey, P., and D. Ligon. 1990. Territory Quality and Dispersal Options in the Acorn Woodpecker, and a Challenge to the Habitat Saturation Model of Cooperative Breeding. *Am Nat* 130: 654–676.

Stanford, C. 1991. *The Capped Langur in Bangladesh: Behavioral Ecology and Reproductive Tactics.* New York: Karger.

Stanford, C. 1992. Costs and benefits of allomothering in wild capped langurs (*Presbytis pileata*). *Behavioral Ecology and Sociobiology* 20: 29–32.

Sterling, E. 1992. Timing of Reproduction in Aye-ayes in Madagascar (*Daubentonia madagascarensis*). *American Journal of Primatology* 27(1): 59–60.

Sterling, E., and A. Richard. 1995. Social Organization in the Aye-ayes and the Perceived Distinctness of Nocturnal Primates. In *Creatures of the Dark*, ed. L. Alterman, G. Doyle, and M. K. Izard, New York: Academic Press.

Storr, G. C. C. 1780. *Prodromus methodi mammalium*. Tubingen.

Strier, K. 2003. *Primate Behavioral Ecology*. New York: Allyn and Bacon.

Struhsaker, T. 1967. Ecology of Vervet Monkeys (*Cercopithecus aethiops*) in the Masai-Amboseli game reserve, Kenya. *Ecology* 48: 891–904.

Sussman, R., and P. Garber, In press. Cooperation and Competition in Primate Social Interactions. In *Primates in Perspective*, ed. S. Bearder, C. Campbell, A. Fuentes, K. MacKinnon, and M. Panger. Oxford: Oxford University Press.

Sussman, R. 2003. *Primate Ecology and Social Structure. Vol. 2: New World Monkeys*. Boston: Pearson Custom.

Sussman, R. 1999. *Primate Ecology and Social Structure. Vol. 1: Lorises, Lemurs and Tarsiers*. Boston: Pearson Custom.

Tamura, N. 1989. Snake-directed Mobbing by the Formosan Squirrel *Callosciurus erythraeus thaiwanensis*. *Behavioral Ecol Sociobiol* 24: 175–180.

Tardif, S., M. Harrison, and M. Simek. 1993. Communal Infant Care in Marmosets and Tamarins: Relation to Energetics, Ecology, and Social Organization. In *Marmosets and Tamarins: systematics, behaviour and ecology*, ed. A. Rylands, Oxford: Oxford University Press.

Tattersall, I. 1988. Cathemeral Activity in Primates: A Definition. *Folia Primatologica* 49: 200–202.

Taub, D. 1984. *Primate Paternalism*. New York: Van Norstrand Reinhold.

Taylor, R. 1970. The Energetics of Terrestrial Locomotion and Body Size. In *Scale Effects in Animal Locomotion*, ed. I. J. Pedley. London: Academic Press.

Taylor, R. 1980. Mechanical Efficiency of Terrestrial Locomotion. In *Aspects of Animal Movement*, ed. H. Elder, and E. Traeman. Cambridge: Cambridge University Press.

Tenaza, R. R. 1975. Territory and Monogamy among Kloss' Gibbons (*Hylobates klossii*) in Siberut Island, Indonesia. *Folia Primatol* 24: 60–80.

Terborgh, J. 1983. *Five New World Primates*. Princeton: Princeton University Press.

Terborgh, J., and A. Goldizen. 1985. On the Mating System of the Cooperatively Breeding Saddle-backed Tamarin (*Saguinus fuscicollis*). *Behav Ecology and Soiobiology* 16: 293–299.

Thompson, S. 1992. Gestation and Lactation in Small Mammals: Basal Metabolic Rate and the Limits of Energy Use. In *Mammalian Energetics: Interdisciplinary Views of Metabolism and Reproduction*, ed. T. Tomasi and T. Horton. Ithaca: Cornell University Press.

Tilden, C. 1993. *Reproductive Energetics of Prosimian Primates*. Ph.D. dissertation, Duke University.

Tremble, M., Y. Muskita, and J. Supriatna. 1993. Field Observations of *Tarsius dianae* at Lore Lindu National Park, Central Sulawesi, Indonesia. *Tropical Biodiversity* 1(2): 67–76.

Trent, B. M. Tucker, and J. Lockard. 1977. Activity Changes with Illumination in Slow Loris *Nycticebus coucang*. *Applied Animal Ethnology* 3: 281–286.

Trivers, R. L. 1971. The Evolution of Reciprocal Altruism. *Quarterly Review of Biology* 46: 35–57.

Trivers, R. L. 1972. Parental Investment and Sexual Selection. In *Sexual selection and the descent of man*, ed. B. Campbell, 136–79. Chicago: Aldine.

Trivers, R. 1974. Parent–Offspring Conflict. *American Zool* 14: 249–264.

Ulmer, F. A. 1963. Observations on the Tarsier in Captivity. *Zoologischer Garten* 27: 106–121.

van Schaik, C. and R. Dunbar. 1990. The Evolution of Monogamy in Large Primates: A New Hypothesis and Some Crucial Tests. *Behaviour* 115: 30.

van Schaik, C. P., P. R. Assink, and N. Salafsky. 1992. Territorial Behavior in Southeast Asian Langurs: Resource Defense or Mate Defense? *American Journal of Primatology* 25: 233–242.

van Schaik, C., and J. van Hooff. 1983. On the Ultimate Causes of Primate Social Systems. *Behaviour* 85: 91–103.

van Schaik, C., and P. Kappeler. 1994. Life History, Activity Period and Lemur Social Systems. In *The Ecological Basis of Lemur Social Systems*, ed. P. Kappeler and J. Ganzhorn. New York: Academic Press.

van Schaik, C., and M. A. van Noordwijk. 1989. The Evolutionary Effect of the Absence of Felids on the Social Organization of the Simeulue Monkey (*M. fasicularis*). *International Journal of Primatology* 6: 180–200.

Vogel, C. 1985. Helping, Cooperation and Altruism in Primate Societies. *Forschritte Der Zoologie* 31: 375–389.

Vogt, J. 1984. Interactions between Adult Males and Infants in Prosimians and New World Monkeys. In *Primate Paternalism*, ed. D. Taub. New York: Van Nostrand Reinhold.

Wallace, A. R. 1869. *The Malay Archipelago*. Oxford: Oxford University Press.

Warren, R. 1994. *Lazy Leapers: A Study of the Locomotor Ecology of Two Species of a Saltatory Nocturnal Lemur in Sympatry at Ampijoroa, Madagascar*. Ph.D. thesis, University of Liverpool.

Waser, P. 1976. *Cercocebus albigena*: Site Attachment, Avoidance and Intergroup Spacing. *American Naturalist* 110: 911–921.

Wasser, S. 1982. *Social Behavior of Female Vertebrates*. New York: Academic Press.

Watanuki, Y. 1986. Moonlight Avoidance Behavior in Leach's Storm-petrels as a Defense against Slaty-backed gulls. *Auk* 103: 14–22.

Watt, S. 1994. Alloparental Behavior in a Captive Group of Spider monkeys (*Ateles geoffroyi*) at the Auckland Zoo. *International Journal of Primatology* 15(1): 135–151.

Weiner, J. 1987. Limits to the Energy Budget and Tactics in Energy Investment in the Djungarian Hamster. *Symp Zool Soc London* 57: 167–187.

White, G., and R. Garrott. 1987. *Analysis of Wildlife Radiotracking Data.* New York: Academic Press.

Whitmore, T. C. 1987. *Tropical Rain Forests of the Far East.* Oxford: Oxford University Press.

Whitten, P. L. 1982. *Female Reproductive Strategies Among Vervet Monkeys.* Ph.D. dissertation, Harvard University.

Whitten, T., M. Mustafa, and G. Henderson. 1987. *The Ecology of Sulawesi.* Yogyakarta: Gadjah Mada University Press.

Wittenberger, J. F., and R. L. Tilson. 1980. The Evolution of Monogamy : A Theoretical Overview. *Annual Review of Ecology and Systematics* 11: 197–232.

Wolfe, J., and C. Summerlin. 1989. The Influence of Lunar Light on Nocturnal Activity of the Old Field Mouse. *Animal Behavior* 37: 410–414.

Wolfheim, J. 1986. *The Distribution, Ecology and Habitat of Primates.* Cambridge: Cambridge University Press.

Wolin, L., and L. Massoupust. 1970. Morphology of the Primate Retina. In: *The Primate Brain*, ed. C. R. Noback and W. Montagna, 1–27. New York: Appleton-Century-Crofts.

Woolard, H. 1925. The Anatomy of *Tarsius spectrum. Proceedings of the Zoological Society London* 1925: 1071–1184.

Woolfenden, G., and J. Fitzpatrick. 1984. The Inheritance of Territory in Group Breeding Birds. *Bioscience* 28: 104–108.

World Wildlife Fund. 1980. *Cagar Alam Gunung Tangkoko Dua Saudara Sulawesi Utara Management Plan 1981–1986.* Bogor, Indonesia: World Wildlife Fund.

Wrangham, R. 1980. An Ecological Model of Female-bonded Primate Groups. *Behaviour* 75: 262–300.

Wright, P. C. 1984. Ecological Correlates of Monogamy in *Aotus* and *Callicebus.* In *Primate Ecology and Conservation*, ed. J. Else and P. Lee. 159–167. New York: Cambridge University Press.

Wright, P. C. 1985. *Costs and Benefits of Nocturnality to the Night Monkey (Aotus).* Ph.D. dissertation, City University of New York, New York.

Wright, P. C. 1989. The Nocturnal Primate Niche in the New World. *Journal of Human Evolution* 18: 635–658.

Wright, P. C. 1990. Patterns of Parental Care in Primates. *International Journal of Primatology* 11: 261–274.

Wright, P. C. 1995. Demography and Life History of Free-ranging *Propithecus diadema edwardsi* in Ranomafana National Park, Madagascar. *International Journal of Primatology* 16: 835–854.

Wright, P. C. 1997. The Neotropical Primate Adaptation to Nocturnality: Feeding in the Night. In *Adaptive Radiations of Neotropical Primates*, ed. M. Norconk, A. Rosenberger, and P. Garber, 89–92. New York: Plenum Press.

Wright, P. C., D. Haring, E. Simons, and P. Andau. 1987. Tarsiers: A Conservation Perspective. *Primate Conservation* 8: 51–54.

Wright, P. C. M. Izard, and E. Simons. 1986. Reproductive Cycles in *Tarsius bancanus*. *American Journal of Primatology* 11: 207–215.

Wright, P. C., L. Toyama, and E. Simons. 1988. Courtship and Copulation in *Tarsius bancanus*. *Folia Primatologica* 46: 142–148.

Wright, P. C., and L. Martin. 1995. Predation, Pollination and Torpor in Two Nocturnal Prosimians: *Cheirogaleus major* and *Microcebus rufus* in the Rain Forest of Madagascar. In *Creatures of the Dark: The Nocturnal Prosimians*, ed. L. Alterman, G. Doyle, and M. K. Izaed. New York: Plenum Press.

Young, A., A. Richard, and L. Aiello. 1990. Female Dominance and Maternal Investment in Strepsirhine Primates. *Am Naturalist* 135: 473–488.

Zullinger, E. M., R. E. Ricklefs, K. H. Redford, and G. M. Mace, 1984. Fitting Sigmoidal Equations to Mammalian Growth Curves. *Journal of Mammalogy* 65: 607–636.

Index

DATE DUE

OhioLINK DEC 0 9 REC'D			
GAYLORD			PRINTED IN U.S.A.

SCI QL 737 .P965 G87 2007

Gursky, Sharon, 1967-

The spectral tarsier